Arms and Oil

ARMS AND OIL
U.S. Military Strategy and the Persian Gulf

THOMAS L. McNAUGHER

THE BROOKINGS INSTITUTION
Washington, D.C.

Library of Congress Cataloging in Publication data:

McNaugher, Thomas L.
  Arms and oil.
  Includes index.
  1. United States—Military policy.   2. Persian Gulf
Region—Strategic aspects.   I. Title.
UA23.M43   1985   355'.0335'73   84-45850
ISBN 0-8157-5624-0
ISBN 0-8157-5623-2 (pbk.)

9 8 7 6 5 4 3 2 1

THE BROOKINGS INSTITUTION is an independent organization devoted to nonpartisan research, education, and publication in economics, government, foreign policy, and the social sciences generally. Its principal purposes are to aid in the development of sound public policies and to promote public understanding of issues of national importance.

The Institution was founded on December 8, 1927, to merge the activities of the Institute for Government Research, founded in 1916, the Institute of Economics, founded in 1922, and the Robert Brookings Graduate School of Economics and Government, founded in 1924.

The Board of Trustees is responsible for the general administration of the Institution, while the immediate direction of the policies, program, and staff is vested in the President, assisted by an advisory committee of the officers and staff. The by-laws of the Institution state: "It is the function of the Trustees to make possible the conduct of scientific research, and publication, under the most favorable conditions, and to safeguard the independence of the research staff in the pursuit of their studies and in the publication of the results of such studies. It is not a part of their function to determine, control, or influence the conduct of particular investigations or the conclusions reached."

The President bears final responsibility for the decision to publish a manuscript as a Brookings book. In reaching his judgment on the competence, accuracy, and objectivity of each study, the President is advised by the director of the appropriate research program and weighs the views of a panel of expert outside readers who report to him in confidence on the quality of the work. Publication of a work signifies that it is deemed a competent treatment worthy of public consideration but does not imply endorsement of conclusions or recommendations.

The Institution maintains its position of neutrality on issues of public policy in order to safeguard the intellectual freedom of the staff. Hence interpretations or conclusions in Brookings publications should be understood to be solely those of the authors and should not be attributed to the Institution, to its trustees, officers, or other staff members, or to the organizations that support its research.

For Leslie

Foreword

IN THE OIL-RICH Persian Gulf, a region crucial to the world's security and economic health, the United States confronts major challenges to its military and diplomatic skills. The Iranian revolution, the Soviet invasion of Afghanistan, and unpredictable turbulence have contributed to declining U.S. influence in the area. In the United States, military questions about force size and strategy have sparked controversy over the proper U.S. role in the Gulf.

In this book Thomas L. McNaugher offers a military strategy for the Gulf that seeks to balance the risks of overinvolvement against the risks of neglect. The author, a research associate in the Brookings Foreign Policy Studies program, believes that the United States must cultivate the traditional security mechanisms of the states on the Arabian Peninsula, and he encourages cooperation with allies like Great Britain and France that historically have been involved in Gulf security. He argues that the United States should focus on protecting the Gulf states from external attack and on deterring further Soviet encroachment in the region, leaving internal security largely to the states themselves.

The author thanks Lieutenant General Richard Lawrence, Harold Saunders, and General Volney F. Warner (Ret.) for thoughtful reviews of the manuscript. Lieutenant Commander William F. Hickman, Lieutenant Colonel Daniel J. Kaufman, John D. Mayer, Jr., and Ted Parker offered timely assistance on key points. Within Brookings, Michael K. MccGwire, William B. Quandt, and John D. Steinbruner gave invaluable conceptual guidance, and Richard K. Betts, Joshua M. Epstein, Edward R. Fried, and Raymond L. Garthoff commented on individual chapters. Nancy A. Ameen provided research assistance, Susan E. Nichols typed the manuscript, and Alan G. Hoden verified the book's factual content. Theresa B. Walker edited the manuscript, Chisolm B.

Hamilton prepared it for typesetting, and Florence Robinson compiled the index.

Financial support for the study was provided by the Ford Foundation and the Department of Energy. The Brookings Institution is grateful for that assistance.

The views expressed in this book are those of the author and should not be ascribed to the organizations that supported the project, or to the trustees, officers, or other staff members of the Brookings Institution.

BRUCE K. MAC LAURY
President

February 1985
Washington, D.C.

Contents

TABLES

FIGURES

CHAPTER ONE

U.S. Security Policy
and the Persian Gulf

OIL PRICES dropped sharply in 1983 after a decade of even sharper rises, cushioning painful but fading memories of long lines at gas pumps. And an oil glut is allaying the fear of price shocks like the ones that rocked the world's economic and financial institutions in the 1970s. Americans who learned painfully of their country's energy vulnerability over the past decade now seem eager to forget the experience and its lessons. Some observers are even asking whether the Persian Gulf, with its large oil reserves and corresponding influence over oil prices, has "passed its prime."[1]

Meanwhile, the crises of the late 1970s that threatened the Gulf and its vital oil lifeline have been weathered, at least for the moment, with surprisingly little strain. The Soviet invasion of Afghanistan now looks more like a bloody morass than a strategic flanking action around Iran to the Gulf. And Iran's revolution, initially believed to be an open invitation to Soviet intrigue, has given birth to an Islamic regime that is almost as anti-Soviet as it is anti-American. Actions taken in 1980 to protect Western interests around the Gulf now seem to have been hasty. One defense analyst has even suggested that "Gulf oil is no longer worth our defense."[2]

No one can predict the future, least of all oil analysts, whose projec-

---

1. Christopher Van Hollen, "Has the Persian Gulf Passed Its Prime?" *Washington Post,* December 27, 1981. See also Eliyahu Kanovsky, "The Diminishing Importance of Middle East Oil: Its Future Implications," *Energy Information Service* (American Jewish Committee), vol. 4 (August 4, 1982); and S. Fred Singer, "What Is Happening to World Oil?" *Wall Street Journal,* March 10, 1982.

2. James A. Nathan, "Gulf Oil Is No Longer Worth Our Defense," *Los Angeles Times,* November 29, 1983.

tions have often been wrong. Yet strong arguments can be made that dismissing the Gulf's importance so casually would be a serious mistake. Barring either unforeseen technological innovations or economic troubles, a comparatively stable oil supply will continue to be of major importance. For this reason alone, the Persian Gulf will remain important. The size of oil reserves and production capacities in the Persian Gulf area will be a dominant factor in the world oil picture for the foreseeable future. Rather than signaling the demise of the oil issue, the present oil glut is producing a welcome respite in which oil consumers like the United States can think seriously about their future stakes in the Gulf.

The United States, in particular, should use the time wisely. The Gulf's political volatility and location just off the Soviet Union's southern flank mark it as a region of potentially great security challenge. Moscow's proximity unquestionably makes the United States an important actor in the area. Yet the Middle East is a remote, politically delicate part of the world; the United States can charge hastily into this region only at considerable expense, perhaps even at its own peril. The linkage between military action and political events in this region is particularly complex. Hence U.S. military policy, defined here to include the provision of arms and assistance to key states as well as planning for the deployment of U.S. forces, must be formulated with special care.

Oil, the Persian Gulf, and U.S. Interests

The United States is interested in the Persian Gulf or, more broadly, the Middle East, for many reasons. For instance, the United States' declared interest in the security of Israel draws on the cultural and political ties between the two countries. And an interest in containing Soviet power draws the United States to the Gulf area simply because of the region's strategic location on the Soviet Union's southern flank and on the road to Africa, South Asia, and the Indian Ocean. Furthermore, given the Soviet Union's concern for threats around its perimeter, it is fair to assume that the superpowers would vie for influence among the Gulf states even if those states did not possess oil in such abundance.

Nevertheless, the dominant cause for concern in the United States, especially since 1973, has been the Gulf's oil resources. Oil has drawn the United States more fully into the area than would otherwise be the case. The Carter Doctrine,[3] the creation of a Rapid Deployment Joint Task Force (RDJTF) in 1980, and the search for access to bases around the Gulf reflect recent and intense interest in the security of oil resources. Without oil, the Iran-Iraq war or the precise fortunes of the Saudi family would probably not cause such pronounced anxiety in the United States.

Why and in what ways is oil so important? Why, in particular, is it important to the United States, which has a fairly large oil production capacity, and which imports only a small portion of its oil from the Gulf? How can events in the Gulf affect the United States? Those questions must be answered before the question of military security in the area can be addressed.

The Once and Future Importance of the Gulf

Only a few decades ago the United States was the world's oil giant. In 1938, the year oil was discovered in Saudi Arabia, 62 percent of the world's oil was produced in the United States.[4] By the mid-1950s the United States still produced twice as much oil as the Middle Eastern and North African oil states combined. U.S. spare production capacity enabled it to dampen modest supply disruptions during the Suez crisis of 1956–57 and the 1967 Arab-Israeli war. During the Suez crisis the United States employed an oil embargo as one way to pressure France and Great Britain into withdrawing their forces from Egypt.[5]

But annual additions to U.S. oil reserves sagged in the postwar era, while discoveries in the Middle East and North Africa boomed because of lower production costs there. Beginning in 1968, additions to U.S. oil reserves fell behind domestic U.S. production; total U.S. proven reserves began to fall from a high of close to 40 billion barrels in 1967 to 32 billion

---

3. Announced less than a month after Soviet troops entered Afghanistan, the Carter Doctrine sought to make clear the importance that the United States attached to the Persian Gulf area: "An attempt by any outside force to gain control of the Persian Gulf region will be regarded as an assault on the vital interests of the United States of America and such an assault will be repelled by any means necessary, including military force." Jimmy Carter, "The State of the Union," January 23, 1980, *Weekly Compilation of Presidential Documents,* vol. 16 (January 28, 1980), p. 197.

4. This and other statistics in the following paragraphs are taken principally from Joel Darmstadter and Hans H. Landsberg, "The Economic Background," *Daedalus* (*The Oil Crisis: In Perspective*), vol. 104 (Fall 1975), pp. 15–37.

5. See Robert R. Bowie, *Suez 1956: International Crises and the Role of Law* (Oxford University Press, 1974), pp. 64, 75.

barrels in 1973, at the time of the first oil price hikes, and then to just over 26 billion barrels in 1983. By contrast, from 1955 onward, almost 80 percent of the annual additions to the world's proven oil reserves came from discoveries in the North African and Middle Eastern states. While crude oil production in other producing areas leveled off or rose only gently after 1965, oil production in the Middle East and northern Africa area more than doubled between 1965 and 1972. Of these states, those around the Gulf were and continue to be by far the largest reserve holders, and most of these reserves are remarkably cheap and easy to tap.

Oil from the Gulf in seemingly limitless quantities led to substantial decreases in the real price of oil over the postwar era. This in turn fueled a boom in oil consumption worldwide, especially in the industrialized states. In the United States, demand continued to rise while new discoveries declined. U.S. oil imports rose from 2 million barrels a day (mbd) in 1962 to almost 5 mbd in 1973, an 8.5 percent annual growth rate.

The effects of oil's price advantage were even more pronounced in Western Europe and Japan. In Western Europe oil imports grew from 37 percent of total energy consumed in 1962 to 60 percent in 1972. Corresponding figures for Japan were 44 percent and 73 percent, respectively. Cheap oil produced fundamental structural changes in the industries of these areas, as firms moved distinctly away from coal in favor of oil. The truly momentous increases in world energy consumption generated by postwar economic growth thus led to still greater increases in the demand for oil.

The oil crisis of 1973–74 can be blamed on an array of specific factors: a simultaneous economic boom in the United States, Western Europe, and Japan in 1972–73, which rapidly increased oil demand; the disappearance of spare capacity in the United States; lower stocks among countries importing oil;[6] and the precipitating event, the 1973 Arab-Israeli war. But the groundwork for the crisis had been laid over the

6. "The steadily increasing weight of American imports on world oil markets probably was an important factor in helping to create conditions for the producer-country price and supply moves of 1973–74; for, at considerably lower levels of United States imports than the 35 percent degree of dependence that we saw developing just before the October, 1973, war, a worldwide supply 'overhang' might have been sufficient to preclude the concerted OPEC actions, or at least their success. Indeed, had conditions in 1973–74 not been substantially different from those prevailing in 1967, the American role as a supplier of last resort would probably have critically altered the situation." Darmstadter and Landsberg, "The Economic Background," p. 27.

entire postwar era and had mainly to do with supply and demand. Market pressures had begun to force the price of oil upward in 1971 and 1972. Although the Arab oil embargo of 1973 did not take much oil off the market, it provoked massive speculative buying by consumer countries and oil firms worried about future shortages. This precipitated a sharp increase in price. Members of the Organization of Petroleum Exporting Countries (OPEC) were able to capture what amounted to a risk premium in the new price structure.[7]

The abrupt fourfold increase in oil prices that occurred in 1973–74 helped precipitate a recession throughout much of the world. But after 1974 the nominal price of oil held fairly steady, and the real price of oil actually fell by about 10 percent between 1974 and 1979. Thus, although demand for oil sagged gently at mid-decade, industrialized economies began to recover in the latter half of the decade, and the demand for oil increased again. This was true especially for the United States, where the process of decontrolling oil prices did not begin until 1979.

The situation changed dramatically in 1979, however, as Iran's revolution temporarily lowered that country's oil output. At the same time oil firms, fearing more price increases, engaged in panic buying to increase their stocks. Competitive bidding for stocks seems to have been the dominant force behind the nearly twofold increase in oil prices that constituted this second price shock.[8] Again, OPEC cashed in on the premium reflected in spot market behavior.

This shock helped produce another economic downturn in the industrialized world, this one the deepest since 1932. And this in turn contributed to the oil glut that began to emerge in 1981. Had the price of oil remained at its pre-1973 level, demand for the substance would surely have outstripped OPEC's maximum production capacity of 32 mbd by the decade's end. Instead, OPEC, the world's residual oil producer, found demand dropping by the end of 1981.[9] Its production fell from the maximum in 1979 to 19 mbd in 1982 and then to less than 18 mbd in

7. See Paul W. MacAvoy, *Crude Oil Prices: As Determined by OPEC and Market Fundamentals* (Ballinger, 1982), pp. 39–46. They were also in a better position to obtain a larger share of the profits on their resources from the oil firms, a process that began at the Tehran conference in 1971.

8. See Edward R. Fried, "Preparing for the Next Oil Shock: The International Dimension" (Brookings Institution, August 1982), p. 4.

9. Non-OPEC oil producers usually operate near full capacity, while OPEC meets remaining world demand. Both increases and decreases in world demand for oil are felt first and most sharply among OPEC producers.

1983. Saudi Arabia, which had raised production from 1979 to 1981 to compensate partially for the loss of Iranian and Iraqi production, cut its production to 6.5 mbd in 1982, and was forced to make further cuts in 1983.[10] Nonetheless, the barrel price of oil fell in March 1983 to $29, nominally $5 less than its peak price in 1980.

The oil glut results from more than simply bad economic performance, however. Its other causes have produced a more cavalier attitude among some observers toward the future importance of oil, particularly the importance of OPEC and the Persian Gulf. Impressive price-induced structural adaptations among the industrialized nations (generally those belonging to the Organization for Economic Cooperation and Development) have helped make them less vulnerable to future oil price shocks. Of the 12 mbd decline in demand for OPEC oil between 1979 and 1982, for example, roughly 7 mbd can be attributed to greater efficiency, conservation, and the substitution of other fuels as their price became competitive with the price of oil. The development of alternative oil sources in the North Sea area and Mexico and massive destocking by oil firms from 1981 to 1983 have also lowered demand for OPEC oil even if they have not signaled reduced dependence on oil in general.[11]

These facts and trends signal a healthy shift away from oil, less dependence on the Persian Gulf in particular as a source of supply, and welcome increases in the efficiency with which oil is used. Whether or not such trends continue depends importantly on the future price of oil, which determines the financial wisdom of investments in conservation, efficiency, and the development of alternative sources, as well as on the pace of economic recovery. Because the price of oil is impossible to predict, so are future levels of demand. But several factors make it probable that oil will regain its critical importance to the world's economy, and that the Persian Gulf states will actually increase in importance as time goes by.

First, worldwide economic recovery will probably lead to increased demand for oil. Although debate continues on this issue, much of it has less to do with whether oil will regain its importance than with when and

10. Saudi oil exports fell from just over 9 mbd in 1981 to 5.6 mbd in 1982. OPEC, *Annual Report, 1982*, p. 67.

11. Fried, "Preparing for the Next Oil Shock," p. 16. For a discussion of the role private sector oil stocks have come to play in oil markets, see James R. Schlesinger, "Crossing the Energy Watershed: Obligations of Public Policy," *Washington Quarterly,* vol. 6 (Autumn 1983), p. 27.

by what amount. Most observers agree that recovery will again produce tight oil markets, though probably not much before the end of this decade. Because oil will remain especially attractive to states lacking elaborate infrastructure or alternative resources, demand for oil will increase relatively more among the industrializing than among the industrialized states. In the OECD states, economic recovery will probably lead to increases in the absolute amount of oil required, though oil's relative importance within these economies may decline.

Once oil markets tighten, supply and price will regain their critical importance to all states. Oil is the world's residual energy source; swings in its price affect all energy markets. Even countries like the United States, whose import dependence is low relative to that of other OECD states, cannot escape the consequences of oil price shocks. The adage that U.S. allies like France and Japan should be held relatively more responsible for security around the Persian Gulf because so much of their oil comes from the Gulf misses the mark when it comes to oil and energy markets. Supply cuts among Gulf producers would force Japan and France to seek oil in other markets, bidding up its price to everyone. And increases in the price of oil would affect the price of other forms of energy. As William W. Hogan puts it, "In the world oil market, no country is an island apart, including the United States."[12]

Finally, in the future the Gulf will grow more rather than less important in the oil market. This area holds 55 percent of the world's proven oil reserves, with Saudi Arabia alone holding 25 percent. Other sources of oil—the Alaskan and North Sea fields, for example—will run down fairly quickly, leaving the Gulf as the long-term source for oil. The Gulf area also holds about one-third of the world's oil production capacity, with Saudi Arabia accounting for about half of that, or 10 mbd. Even under slightly loose market conditions, loss of output from the Gulf or Saudi Arabia would have momentous consequences for the world's oil markets, and hence for the world economy.

More important, key Gulf oil states, particularly the oil kingdoms of the Arabian Peninsula, have relatively large oil production capacities and reserves, small populations, and large financial reserves. These states will be more capable of adjusting their production levels to accord with market realities. This will grow more true in the future, as states

12. "Import Management and Oil Emergencies," Harvard University, John F. Kennedy School of Government, Energy and Environmental Policy Center, June 1980.

with smaller reserve holdings and larger populations—Nigeria, Mexico, and Venezuela, for example—find themselves with less and less room to vary production rates. Thus while the Gulf states may well become slightly less important as contributors to global energy supplies, they will grow more important as potentially stabilizing or destabilizing influences on the oil market and hence on all energy markets.

Oil and U.S. Interests

Ultimately, the U.S. interest—indeed, everyone's interest—in oil focuses on its price. Especially dangerous are abrupt price changes, so-called price shocks. Structural rigidities in industrial economies, though partially mitigated by adaptations forced on industries by the price shocks of the 1970s,[13] still hamper rapid adaptation to sharp changes in factor prices. The indexing of labor contracts tends to keep real wages relatively unchanged even during periods of inflation. Factories cannot be converted overnight to other fuels, and rapid changes in balance-of-payment positions affect investment and other financial policies.

Although the economic costs of the sharp price increases that occurred over the course of the 1970s are difficult to pin down, unquestionably those costs have been high. As Edward Fried puts it,

Since 1973 OECD economic growth averaged only half as much as during the preceding decade, inflation doubled, and unemployment as a percent of the labor force on average also doubled. Only a share of this comparative misfortune is attributable to the oil shocks but that share is certainly large.[14]

Significantly, one set of authors speculates that, had the oil price increase of the 1970s been spread evenly over twenty years, the loss in U.S. output would have been considerably lower than it was.[15]

The political importance of oil derives from the effects of changes, or

---

13. As noted earlier, oil is likely to remain somewhat less important to the industrialized world in the future than it would have had its price remained at pre-1973 levels. Moreover, some industries have acquired dual-fired burners or alternate fuel sources that improve their adaptability to changing energy prices. Structural rigidities remain, however. And it may be that the elimination of lower-value uses of oil as a result of earlier price shocks will only make adaptation more difficult in the future. See Fried, "Preparing for the Next Oil Shock," p. 34.

14. Ibid., p. 9.

15. See Robert E. Hall and Robert S. Pindyck, "Energy and American Economic Policy," Energy Laboratory Working Paper 81-035 (Massachusetts Institute of Technology, June 1981).

feared changes, in its price. Earlier price shocks introduced a host of domestic political problems for oil-consuming states—inflation, recession, dislocations within the labor force, and unemployment. Price changes also raised problems among nations, as the reaction called forth debate about appropriate solutions. Although the OECD states have developed cooperative approaches to possible future price shocks, many are skeptical about how much they will actually cooperate in sharing the burden.

Even the mere threat of a price shock can be important. Those who possess power to impose steep costs on oil consumers possess considerable leverage. This realization gave rise after 1973 to fear of OPEC extortion or strangulation of the industrialized world. Such thinking also underlies fear of a Soviet invasion or of expanding Soviet influence in the region. By itself, forcible Soviet capture of Iran's oil would have about the same effect on supply and demand as would Soviet purchase of the same amount of oil. But if an invasion of Iran were to put the Soviets in control, or in apparent control, of the Gulf's production capacity, they could gain great leverage over oil-consuming states.

Thus it is not quite enough to say that the U.S. interest is only in the smooth flow of oil at reasonable prices. Should Moscow gain control of the Gulf, cut prices, and guarantee oil supplies to key OECD states, many in the OECD might still feel uneasy about Soviet intentions over the long run. The United States must worry about who gains control of the flow and price of oil, whatever the immediate effects of the situation on supply and price may be.

U.S. Interests and the Gulf

The presence of so much of the world's oil in a politically volatile region just off the Soviet Union's southern border gave rise over the 1970s to visions of truly worrisome threats to U.S. interests in the Gulf. In the aftermath of the 1973 embargo, fears were raised of an OPEC attempt to strangle the West. During Iran's revolution, and even more so after Soviet forces entered Afghanistan late in 1979, many feared a Soviet drive to Iran's oil region around Abadan. The second scenario figured prominently in U.S. military planning for Gulf contingencies.

Both scenarios may be plausible, and both may be necessary grist for the military planner's mill. Yet neither is probable at the moment. As will become clear in chapter 2, Soviet troops simply are not poised and ready to invade Iran, though mobilization could bring them to the ready over some period of time. In any case, historically, the Soviets have preferred to deal with this area on the diplomatic and political level, focusing their military planning on other contiguous areas such as Europe and the Sino-Soviet border.

Meanwhile, Gulf rulers have learned over the past decade that their interests are often compatible with those of the United States and its allies. To the extent that previous shocks induced a surprising degree of adaptation in industrialized economies, oil producers must worry that future shocks will undermine the value of unexploited reserves. Declining demand for oil since 1981 reminds rulers in these states that the market can work against them as well as for them. And after a decade of economic boom, most of these states have investments in domestic and foreign projects that tie their fortunes more firmly than ever to a stable world economic regime. Reasonable governments, especially in swing producing states like those around the Gulf, face growing incentives to stabilize rather than to disrupt the oil market.

Events of the past decade nonetheless suggest various ways in which events around the Gulf could harm U.S. interests. As occurred in 1973, domestic and regional pressures emanating from another Arab-Israeli confrontation might move Gulf rulers to disregard market conditions and seek to use oil to influence world opinion and U.S. foreign policy. Conservative religious leaders opposed to the massive social changes that come with increasing oil revenues might successfully pressure existing regimes to cut production, or they themselves might come to power and seek the same end.[16] In these cases sovereign governments might choose a course different from one recommended by common notions of economic rationality.

Alternatively, otherwise rational governments in the region might be coerced into adopting policies harmful to U.S. interests. No recent examples of this phenomenon have occurred, but it is not difficult to conceive of a set of events in the ongoing Iran-Iraq war that could place Iran in a dominant position in the Gulf. Iran would then gain substantial leverage over the small sheikhdoms of the Arabian Peninsula. A Soviet

16. The willingness of the Khomeini regime to sell its oil to all comers is no proof that all conservative religious leaders would act this way, or that Khomeini himself would be so respectful of Western interests if he were not at war with Iraq. Nor is it clear that a leader like Khomeini would be as moderate as King Faisal of Saudi Arabia in a future Arab-Israeli conflict like that which precipitated the 1973 embargo.

invasion might produce a similar situation. Although some of these scenarios might be difficult to distinguish from those involving deliberate choice by the governments, the difference would crucially affect the courses of action open to oil consumers.

Chaos, violence, and confusion could also produce a damaging price shock. Iran's revolution led to a sharp drop in production and great uncertainty about future oil supplies. Those events contributed to increasing prices in 1979–81. The symbolic and economic importance of oil facilities makes them a likely target for terrorist attacks. Interstate as well as intrastate violence could lower oil production, as has been true in the Iran-Iraq war. Governments do not have to choose to cause trouble for trouble nonetheless to affect the flow and price of oil.

Finally, even events not deliberately marked by violence or chaos could harm U.S. interests in the Gulf. For instance, key Gulf oil producers might be unable or unwilling to adjust their production in ways that stabilize oil markets over the long run. Failure to do so under future conditions of energy scarcity could initiate price shocks and painful economic adjustments in consuming states that might wreak havoc throughout the world's economy.[17]

The same can be said with regard to the Soviet Union. Whatever its designs on the Gulf's oil, Moscow worries first about the security of its borders. The emergence of a perceived threat from the south would very likely prompt Moscow to increase the readiness of its forces and perhaps to deal more aggressively with the area than it has thus far. Meanwhile, the importance of the Gulf's oil to the United States and its allies has raised pronounced concern in the United States for Soviet activity in the area. With the Gulf region itself notoriously unstable and beyond the full control of either superpower, the possibilities for misperception, confrontation, and escalation are high.

The Dilemma of U.S. Security Policy in the Gulf

Military security instruments are especially important in a region so close to the Soviet Union and so marked by local and regional turbulence. Yet it is easier to talk about the role of military instruments than to implement useful security policies. Indeed, the problems confronting

17. See Schlesinger, "Crossing the Energy Watershed," pp. 27–28.

U.S. security planners have worsened in recent years, as Iran's revolution has both increased the level of threat in the area and decreased U.S. access to the area.

The Deteriorating Security Situation

Until 1979 the United States could rely on others to carry the primary burden for securing its interests in the Gulf. Although the United States emerged from World War II with a close relationship with Saudi Arabia, the British remained the dominant Western power in the Gulf after the war, leaving it only in 1971. With attention at that point on the war in Vietnam, the United States turned to the shah of Iran as its regional police officer, the most important and powerful "pillar," at least where military security was concerned, of a "twin pillar" strategy that included Saudi Arabia. Beginning in 1971 U.S. arms flowed in increasing numbers to Iran, while the number of U.S. citizens in that country grew to more than 40,000 in 1978.

Whatever the shah's failings, reliance on Iran had considerable strategic and political value. Iran was and remains far and away the largest of the Gulf states, with a population three times that of Iraq, the second largest Gulf power. This, combined with Iran's comparatively greater industrial and technical sophistication, made it an obvious candidate for regional police officer. Iran's strategic position between the Soviet Union and the Gulf added to its value; Iranian forces could act as a first-line deterrent to Soviet aggression, while U.S. forces could expect to deploy to Iran's bases in the event of a crisis.

The shah's fall was chiefly responsible for the crisis atmosphere that gripped U.S. decisionmakers in 1979–80. Besides triggering an increase in the price of oil, Iran's revolution created instability along the Soviet Union's southern flank and abruptly curtailed U.S. access to the area. The Soviet invasion of Afghanistan in December 1979 seemed only to confirm fears that Moscow had aggressive designs on the West's oil supplies. Finally, Iran's revolution gave birth to an Islamic republic opposed to the United States as well as to U.S. friends around the Gulf, notably Saudi Arabia. Threats seemed to be multiplying while the means for countering them evaporated.

The oil glut, the Soviet quagmire in Afghanistan, and Moscow's failure to acquire a strong position in Tehran have calmed the situation since

1979. Yet there is no escaping the fact that Iran's revolution presents the United States with a fundamentally new and worse security challenge in the Gulf. The collapse of a U.S. ally in Iran has been a net gain for Moscow, whatever the complexion of the new Iranian regime. Another phase in Iran's revolution may yet toss up opportunities for Soviet intrigue or military action. Iran's revolution has also worsened security on the Arabian Peninsula. Not only does Iran possess the largest military potential in the Gulf but the Khomeini regime also wields the banner of Islamic fundamentalism with a fervor most discomforting to traditional peninsular rulers.

Since 1980 the United States has sought to adjust its military security policy in the Gulf to these new realities. Yet the adjustment has been plagued by military and political problems frustrating U.S. military planners and hampering the development of a coherent approach to the region.

The Military and Budgetary Problem

Driven chiefly by fear of Soviet military action, the United States moved early in 1980 to shore up its military position around the Gulf. Within weeks of the Soviet invasion of Afghanistan, President Jimmy Carter enunciated his doctrine. On March 1, 1980, he established the command headquarters for the RDJTF, housing it under the U.S. Readiness Command (REDCOM), a major unified command with responsibility for contingency operations worldwide.[18] One marine amphibious force, three army divisions, a variety of smaller combat and supporting units, and seven tactical fighter wings (approximately 500 aircraft) from the air force and the Air National Guard were allocated to

18. The conceptual origins of the RDJTF can be traced at least as far back as Presidential Directive (PD) 18, written early in the Carter presidency. In fact, the problem of projecting U.S. forces to distant areas has been a hardy perennial in U.S. defense thinking since the early 1960s. But thinking about the subject has rarely yielded actual programs, especially in the area of strategic lift. In this sense, the several crises of 1979 may be said to have created the political opportunity in the United States to add lift assets rarely procured under less worrisome international conditions. On the general problem of force projection, see William W. Kaufmann, *Planning Conventional Forces, 1950–80* (Brookings Institution, 1982). On PD 18, see Zbigniew Brzezinski, *Power and Principle: Memoirs of the National Security Adviser, 1977–81* (Farrar, Straus, Giroux, 1983), pp. 455–56.

RDJTF headquarters for planning and for operational control as required during a crisis. Elements of a carrier task force were also made available to support the force.

Resource constraints brought the RDJTF under fire from the start. No new U.S. forces had been created; the RDJTF instead had to borrow units otherwise slated for Europe or Asia. Critics argued that this amounted to robbing Peter to pay Paul.[19] They also noted the absence of air- and sealift—so-called strategic lift assets—to get enough units to the Gulf quickly enough to meet the Soviet invasion threat then under discussion. Past U.S. efforts to develop "projection forces," they noted, had foundered on the army's tendency to buy equipment too heavy to be easily carried, while the air force and navy ignored lift in favor of front-line combat systems. Former Secretary of Defense James R. Schlesinger was not alone in suggesting that the RDJTF was neither rapid, deployable, nor indeed a force.[20]

Steps taken since 1980 have only partially addressed these problems. More strategic lift is now in the budget. An air force program to purchase fifty C-5Bs between 1982 and 1988 will increase by more than 60 percent the size of its fleet of "outsize" cargo aircraft. The air force has accelerated the purchase of KC-10 tankers and has also completed a program to stretch its fleet of C-141 cargo aircraft. Meanwhile the U.S. Navy has purchased eight SL-7 fast deployment container ships to be on line by 1986. It has also begun to purchase maritime prepositioning ships capable of housing equipment and thirty days' supplies for three marine brigades, making it possible to deploy a marine division to the Gulf in about ten days. These changes are more impressive in percentage than in absolute terms, however, and little will be in place before 1986.[21]

In January 1983 the RDJTF was removed from REDCOM and converted to the U.S. Central Command (CENTCOM), a "unified" command reporting directly to the secretary of defense. Still, no new forces were created, suggesting that with the creation of CENTCOM U.S. policymakers were not facing reality. Indeed, even the relatively high

19. See, for example, Jeffrey Record, *The Rapid Deployment Force and U.S. Military Intervention in the Persian Gulf* (Cambridge, Mass.: Institute for Foreign Policy Analysis, 1981), pp. 33–35, 54.

20. See his "Rapid(?) Deployment(?) Force(?)" *Washington Post,* September 24, 1980.

21. For a full review of U.S. procurement initiatives, see "Rapid Deployment Forces and the Persian Gulf," in International Institute for Strategic Studies (IISS), *Strategic Survey, 1982–1983* (London: IISS, 1983), pp. 135–36.

defense budgets of the Reagan presidency have not appreciably increased the strength of U.S. ground forces. Moreover, the preference among some members of the Reagan Defense Department for bringing forces to bear around the Soviet periphery may have distracted attention from demanding force and lift requirements for the Gulf. After an initial burst of energy in 1980–81, for example, strategic lift programs have received little additional attention.

The possibility of military action in the Gulf raises a maze of operational questions. These concern the tactics, training, logistics, and command and control requirements for fighting in a remote area with a host of rigorous terrain and weather conditions, from the heat and sand of Saudi Arabia to the rugged mountains and extreme temperatures of northern Iran. Yet the broader issue of resources overshadows such questions. U.S. military planners have had to formulate answers to operational questions within a fairly constricted framework. The U.S. force posture has not grown appreciably in response to the new security situation in the Gulf.

The Political Problem

An obvious path around some of these budget and force posture constraints is to position U.S. forces and materiel in the region itself and to help local states defend themselves.[22] U.S. policy has moved in both directions. Yet local rulers have been no more tractable than the defense budget. The United States has obtained access rights to certain bases, but those rights have been carefully restricted. None of its remaining friends in the Gulf area has been as willing as the shah was to provide the United States with military resources.

Arab rulers have made clear their concern for the Palestinian issue, for the embarrassment they endure in dealing with Israel's chief ally, and for the basic unreliability that U.S.-Israeli ties impart to U.S.-Arab relations.

---

22. More strident critics called for positioning U.S. forces in or near the Gulf. See, for example, Robert W. Tucker, "American Power and the Persian Gulf," *Commentary*, vol. 70 (November 1980), pp. 25–41. Officials in the RDJTF may have wanted the same thing but confined public discussion to obtaining basing for a forward command element in the region. A very small (fewer than twenty people) headquarters was in fact established on board ships of the U.S. Navy's Middle East Force, stationed off Bahrain, in December 1983. See "Persian Gulf Force Gets Headquarters in Mideast," *Chicago Tribune*, December 1, 1983.

These concerns have acquired substantially greater urgency with the rise of a fundamentalist Islamic regime in Tehran. Arab rulers also make clear their fear of the United States as a genuine threat to them. They point out, especially to Americans portraying the Soviets as the major threat in the region, that only the United States has extensively discussed the possibility of invading the Gulf's oil fields to destroy OPEC's power over oil prices. Only in the United States have a president and two cabinet secretaries broached the prospect that force might, under extreme conditions, be used against the Gulf states. Finally, rulers of the small but rich Gulf oil sheikhdoms worry that involving the United States military more directly in their affairs will only increase the attention shown them by the Soviet Union, ultimately reducing the diplomatic leeway available to local states.

Although some Western observers view these protestations with cynicism, most Americans sensitive to regional political dynamics are sympathetic to Arab concerns. These people were alarmed by the Carter Doctrine and the creation of the RDJTF. Many argued that a larger U.S. presence in the Gulf area would be dysfunctional: "In the Gulf, an obtrusively large U.S. military presence may increase the risks to friendly regimes of domestic and intraregional challenges from nationalist forces opposed to close association with external power blocs."[23] These warnings were neatly captured in the epitaph, "Don't engulf the Gulf."[24]

U.S. military analysts did not need to be sensitive to these arguments or well schooled in regional politics to realize that the Gulf states were reluctant to forge closer military ties to the United States. Ultimately a U.S. military presence was up to Gulf rulers themselves, and these rulers were blocking the elaborate buildup many U.S. strategists felt was essential to meet the new threats created by Iran's revolution. The United States has been given no secure basing or prepositioning rights in the Gulf itself. Both Oman and Egypt have allowed some degree of prepositioning, but neither has been willing to offer the United States more than uncertain access to their bases. The Omani and Egyptian militaries have run joint exercises with U.S. forces, but these have been

23. Paul Jabber, "U.S. Interests and Regional Security in the Middle East," *Daedalus*, vol. 109 (Fall 1980), p. 80.

24. From Christopher Van Hollen, "Don't Engulf the Gulf," *Foreign Affairs*, vol. 59 (Summer 1981), pp. 1064–78.

kept low key. Military planners have done somewhat better outside the Gulf itself, acquiring access to ports in Kenya and Somalia. But the only guaranteed U.S. access is to the tiny island of Diego Garcia, about 2,500 miles from the Strait of Hormuz. Although some analysts might have argued that the United States could not respond properly to the new situation *without* engulfing the Gulf, the United States was not being given a choice.

From 1971 to 1979 the shah of Iran buffered the United States from the competing demands of its policies in the Middle East. During the shah's reign Iran supplied Israel with about 50 percent of its oil. Israel maintained a technical mission in Tehran, and Israel's intelligence services helped train the Savak, the shah's secret police.[25] Because Israelis saw Iran as a strategic counterweight to Iraq, they welcomed U.S. arms shipments to the shah. Contrast the controversies surrounding the sale of F-15s or airborne warning and control system (AWACS) aircraft to Saudi Arabia, for example, with the ease with which F-14s were sold to Iran. With the shah's fall the United States was no longer easily able to square the circle of policies designed to support Israel while also protecting Arab friends in the Gulf.

Toward a Military Policy

Events since 1981 have given the United States and its allies an unexpected but welcome opportunity to rethink issues of Gulf security. It is prudent to assume that the U.S. stake in this region will rise slowly in coming years and remain high for some time to come. Threats to U.S. and allied interests in the region can now be assessed more carefully than they were just after the Soviets invaded Afghanistan. Can the United States handle the new security problems in the region within prevailing budgetary and regional political constraints? If not, can it find ways around those limitations that nonetheless are sensitive to regional political dynamics? In what ways can the United States best apply the instruments of military policy to secure its interests around the Gulf?

This book seeks to answer these questions. Part 1 treats the problem of Soviet military power in the region in the wake of Iran's revolution.

---

25. See Rinn-Sup Shinn, "Foreign Relations," in Richard F. Nyrop, ed., *Iran: A Country Study* (Government Printing Office, 1978), p. 238.

After a detailed examination of Soviet military threats to the region, questions of military strategy are addressed: how can the United States apply or maintain force most effectively to achieve its political objectives?[26] I suggest that the most appropriate use for U.S. forces in this case is also the most demanding one: deterring Soviet entry into any part of Iran. A second chapter in part 1 outlines the implications of this assessment for U.S. force posture, tactics, and training.

Part 2 turns to the other side of the Gulf and focuses especially on Saudi Arabia. Here the demands on U.S. forces are likely to be less pressing than those associated with the Soviet threat, but the demands on U.S. political sensitivities are likely to be far greater. Moreover, the United States is but one of several external powers engaged in helping the peninsular oil states manage their security problems. Although this poses demanding political requirements on U.S. military security policy, the section suggests that it is in the U.S. interest to encourage cooperation among these powers as a means of bypassing some of the restrictions that hamper American dealings with peninsular states. There is a crucial role for U.S. arms and assistance as well as for U.S. forces but only within the broader context of a multilateral security framework.

A region as volatile as the Persian Gulf will always present risks and uncertainty to those whose interests lie there. U.S. military policy must be structured to allow for such uncertainty. Significantly, the United States is not far from having the military capabilities to support such a policy. The more important question is, can the United States muster the political sensitivity needed to use its capabilities to the best possible advantage?

26. I borrow here from Alastair Buchan's definition of military strategy as something that specifies how "the application or maintenance of force [can contribute] most effectively to the achievement of political objectives." *War in Modern Society: An Introduction* (Harper and Row, 1968), pp. 81–82.

PART ONE

Balancing Soviet Power in the Gulf

SOVIET PROXIMITY to the Gulf and the sheer size of the Soviet force posture are legitimate causes for worry in the United States. The collapse of the U.S. position in Iran in 1979, and more immediately the Soviet invasion of Afghanistan in that year, intensified that worry. Oil vital to the United States and its allies sat a scant 850 miles from Soviet territory, while U.S. forces, small in comparison with Soviet conventional forces near Iran, were robbed of their principal route of access to the region. The Rapid Deployment Joint Task Force looked hopelessly outmanned and outpositioned.

The intractability of the problem facing the United States in 1980 spawned various simple but extreme solutions. Some suggested strategies involving the threat of horizontal escalation. Some of these strategies aimed to deter Soviet military action around the Gulf by threatening things of value to Moscow in areas that were more accessible to U.S. forces (threatening Cuba, for example). Others sought to deter by threatening to retaliate all around the Soviet periphery. Still others argued that the United States should seek to deter by threatening nuclear, or vertical, escalation.[1] Besides the need in some of these cases

---

1. On nuclear escalation, see Kenneth N. Waltz, "A Strategy for the Rapid Deployment Force," *International Security*, vol. 5 (Spring 1981), pp. 49–73. For a conventional escalation strategy, see F. J. West, Jr., "NATO II: Common Boundaries for Common Interests," *Naval War College Review*, vol. 34 (January–February 1981), pp. 59–67. West explicitly rejects the notion of nuclear escalation in favor of horizontal escalation at sea. The point remains that besides a "toehold somewhere in the Gulf," the purpose of which is to justify a U.S. decision to escalate, there is little discussion of military objectives in the Gulf region itself.

to place a small force (often called a trip-wire) somewhere in the Gulf, military objectives there were unimportant. The overriding aim of these strategies was to relieve the disadvantaged position of the United States by taking military action to a more accessible area, or to a level of weaponry where the United States was not inferior.

None of these strategies is very attractive, however. It may be easier militarily to attack targets close to the United States, but it is hard to find a target that is more valuable to Moscow than control of the Persian Gulf. Moscow would probably be happy to trade Cuba for the Persian Gulf, for example. Taking the war to the Soviet periphery, even with conventional weapons, is likely to involve a high risk of nuclear war. Futhermore, such a strategy is based on the questionable premise that a big war is preferable to a small one. Finally, strategies involving the threat of nuclear escalation face the problem that has plagued the North Atlantic Treaty Organization (NATO) for over a decade; it makes no sense to place obvious reliance on escalation in an era of nuclear parity. Kenneth Waltz argues for reliance on the threat of nuclear escalation, for example, on the assumption that the balance of resolve favors the United States, which clearly has a vital interest in the Gulf's oil.[2] But the balance of resolve is more important than the balance of nuclear or conventional force only if both sides can clearly understand each other's interest in the Gulf. Unfortunately, it is easy to imagine scenarios where the United States and the Soviet Union could misunderstand each other's stakes, resolves, and willingness to escalate conflict.

Escalatory strategies lack flexibility as well as credibility. They allow in this case for one scenario, a Soviet invasion of Iran's oil area that would bloody a small U.S. force designed principally to seize oil wells along the Gulf's shores.[3] These strategies assume that seizing oil wells is the only Soviet military action that could conceivably harm U.S. interests. Yet there are a number of Soviet interests in the Gulf area and a number of ways in which Soviet military action can serve those interests. Whether or not such military action would threaten U.S. interests is a matter for analysis that trip-wire strategists have not performed.

There appears to be a need for the United States to meet Soviet power in the Gulf with conventional forces that would play the same role in the Gulf that they play in Europe. Such forces would allow the United States

2. Waltz, "A Strategy for the Rapid Deployment Force," pp. 66–67.
3. Ibid., p. 63.

to signal resolve and commitment; prevent rapid moves that preempt or avoid escalatory responses; and promise a prolonged and potentially costly conventional battle that would remove the immediate need for escalation and buy time for negotiations. Such forces would also permit the United States to have some flexibility in selecting objectives and responding to various Soviet actions. U.S. rapid deployment forces could serve these purposes; their overall size is less important than their agility, training, and support. But to understand issues of U.S. force posture it is first necessary to examine how Soviet forces might be used to extend Soviet control over U.S. interests in the Gulf.

CHAPTER TWO

The Soviet Military Threat
to the Gulf

SOVIET INTEREST in the Gulf area predates the discovery of oil there, and oil remains but one of several interests drawing Moscow's attention southward. A common border with the Soviet Union brings the Gulf in for a share of the concern Moscow extends to all bordering areas. Importantly, many of the ethnic and religious groups in the Soviet Union's southern republics have counterparts in Iran, Afghanistan, and Turkey, raising the possibility that events in these countries could cause repercussions within the Soviet Union itself. Many observers speak of a long-standing Soviet ambition to obtain warm water ports besides those on the Black Sea. Only recently has the desire to control oil been added to the list of Soviet objectives.

Notwithstanding solid grounds for Soviet concern with the Gulf area, the region has tended to fall in third, behind Europe and China, on Moscow's list of security priorities.[1] The Soviet postwar policy toward Iran has been primarily defensive, designed to prevent the emergence of an Iranian-U.S. alliance or the use of Iran as a U.S. base.[2] The shah's announcement in September 1962 that he would not allow any nation to base missile forces on his territory ushered in sixteen years of healthy Soviet-Iranian relations, despite the shah's pro-American tilt and the

---

1. See George W. Breslauer, "The Dynamics of Soviet Policy toward the Arab-Israeli Conflict: Lessons of the Brezhnev Era," Working Paper 8 (Brown University, Center for Foreign Policy Development, October 1983), pp. 2–3.

2. Moscow's concern for threats emanating from Iran dates from the early years of the Soviet Republic. In 1920 Lenin supported the "Socialist Republic of Gilan" in northern Iran to undermine the British position in Iran and to limit British support to White Russian forces operating out of Iran. When a coup brought Reza Khan to power in Tehran

presence of U.S. military personnel in Iran.[3] During Iran's revolution the Soviets were quick to assert that foreign intervention in Iran would be perceived as a threat to the Soviet Union. But Moscow has been reluctant to tamper aggressively with Iran's minorities or to bring obvious military pressure to bear on Tehran.[4]

Major force deployments in Eastern Europe and along the Sino-Soviet border have far exceeded military activity along the Soviet Union's southern flank, where the Soviets have tended to use force sparingly. Soviet forces did occupy Azeri and Kurdish portions of Iran in 1946 in an effort to extract energy concessions from Iran's ruler but also because of a desire to acquire a deeper buffer zone to the south. Soviet forces were withdrawn later in that year, primarily in response to U.S. pressure (but also after Tehran had granted Moscow its oil concessions).[5] In the Middle East as a whole, the Soviets threatened to intervene in the Arab-Israeli wars in 1967 and 1973, but they did so only when it was fairly certain that they would not have to act; they have not been high risk-takers.[6] The invasion of Afghanistan appears to contrast sharply with these low-key, cautious, and defensive policies. Yet the principal goal of the invasion was to prevent the collapse of a communist regime which the Soviet Union had sought without success to control by political means.[7]

---

in 1921, Moscow dropped its support for the Gilanis and signed a treaty with the new Iranian regime, principally to undercut any pretext for a British presence in Tehran. Articles 5 and 6 of this treaty gave Moscow the right to intervene in Iran should foreign powers seek to use Iranian territory as a base from which to threaten the Soviet Union. Although Iran has since declared the treaty void, the Soviets hold articles 5 and 6 valid. They would probably refer to the articles again to justify any future military action against Iran. See Alvin Z. Rubinstein, *Soviet Policy toward Turkey, Iran, and Afghanistan: The Dynamics of Influence* (Praeger, 1982), pp. 60–61.

3. Ibid. pp. 67–69.

4. See Muriel Atkin, "The Islamic Republic and the Soviet Union," in Nikki R. Keddie and Eric Hooglund, eds., *The Iranian Revolution and the Islamic Republic*, Proceedings of a conference at the Woodrow Wilson International Center for Scholars (Washington, D.C.: Middle East Institute, 1982), pp. 141, 145.

5. See Bruce Robellet Kuniholm, *The Origins of the Cold War in the Near East: Great Power Conflict and Diplomacy in Iran, Turkey, and Greece* (Princeton University Press, 1980), pp. 270–382.

6. Breslauer, "The Dynamics of Soviet Policy," p. 15.

7. The last major Soviet effort to employ political means to solve the Afghanistan problem came in September 1979, when Moscow sought unsuccessfully to unseat the aggressive and scheming Hafizullah Amin. In the months that followed, Amin tried to make contact with the West through Pakistan. By the time Soviet troops moved into Kabul in December they were not only preventing the collapse of a communist regime but also preventing what appeared to Moscow to be an abrupt turn to the West by Afghanistan's

Furthermore, the invasion unfolded only after it was fairly clear to the Soviets that the United States would not respond militarily to it.

The fact remains, however, that the Soviet Union shares a border with the Gulf region, and along that border Moscow has deployed forces that could be used to support any of its interests in the Gulf. Moreover, even the defensive use of force might yield increased influence over the flow of oil. Thus military issues cannot be ignored. What could the Soviets do with their forces? What are the constraints on their military operations in the Gulf area? How should the United States think about the Soviet military threat to the Gulf?

Soviet Capabilities

Concern for the Soviet military threat to Iran springs primarily from the ground and air forces deployed along the Soviet Union's southern flank: in the North Caucasus, Transcaucasus, and Turkistan military districts; and in Afghanistan. According to the Defense Department, there are twenty-nine divisions in the southern Soviet Union, including roughly 105,000 troops in Afghanistan.[8] The International Institute for Strategic Studies cites one fewer division but gives a clearer sense of their deployment (table 2-1).

These forces vary in readiness level. Soviet divisions in Afghanistan are combat ready but are fully engaged there; a ground force threat to Iran or Pakistan from Afghanistan may someday be realized, but not soon. Two or three of the motorized rifle divisions in the Soviet Union's southern military districts are said to be fully combat ready, but the remaining units are quite the opposite. Old equipment apparently is being modernized,[9] although it is not clear whether this is the result of the normal modernization cycle, a response to revolution in Iran, or adaptation to lessons learned in Afghanistan. Full-time manpower remains low. These units could be deployed only after being fully manned, maintained, and trained.

---

leadership. See in particular Thomas T. Hammond, *Red Flag over Afghanistan: The Communist Coup, the Soviet Invasion, and the Consequences* (Boulder, Colo.: Westview Press, 1984), pp. 49–94.

8. U.S. Department of Defense, *Soviet Military Power*, 2d ed. (Government Printing Office, 1983), p. 34.

9. Ibid., p. 50.

Table 2-1. *Soviet Ground Forces near Iran*

	Type of division		
Military district	*Tank*	*Motorized rifle*	*Airborne*
Transcaucasus	0	11	0
North Caucasus	1	7	0
Turkistan	0	5	0
Afghanistan	0	3	1

Source: International Institute for Strategic Studies (IISS), *The Military Balance, 1983–1984* (London: IISS, 1983), p. 16. David C. Isby counts elements of seven motorized rifle divisions and one airborne division in Afghanistan, some of them pulled from the Turkistan military district. See his excellent "Afghanistan 1982: The War Continues," *International Defense Review*, vol. 15, no. 11 (1982), p. 1524.

The concern for major Soviet military action raises questions about the time required to mobilize these units, with estimates varying from two to several weeks.[10] But it makes little sense to focus on a single estimate. Mobilization time is likely to vary substantially with how far Soviet commanders expect to go, how many units they expect to use, and how much resistance they expect to meet. It may also vary with the circumstances. Confronted with a surprise invitation to occupy Iranian Azerbaijan, for example, Moscow might, within limits imposed by the readiness of available forces, try to deploy forces more hurriedly (if it wanted to deploy them at all) than it would if it were choosing the time and direction of attack.

Little data support the debate about mobilization. The Soviets mobilized reserves about a month before they invaded Afghanistan. They apparently took three months to prepare more units for a riskier operation in Czechoslovakia in 1968. Afghanistan may represent the best case. The number of units mobilized was small (four to five divisions); Soviet troops were already in place in Kabul; the Afghan army could be and was ingeniously disarmed; the United States seemed usefully distracted by events in Iran; and the Afghanis themselves were not expected to resist. That the Soviets had to rotate reservists out of Afghanistan about three months after the invasion occurred, and replace them with better trained regulars, suggests that in this case mobilization time was not sufficient. Thus a month may be a bare minimum for mobilization of even small contingents where the Soviets have some degree of choice, and a month allows little time for training of units as

10. Ibid. Joshua M. Epstein argues that it is "perfectly plausible" that mobilization would take about three months, although he assumes one month for his analysis. See his "Soviet Vulnerabilities in Iran and the RDF Deterrent," *International Security*, vol. 6 (Fall 1981), p. 140 (Brookings Reprint 401).

Table 2-2. *Soviet Military Transport Aircraft*

Aircraft	Inventory	Range with maximum payload (nautical miles)	Maximum payload (tons)	Troops	Paratroopers
AN-12 (Cub)	500	750	22	90	60
AN-22 (Cock)	50	2,260	88	175	175
IL-76 (Candid)	130	2,850	44	140	140

Source: Dennis M. Gormley, "The Direction and Pace of Soviet Force Projection Capabilities," *Survival*, vol. 24 (November–December 1982), p. 272.

they flesh out. If the unexpected opposition of Afghanistan's rebels makes the Soviets more cautious in the future, even a month may be a conservative estimate.

Soviet airborne divisions are smaller in size than regular units—about 8,500 soldiers as opposed to 12,000 soldiers in a motorized rifle division—but they have a surprising amount of firepower for air-delivered forces and are fully combat ready. Although they are deployed all around the Soviet Union, these units are centrally controlled from Moscow and constitute the core of Soviet force projection capabilities. They have been among the lead elements of virtually every Soviet military action in the postwar era. There are eight airborne divisions in all; one is a training unit and one is in Afghanistan, leaving six currently available for rapid deployment.

Aircraft available for lifting airborne units are outlined in table 2-2. These could be supplemented by mobilizing Aeroflot, the Soviet civil air fleet. Ultimately, however, the reach and speed of deployment of these units are a matter of receiving airfields, en route transit points, and the absence or presence of opposition, either on the ground or in the air.[11] But the range and payloads shown in table 2-2 suggest that, in theory at least, Soviet airborne forces can reach virtually any important point around the Gulf.

Soviet ground forces in the southern area (including Afghanistan) are supported by about 845 aircraft of all types, along with 400 helicopters.[12] The quality of aircraft and airfields apparently has improved since 1979, with an increasing number of SU-24 (Fencer) deep-strike aircraft replac-

11. See the excellent discussion in Kenneth Allard, "Soviet Airborne Forces and Preemptive Power Projection," *Parameters*, vol. 10 (December 1980), pp. 45–48.
12. Department of Defense, *Soviet Military Power*, p. 50.

Table 2-3. *Soviet Air Power: Missions and Capabilities*

Aircraft	Mission	Combat radius (miles)	Ordnance load (tons)
MIG-23 Flogger B	Air combat	525	2.2
MIG-27 Flogger D	Ground attack/strike	600	2.2
SU-17 Fitter C	Ground attack/strike	600[a]	3.0
MIG-21 Fishbed J	Air combat	400	1.0
SU-24 Fencer	Ground attack/strike	970[b]	2.2
TU-26 Backfire	Interdiction (medium bomber)	1,900[c]	10.0

Source: Robert P. Berman, *Soviet Air Power in Transition* (Brookings Institution, 1978), pp. 26, 32; and *Jane's All the World's Aircraft, 1983–84* (London: Jane's Publishing Co., 1983), pp. 233, 240.

a. *Jane's* posits a radius of 195 miles for low-low-low mission profile, 340 miles for high-low-high (p. 233).

b. As given in *Jane's*, p. 233, for a high-low-high mission profile carrying two external tanks. *Jane's* posits a 200-mile radius for low-low-low profile.

c. For high-low-high flight profile. Berman (p. 26) notes radius of 900 miles for low-low-low profile, and a maximum radius at high altitude of 2,750 miles. *Jane's* cites a maximum unrefueled combat radius of 2,950 miles (p. 240).

ing older air defense regiments. Some of these aircraft are currently in Afghanistan, but presumably all could be made available for operations against Iran. Within the limits of available support facilities still more aircraft could be transferred to the southern military districts, if required, from other areas of the Soviet Union.

The missions and capabilities of major Soviet fighter and attack aircraft are outlined in table 2-3. The radii of these aircraft are critical but vary substantially with mission profile. Although the Fencer's combat radius is listed nominally as about 800 miles, *Jane's* lists its radius in the "lo-lo-lo" mission—the most demanding profile, flown completely at low altitude—as only 200 miles.[13] This makes Soviet strike coverage very much a function of the opposition they meet, their planning a function of the opposition they *expect* to meet.

Fighter aircraft that engage in combat maneuvering will experience a similar decline in range. The radii of Soviet fighter aircraft, which are usually controlled by ground radar that guides them like missiles to their targets, are likely to be constrained as well by the deleterious effects of mountainous terrain on their ground radars.

Figure 2-1 illustrates the coverage of the principal Soviet interdiction and fighter aircraft, the SU-24 Fencer and MIG-23, respectively, flying from bases at Kirovabad and Ashkhabad, and from Shindand in Afghanistan. Fencers can reach the north end of the Gulf, but only by flying

13. *Jane's All the World's Aircraft, 1983–84* (London: Jane's Publishing Co., 1983), p. 233.

Figure 2-1. *Estimated Maximum Radii, Selected Soviet Aircraft*

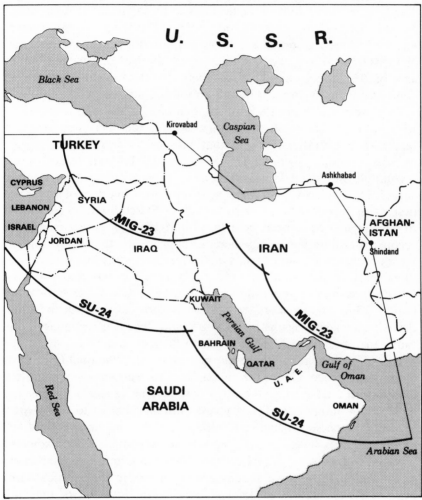

an almost ideal flight profile and leaving fighters behind. Forced by hostile air defenses to fly more demanding flight profiles, Soviet aircraft would probably not be able to cover the Gulf at all. Thus any Soviet move to the north end of the Gulf would probably require a shift of aircraft, base support, and petroleum, oil, and lubricants (POL) into Iran itself.

Soviet naval deployments to the Indian Ocean grew substantially just after the revolution in Iran, then fell to just below thirty ships in 1981.[14] The fleet enjoys main docking facilities in Ethiopia and at Aden in the People's Democratic Republic of Yemen (PDRY). On occasion naval forces have been accompanied by an amphibious transport vessel and about 400 naval infantry. The latter forces are part of a naval infantry arm of the Soviet navy totaling about 16,000 soldiers split among deployments to the Soviet Union's various coastal areas.

The forces just listed are formidable in broad outline in comparison with local or U.S. rapid deployment forces. But their structure and readiness levels do not suggest that Moscow is preparing to initiate aggressive military action. The Soviet naval buildup trailed Iran's revolution and the U.S. naval buildup in the Indian Ocean, more suggestive of Moscow's concern for its southern flank than of aggressive designs on the interests of Iran or the United States. Soviet deployments to Afghanistan have been held to around 105,000, barely enough to accomplish military missions there, let alone secure the area to support force projection south or west. Finally, the continuing low readiness of most units in the southern military districts suggests that this area remains less important in military terms than Europe or the Sino-Soviet border. Thus far, in short, Soviet forces seem to be structured and deployed to hedge against uncertainty and defend a secondary flank rather than to impose Moscow's will on the situation.

It is difficult to predict whether or how quickly the quality of these forces will change. Given the similarities between terrain in northern Iran and in Afghanistan, the Soviets should be expected to alter the structure of units in the Transcaucasus military district to accord with lessons learned in Afghanistan, although this need not substantially affect readiness levels. At the very least, weapons will probably be replaced with newer models in accord with standard Soviet modernization policies. There have already been exercises in the Transcaucasus area, some apparently suggesting plans for an invasion of the Gulf

14. The buildup from eighteen to twenty ships in December 1979 to more than thirty ships by February 1980, "may have been partly defensive, for it followed shortly on the heels of the American deployment of two, and sometimes three, carrier battle groups in the Indian Ocean. . . . [T]he Soviets also may have wanted to insure that they had sufficient forces to take advantage of any opportunity to show themselves friends of the Khomeini regime." Donald C. Daniel, "The Navy," in David R. Jones, ed., *Soviet Armed Forces Review Annual*, vol. 5: *1981* (Gulf Breeze, Florida: Academic International Press, 1981), p. 145.

region, though these exercises appear to have involved command and control more than troops themselves.[15]

It is even more difficult to know whether the priority of Iran in Soviet security policies will change, or whether in fact it has changed. While the Soviets have learned much about mountain fighting in Afghanistan, it hardly follows that they are eager to do more of it in Iran. Indeed, the brutality and indecisiveness of fighting in Afghanistan must surely make the Soviets all the more wary of intruding into the states along their southern border without first seeking to co-opt the population of the area they wish to occupy. It is worth remembering that the substantial expertise in jungle warfare that U.S. forces acquired during their years in Vietnam hardly increased their desire to apply those skills elsewhere.

Concern about turbulence in Iran or a desire to exploit the West's dependence on oil may prompt the Soviets to bolster the quality of units deployed along their southern flank, as a precursor to using force more aggressively in the Gulf region than they have in the past. Conversely, if Moscow senses the emergence of a clear military threat to its south, it will take steps to improve its military capabilities in the area. In either case the result will be the same—a more serious Soviet military threat to the Gulf. In the case of a perceived threat to the Soviets' southern border, the quality of their forces is likely to be determined as much by U.S. action as by Soviet initiative.

From Capabilities to Threats

The forces described give the Soviets the capability to do virtually all that has been ascribed to them. They could put small airborne deployments at key points around the Gulf and follow up with more units and support. Soviet naval infantry could be deployed in similar fashion to points along the region's shoreline. Backfire bombers could destroy oil facilities or threaten tanker traffic in the Strait of Hormuz and U.S. naval forces in the Indian Ocean. Finally, main force Soviet units could march

15. See Jack Anderson, "Iran Brought Superpowers Close to Blows," *Washington Post,* June 28, 1983. Lieutenant General Robert C. Kingston, commander of the U.S. Central Command, later confirmed that Soviet activities in August 1980 raised fear in Washington of an imminent Soviet invasion of Iran. See the interview with him by Benjamin F. Schemmer in *Armed Forces Journal International,* vol. 121 (July 1984), p. 68.

toward the Gulf from positions east or west of the Caspian as well as from Afghanistan, assuming that the units had time to mobilize.

Some of these threats make little sense. Disrupting oil traffic or destroying Gulf oil facilities might be useful in the context of a major conventional war with the West, but it would be senselessly provocative in lesser circumstances. The Soviet navy could harass U.S. naval operations in the area, and it could support offensive Soviet actions emanating from Soviet territory. The navy is not of a size or structure to carry out offensive missions independently. Soviet naval infantry has been structured for use in tactical situations close to the Soviet periphery, and events since 1979 have not produced fundamental changes in this structure. While naval infantry could respond to an invitation or show the flag, more aggressive actions would require more and larger ships, more support, and more naval infantry than the Soviets now have.[16] Soviet interest in amphibious warfare has grown and may yet produce these things. But for the foreseeable future Soviet airborne units are far more likely than naval infantry to be used to respond to events around the Gulf.

By contrast, the Soviet airborne threat deserves attention. In Angola (1975) and Ethiopia (1978) the Soviets demonstrated an impressive ability to sustain a massive airlift of weaponry to distant areas when their help had been requested, and when a U.S. response could be discounted. Similar circumstances around the Persian Gulf would present even less challenge to Soviet capabilities, given the Gulf's proximity.

Should the Soviets face enemy countermoves—either U.S. or local—airborne operations would become much more risky and difficult. They would unfold outside Soviet air cover unless and until the Soviets moved aircraft and their support south. But this would require airlift, lowering the number of air transports available for airborne units, and slowing the troop buildup on the objective. The possibility of a U.S. response would probably make Moscow reluctant to commit all or even most of its airborne units to a single theater, especially the Gulf, since these elite units have important roles to play in Europe. Similar considerations might lead the Soviets to withhold some of their airlift. Thus,

---

16. Dennis M. Gormley notes that the Soviet Union's "lack of large-deck aircraft carriers and sufficient strategic amphibious assault forces" prevents her from projecting naval power ashore. See his "The Direction and Pace of Soviet Force Projection Capabilities," *Survival*, vol. 24 (November–December 1982), p. 268.

under conditions of substantial risk in the Gulf, it is unlikely that the full weight of the airborne threat, in units or deployment rate, would be available.

Even local air defenses could threaten the initial waves of the assault, and local forces could threaten initial troop deployments. U.S. air defense capabilities along the path of delivery could do the same thing, while adding a considerable risk of escalation. If such a rapidly deployable U.S. capability existed, then the Soviet airborne threat would be less a matter of capabilities than of nerve and resolve. This aspect of the issue is aptly captured in the adage that getting a battalion to the Gulf first is better than getting a division there second.

It is unlikely that the Soviets would try to sustain an offensive airborne operation solely by air. They would have to reach out to the airhead with ground forces, in which case their assessment of the airborne operation would depend on their assessment of the overland attack linking them to it. That raises the main force invasion not only as a threat in its own right, but also as crucial to other actions, especially airborne force projection.

The main force threat, whether launched from west of the Caspian or, after pacification and a force buildup, from Afghanistan, would also run the risk of a U.S. response. Operationally, however, the main force invasion would not be as tenuous and vulnerable as airborne force projection. Indeed, such operations would begin from the homeland itself, or from extensions of it, and would draw on the full range of the Soviet Union's ponderous conventional force posture. How would Soviet commanders see their prospects in Iran? How quickly could they expect to move south toward the Gulf? What could go wrong? There are no precise answers to these questions, but rough estimates can be made by examining Soviet doctrine—what they would want to do—and by studying the operational environment in Iran.

The Invasion Threat: Doctrine

The Soviets have presumably learned much about mountain warfare from fighting in Afghanistan. Many of these lessons seem to have challenged their doctrinal and organizational tenets, notably their tendency to centralize planning and command at fairly high levels. We should expect to see these lessons applied to units in the southern military districts, especially the North Caucasus and Transcaucasus military districts, which face extremely rugged terrain in Iran. Still, Afghanistan has principally been an exercise in area control, not an invasion. Search-and-destroy techniques developed there might be useful in the wake of a Soviet invasion of Iran, but such techniques would hardly serve to spearhead an invasion, especially if the expected enemy were the United States. Thus the basic doctrinal tenets that have been developing since well before the Soviets moved into Afghanistan are likely to be the prevailing ones for a march into Iran.

Soviet doctrine ascribes great importance to surprise, and the Soviets may go to some lengths to achieve it. But there are limits to how far they can go in this direction. Doctrine provides the basis for organizational routines and training patterns and thus constrains the ability of large military organizations to change, especially in a hurry. These constraints are likely to be still more pronounced when doctrine is reified in the structure and capabilities of military organizations. This is true with the more important tenets of Soviet tactical doctrine.

That doctrine stresses massing fires to break through enemy resistance and thereafter moving at unprecedented speeds toward objectives and victory. This thrust is clearly visible in the high firepower and mobility of Soviet tactical units. Logistical support is pushed down from higher units to allow Soviet divisions to concentrate on the battle alone. Although Soviet logistical support has grown over the past decade, it remains light compared with U.S. Army units. In any case, many of the logistics improvements applied to Soviet forces in Europe have yet to work their way into those forces in the southern military districts. Thus, speedy victory tends to be required; Soviet divisions are not well structured to accommodate much sacrifice of doctrine in this area.[17]

The doctrinal demand for massed fire and rapid advance is also

17. The validity of Soviet doctrine on logistics appears to be a matter of faith with the Soviets, as well as with Western observers who envy the Red Army its lean, high-firepower divisions. The system did not work well during the invasion of Czechoslovakia, even though this operation was unopposed; Soviet divisions were left without many basic supplies on the third day of the occupation. That experience probably prompted the Soviets to focus more attention on logistics in the years since, especially in the latter half of the 1970s. Whether or not the additional attention has improved performance, however, remains a moot point; some reports indicate that serious logistical problems hamper operations in Afghanistan today. On the Czechoslovakian operation, see Leo Heiman, "Soviet Invasion Weaknesses," *Military Review,* vol. 49 (August 1969), pp. 38–45. On Afghanistan, see David R. Griffiths, "Afghan Problems Stall Soviets," *Aviation Week & Space Technology,* vol. 112 (April 21, 1980), pp. 18–19.

evident at levels above the division. The Soviet Combined Arms Army, and the important role given the combined arms concept in Soviet military thought, bear witness to the Soviet effort to confront enemy forces with the combined firepower of all arms. Air armies of Soviet Frontal Aviation, the Soviet air component that would support an invasion, are controlled by military district commanders. Ground attack aircraft reinforce the firepower of ground units, while fighter aircraft reinforce the Soviet army's well-developed ground air defense assets in seeking to insure air superiority over the battlefield.

This last point receives special emphasis in Soviet doctrine. Although the presence of air defense assets in Soviet ground forces may free Frontal Aviation aircraft for independent missions, the primary independent mission is likely to be the destruction of enemy aircraft on the ground.[18] Whatever the circumstances, Soviet doctrine demands the achievement of air superiority. The use of airborne units in advance of invading forces, for example, is contingent on the assumption of Soviet air superiority.[19] Without it the Soviets' willingness to encircle enemy forces or secure key assets declines, as do the speed and surprise of the overall operation.

Another doctrinal tenet around which unit structure and technologies revolve is the emphasis on centralized control in the hands of army commanders. This emphasis is embedded, first, in the routines of the organization. The army commander's plans tend to govern actions of lower level subordinates, leaving them little room for initiative.[20] Requests for close air support must rise through the chain of command and then over to Frontal Aviation units before being effected, leaving little room for altering air support plans as combat ebbs and flows.[21] The tenet is also embedded in unit rank structure. Soviet battalion commanders tend to be of lower rank than their U.S. counterparts, reflecting a lesser

18. Robert P. Berman, *Soviet Air Power in Transition* (Brookings Institution, 1978), p. 57.

19. See the essays by Peter Vigor, "The 'Forward Reach' of the Soviet Armed Forces: Seaborne and Airborne Landings," and John Hemsley, "The Soviet Ground Forces," in John Erickson and E. J. Feuchtwanger, eds., *Soviet Military Power and Performance* (Hamden, Conn.: Shoe String Press, 1979).

20. See Hemsley, "Soviet Ground Forces," p. 70; and C. N. Donnelly, "Tactical Problems Facing the Soviet Army," *International Defense Review,* vol. 11, no. 9 (1978), p. 1410.

21. Berman, *Soviet Air Power in Transition,* p. 10.

degree of reliance on their independent initiative.[22] Finally, centralization is reflected in the technology of Soviet weaponry. Soviet fighter
aircraft, for example, are controlled by ground radar, leaving the pilot
with little independence.[23]

The Invasion Threat: Operational Environment

The Soviets must project their forces, whether out of their southern
military districts or Afghanistan, into some of the most rugged terrain in
the world. Mountains stretch from the "Armenian Knot" of mountains
in Iran's northwest corner, through the sharply etched Elburz to the
Zagros, which run down Iran's western edge to the Strait of Hormuz,
leaving only a small plain around the oil region at Abadan.[24] To the east
of the Caspian, the Golul and Koppeh Dagh rise as high as 12,000 feet
but generally are narrower and less rugged than other Iranian ranges
(figure 2-2).

Weather in these ranges is "intolerably hot and arid in summer and
bitterly cold in winter—possibly with the most extreme climate of any
part of the world."[25] Rainfall in these ranges runs eight inches to twenty
inches per year, with rain falling earlier further south; where in the north
March is the month of heaviest rain, closer to the Persian Gulf precipitation peaks in December and January. This level of precipitation has over
the years created rivers that often cut east to west in a transverse pattern
that makes them a real hindrance to travel.

Soviet ground forces moving out of Afghanistan would face fundamentally different terrain and weather conditions in Iran. Still, although
flat in comparison with Iran's mountains in the north, the plateau
country of central and southeastern Iran is marked by large boulders,
knife-like ravines, and lines of low mountains rising 3,000 feet to 5,000

22. On this point see Peter W. Vigor and Christopher Donneliy, "The Manchurian
Campaign and Its Relevance to Modern Strategy," *Comparative Strategy,* vol. 2, no. 2
(1980), pp. 159–78.

23. Berman, *Soviet Air Power in Transition,* p. 9.

24. Information in this section is taken mainly from four sources: W. B. Fisher, *The
Middle East: A Physical, Social, and Regional Geography* (London: Methuen, 1950); W. B.
Fisher, ed., *The Cambridge History of Iran,* vol. 1: *The Land of Iran* (Cambridge
University Press, 1968); Peter Mansfield, ed., *The Middle East: A Political and Economic
Survey,* 4th ed. (Oxford University Press, 1973); and Harvey H. Smith and others, *Area
Handbook for Iran* (GPO, 1971).

25. Fisher, *Middle East,* p. 258.

Figure 2-2. *Iran*

feet above the surrounding plateau. Temperatures are extreme, reaching 130°F in summer. The so-called wind of 120 days blows continuously in this province from May to September, often reaching speeds of seventy miles per hour, and driving dust and gravel before it with "tremendous destructive force."[26]

Few paved, two-lane roads connect Iran with the Soviet Union, although a reasonably good network connects west and east with Tehran, and two paved roads head south from the Armenian Knot to the oil area of Khuzistan. These roads twist along the edges of mountains, often leaving even the improved roads without shoulders. Unpaved roads are

26. Smith and others, *Area Handbook for Iran*, p. 19.

often cut by landslides and swollen rivers and streams; many of the unimproved roads may be impassable from November through May. One road connects Afghanistan with Iran through Saranj, but this road is undeveloped and without infrastructure.

Iran is liberally sprinkled with airfields that can accept major Soviet transport aircraft. Most of these are unimproved, however. The few rail lines running north to south are often carved, like the roads, into the mountains. Though of obvious strategic value to a Soviet invading force, the Soviet and Iranian portions of this line differ in width, requiring a switch of trains at the border town of Jolfi.

Finally, of potential strategic significance from a logistics point of view is the oil infrastructure on the western side of Iran. Two oil refineries are located along the route south from the Transcaucasus military district. One at Tabriz has a capacity to refine 80,000 barrels of oil daily, while a smaller one capable of handling 18,000 barrels a day is in Kermanshah. One would expect each to have storage facilities nearby, presenting an invading (or a resisting) force with the opportunity to ease its logistical problems by acquiring POL on the move.

The Invasion Threat: The Mountain Campaign

That rugged terrain is not kind to Soviet doctrine or equipment has been made plain in Afghanistan. Moving into Iran would present an even greater problem. Rather than operating concentrically from fixed bases, Soviet units would be pushing forward into new territory. The effects of this would be especially visible in four areas: the effort to mass fires, the effort to move rapidly, the need to centralize control, and the need to resupply the operation.

Soviet commanders would find it difficult to mass fires on narrow mountain roads that string out advancing forces. The Soviets would have to spread artillery, air defense, and support units throughout their advancing columns, in units small enough and spread thinly enough to provide effective fire and support to any point on the line that comes under attack. Mountains constrain the effectiveness of some systems and encourage the use of others but overall would probably diminish the firepower the Soviets could bring to bear. Soviet tanks would lack wide fields of fire.

Mountainous terrain would restrict the capabilities of fixed-wing, high-speed close air support aircraft, forcing the Soviets to rely more heavily on helicopters for close air support.[27] The effectiveness of Soviet ground-based air defense systems and fighter aircraft, both of which are radar directed, would suffer.[28] The Soviets might compensate by taking (probably with heliborne assault forces) key high ground as they advance, for use as surface-to-air missile (SAM) and ground control radar sites. But for air defense weapons like the ZSU-23/4, this would not be an option; the Soviets would have to assume reduced effectiveness for these systems in the more rugged mountain areas.

The Soviets realize that mountain operations are not likely to achieve the high rates of advance that their doctrine calls for on flat terrain. "The normal speed of a vehicle column in low mountain or hilly areas will fall to 18–20 km/h," Christopher Donnelly notes in his assessment of Soviet mountain doctrine, "and the daily rate of advance may be halved. The effect of poor weather . . . will slow down a column to 5–8 km/h in hilly country."[29] Technical problems with weapon systems may slow it still further.[30] On many of Iran's one-lane unpaved tracks, vehicles with thrown tracks cannot be moved to the shoulder for repair. In emergencies, downed vehicles can be pushed off the road and forgotten. Otherwise, their repair will slow the entire column. Opposition, whether air interdiction or resistance on the ground, would also lower the overall rate of advance.

Still, the Soviets would try to maintain a relatively fast pace, and can shape their operations in various ways to achieve that end. First, if the Soviets are in a position to choose the season of their attack they would probably choose late spring, after winter snows have melted and run off,

27. For problems with close air support in Afghanistan, see Griffiths, "Afghan Problems Stall Soviets," pp. 18–19. See also Graham H. Turbiville, Jr., "The Attack Helicopter's Growing Role in Russian Combat Doctrine," *Army,* vol. 27 (December 1977), p. 30; and C. N. Donnelly, "Soviet Mountain Warfare Operations," *International Defense Review,* vol. 13, no. 6 (1980), pp. 829, 833.

28. Donnelly, "Soviet Mountain Warfare Operations," pp. 829–32.

29. Ibid., p. 828.

30. Ibid., p. 827. Donnelly notes that Soviet T-55 and T-62 tanks "experience frequent clutch problems in hilly terrain; are subject to track casting on rocky ground; and overheat readily occasioning unpopular delays." Douglas M. Hart notes that "BMPs [Soviet infantry fighting vehicles] are often employed on mountain trails barely capable of supporting these vehicles. Breakdowns are frequent, and crews have been criticized for poor preventive maintenance and their inability to repair vehicles on the march. BMP exhaust is more observable in the mountains, because the altitude causes overenrichment of the fuel mixture." See his "Low-intensity Conflict in Afghanistan: The Soviet View," *Survival,* vol. 24 (March–April 1982), p. 62.

or early fall, after the hottest part of summer but well in advance of the winter snow. If the Soviets do not expect quick victory, late spring may be the only appropriate time to begin operations.

Second, the Soviets would try to stay on major roadways.[31] If the advance were unopposed, as it was in Afghanistan, their columns would move over the best paved roads available. Where the Soviets expect or receive ground opposition, they would spread their columns over a wider front, using secondary and less developed roads to allow simultaneous approaches to enemy positions from several directions.[32] Spreading the advance over a wider front would also complicate the problem of air interdiction. Even paved roads, however, may not remain paved as operations progress; Soviet tanks shredded many paved roads during the invasion of Czechoslovakia.[33] Although a similar decay in Iran's paved road network might not slow the initial Soviet assault, it might severely hamper resupply.

Third, the Soviets would try to move during daylight whenever possible. This will be especially true if they expect to meet resistance on the ground.[34] If the major threat is air interdiction, possibly the best defensive tactic is to move at night and accept a slower but safer advance as the lesser of two evils. Meeting both air and ground opposition will present Soviet commanders with a quandary that they must settle on the basis of experience and immediate needs.

Finally, the Soviets are likely to run advance detachments of regimental size up to a day's march ahead of their main columns in an effort to dispose of ground resistance in advance of their main task force. This practice helped speed the Red Army's advance on the Trans-Baikal front

31. Donnelly, "Soviet Mountain Warfare Operations," p. 828.

32. Ibid., p. 830. Iran's mountains seem to be crossed by many unpaved tracks that might permit multiple approaches. See *Paiforce: The Official Story of the Persian and Iraq Command, 1941–46* (London: His Majesty's Stationery Office, 1948), chap. 13, especially the map on p. 68. The British called these tracks "motorable" but were referring to the light vehicles organic to mountain infantry units. Soviet armored vehicles are likely to be too heavy for such tracks. Light infantry would be able to exploit them, but at a much slower pace than that called for in Soviet doctrine. In any case, as Douglas M. Hart notes, the need to adopt "look-move-look" tactics against Afghani rebels has slowed the pace of Soviet movement in that conflict substantially. See his "Low-intensity Conflict in Afghanistan," p. 63.

33. Heiman, "Soviet Invasion Weaknesses," p. 41.

34. As Donnelly puts it, "Major night marches are considered to be unlikely, therefore, in any mountainous or hilly area where a meeting with the enemy may occur." See his "Soviet Mountain Warfare Operations," p. 830.

during its successful Manchurian campaign in the final months of World War II.[35] A modern equivalent would probably employ helicopter assets for mobility and close air support, tactics widely used in Afghanistan.

Mention of advance units raises the question of how Soviet airborne units might be used. If the Soviets expect to advance with minimal resistance and under their own air cover, one would expect to see airborne units used as they were in Czechoslovakia and Afghanistan, air landed in the capital and at other key airfields and facilities. Lacking air superiority, however, the Soviets would probably be more conservative with these units, using them in the advance but much closer to main forces. A landing at Tabriz to secure the airfield and possibly the oil facilities there is possible in any case, given the proximity of this city to the Soviet border. Beyond that, airborne advances are likely to go no further than a day's march ahead of the main attack and will be designed to deal in advance with pockets of enemy resistance. For these missions airborne troops may move by helicopter or in their organic ground vehicles.

Even unopposed mountain operations are likely to challenge the Soviet requirement for centralized control. Such problems are multiplied by the presence of opposition. To meet ground resistance the Soviets would spread advancing units over several roads and tracks, thereby increasing both the breadth of their control problem and the risk that units will become isolated, lost, or stalled. If the threat of air interdiction forces the Soviets to move at night *and* spread the assault, everything gets worse. Using helicopters for command and control may alleviate some of these difficulties. But to the extent that centralized control is built into Soviet routines and systems, to the extent that it may be a cultural as well as an organizational phenomenon,[36] command and control problems may remain an intrinsic difficulty to Soviet units operating in mountainous terrain, producing slower, less coherent, and more vulnerable operations than those envisioned in Soviet doctrine.

The problems of resupply in the mountains are readily apparent. Iran's narrow roads will not support two lanes of traffic. Even two-lane

35. See Col. Z. Shutov, "In Deserts and Mountains," *Soviet Military Review*, no. 11 (November 1980), pp. 41–43.
36. "One of the main problems is the Russians' tendency to sit and do nothing until an order is given. Making preparations in anticipation of an order so as to speed up its implementation is just not generally done." Donnelly, "Tactical Problems Facing the Soviet Army," p. 1410.

paved roads without shoulders might not support two lanes when one consists of tanks and other wide vehicles. If trucks constitute the major resupply vehicle, they would not be able to move to the front of a Soviet advance unless the column closes and consolidates on some objective and awaits the resupply convoy. Pipelines for fuel can be laid with remarkable speed, but these would take up a portion of the roadway and are likely to give rise to queuing problems if refueling is to take place on the road itself rather than at a major base camp. Resupply would be difficult if not impossible on the move; it would require forces to halt and consolidate.

Because any such halt is going to create vulnerabilities, especially for interdiction bombers, and provide time for enemy forces to dig in and position themselves to meet further Soviet advances, it is in the Soviets' best interests to avoid resupply for as long as possible. They can avoid stops by carrying as many supplies as possible. What they carry, and how far they travel with supplies, depends primarily on whether they expect and meet enemy opposition.

If the Soviets expect no resistance they can carry a basic load of ammunition, pick up food and water as they advance, and use most of their organic transport to carry POL. In the western side of Iran they may also be able to secure POL as they advance by using refinery facilities at Tabriz and Kermanshah. They could run small airborne and engineering units to those refineries to prepare the way in advance of the main column. Optimally, this kind of an advance is nothing but a road march and can move slowly but surely toward its objectives.

If the Soviets expect resistance, especially ground resistance, they will have to trade POL capacity for more ammunition in their initial supplies. If they meet resistance, fuel consumption will rise as vehicles in the rear idle at the halt while vehicles at the front try to maneuver against enemy forces. Overall fuel consumption increases as other weapon systems are brought into play. Helicopter gunships, for example, are likely to require local refueling, placing an additional burden on POL trains. If ground operations move beyond the range of home-based Soviet aircraft, a major need for POL, ammunition, and spare parts arises as tactical air units move south into Iran itself to support further operations.

The resupply problem can be mitigated, even under duress. Iran's oil infrastructure takes on enormous importance under these conditions, both to the Soviets, who could use it for resupply, and to the opposition, who can easily destroy it, or capture facilities and use them. Because the Tabriz refinery is close to the Soviet Union, the Soviets may risk an airborne operation to capture it. By the same token, however, that refinery is not likely to be of much help once Soviet operations move farther south. The refinery at Kermanshah is too far for airborne operations unless the Soviets are certain of only light resistance.

The simplest way to alleviate the resupply problem, however, would be to limit objectives. Estimates place the range of Soviet T-72 and T-62 tanks on a single tank of fuel at about 300 miles;[37] in mountainous terrain this would probably drop to about 200 miles, and in the presence of enemy resistance the range would drop still further. If supply vehicles organic to the advancing column can carry one full refill for all vehicles, then the column can go about 400 miles. These are rough calculations, but they suggest that the oft-mentioned Soviet move into Azerbaijan and Kurdistan would probably not be hampered by the need for major resupply unless strong resistance were met soon after the Soviet advance entered Iran.

If a combination of Soviet ambition and strong resistance made it impossible to avoid resupply, the Soviets would probably have to sacrifice the blitzkrieg-like race to the final objective demanded by their doctrine. Instead the Soviets would have to mount a campaign of discrete steps to intermediate objectives, with major halts at each step for the construction and stocking of logistics depots and possibly air bases. Each depot would have to be secured before the main assault elements moved on to the next objective. The distance between intermediate objectives, and the size and composition of the security forces required to protect each depot, would be determined by the nature of enemy resistance. This rough assessment suggests that the Soviets could not race to Abadan, nor could they support more than a few operating divisions in their final assault.

The Invasion Threat: The Potential of Afghanistan

A variety of Soviet operations out of Afghanistan can be imagined. A Soviet armored thrust across the southeastern part of Iran might at least resemble the race that their doctrine calls for. Soviet forces would have

37. Taken from *The Soviet War Machine* (London: Hamlyn, 1977), p. 178.

more room here than in Iran's mountains to flank enemy ground
resistance and to bring the full force of their weaponry to bear in front of
their advance. At the very least, a Soviet move toward the Strait of
Hormuz might constitute an important component of a Soviet invasion
of Iran, since forces lodged on the strait would be in a position to
interdict the shipment of U.S. forces and supplies to the Gulf. Soviet
operations into southern Pakistan might stem from political decay or
turbulence within Pakistan itself. Given the presence of growing numbers of Afghani refugees in Pakistan and the prevalence of separatist
elements among the Baluch, it is easy to see that the Soviets could be
presented with opportunities they may be reluctant to ignore.[38]

Military operations south out of Afghanistan would unfold much
closer to U.S. air power, namely carrier-based air, than operations into
northern Iran. U.S. Marines would have fairly easy access to objectives
along the Indian Ocean littoral. Thus in contemplating such action the
Soviets would have to be willing either to discount the possibility of a
U.S. response—to assume, in short, that a preemptive move on their
part would effectively deter U.S. counteraction—or to accept the risk of
a direct clash with U.S. forces.

These operations would also be strained logistically, owing primarily
to the distances involved. The Soviets might try to stock spares and
ammunition in Afghanistan, though Afghanistan is likely to remain an
insecure rear area for some time to come. But over the long haul
operations out of Afghanistan would have to be supported out of the
Soviet Union itself, and in particular out of the Soviet Union's central
military districts. Seen from this perspective, such operations would be
supplied along two long lines, one swinging east from around Moscow to
Afghanistan and then south toward the Indian Ocean, the other reaching
west from points along the Sino-Soviet border and then south again
toward the Gulf.

Thus, despite Afghanistan's proximity to the Strait of Hormuz and the

38. Significantly, the Soviets have not tried in recent years to provoke minority groups
in either Iran or Pakistan. Instead, "the Soviets have been cool toward Arab, Turkmen, and
Baluch nationalists, linking them with American and monarchist conspiracies and other
pejorative labels, including feudal reactionaries and Afghan drug smugglers." See Muriel
Atkin, "The Islamic Republic and the Soviet Union, " p. 145. See also Alvin Z. Rubinstein,
Soviet Policy toward Turkey, Iran, and Afghanistan, p. 115. This does not mean the Soviet
policy could not change, however, or that minorities within either country could not break
with central authorities without Soviet help.

Indian Ocean, military operations out of that country might not appear to be as attractive to Moscow as operations out of the Soviet Union itself into northern Iran. If opportunity knocked in Pakistan, the Soviets would have no choice but to consider the risks, costs, and potential benefits of military action there. But if the goal were to exploit turbulence in Iran, to acquire a buffer off their southern border, or to acquire some influence over the flow and price of oil from the Gulf, Soviet commanders would have greater leeway in which to shape their operations. In these circumstances the Soviets would probably prefer to avoid the risks of a U.S.-Soviet clash, as well as the logistical problems of moving out of Afghanistan, if these could be avoided. Afghanistan thus appears to offer only limited potential for operations into Iran and risky, though perhaps tempting, possibilities for operations into Pakistan.

Conclusions

The low readiness of ground forces in the Soviet Union's southern military districts and the reactive mode of the Soviet naval buildup in the Indian Ocean suggest that Moscow's interest in its southern flank thus far has not been driven primarily by lust for control of the Gulf's oil. Rather a prudent concern for the area's turbulence and possible U.S. buildup there motivates the Soviets. Nothing in their present force posture suggests that they are poised to impose their will on the area. Rather, the Soviets are best prepared to respond to opportunities, which they have done in the past in other parts of the world, but only when they expected no opposition.

Soviet capabilities do not rule out offensive military action around the Gulf. Although the potential military power the Soviets could wield to their south is impressive in theory, in reality Soviet commanders are probably more impressed with the constraints they face. Soviet forces themselves are the first constraint. Soviet divisions above Iran are generally low-grade and light on logistics. Soviet air cover falls short of the Gulf, shorter still if the limits imposed by Soviet ground control radar and the need to maneuver in the face of an enemy air threat are considered. And Soviet tanks and personnel carriers have a poor record for reliability in rugged terrain. Iran's terrain is a second constraint—the rugged mountains, limited network of narrow roads, and extremes of weather pose serious obstacles. Combined, these two sets of constraints offer opposing forces a high degree of leverage over Soviet operations, whether air, ground, or both.

If the Soviets nonetheless consider military action, they face incentives to be content with less ambitious goals than taking all of Iran. A move into the northwestern portion of Iran could be mounted with considerably less time for mobilization, could be resupplied from bases in the USSR itself, and could be covered by aircraft based in the Soviet Union. Even strong local opposition would have difficulty stopping this attack, although the opposition could tie down occupying units. Unlike operations out of Afghanistan, should these become possible, the attack into northwestern Iran would unfold far from the principal locus of U.S. power in the area, which is U.S. carriers in the Indian Ocean. Historic precedent for such a move does exist in the 1946 invasion, and political rationale can be drawn from the 1921 Soviet-Iranian treaty, parts of which the Soviets refuse to renounce despite Iran's having done so.

Although limited in scope, such an operation appears to have genuine value to the kind of goals Moscow might pursue to its south. Defensively, limited operations in northern Iran would open a buffer area along Moscow's southern flank. By bringing Soviet forces into the most populous area of Iran and by placing them next to Iraq, Moscow could probably bring both countries under greater Soviet influence. The Soviet air umbrella would extend over the northern Gulf, complicating U.S. military operations into the area. Offensively, a limited move to the south could represent the first step in Soviet operations aimed at the Gulf. Soviet divisions would move past the first hurdle of mountains in Iran and bring logistical and air cover into position for another step at another time. The weight of Soviet power thus would fall more heavily on all the Gulf states, putting the states in the uncomfortable position of having to choose between greater accommodation with Moscow or closer relations with the United States. The Arab states have sound political reasons for keeping both superpowers at arm's length; a Soviet move into northern Iran would limit their ability to do so.

There has been too facile a tendency in the United States to connect U.S. interests in oil to oil wells as military objectives. A short Soviet jump into northwestern Iran could leave oil wells unmolested, but it would surely extend Soviet influence over the flow of oil. For this reason, and because such an operation would be both easier for the Soviets to mount and more difficult for the United States to stop, the limited invasion represents the most realistic worst case scenario on which to base U.S. military planning.

CHAPTER THREE

Toward a U.S. Strategy and Force Posture

IF THE SOVIETS do not have to capture oil wells to acquire influence, or the appearance of influence, over the flow and price of oil, then the United States should think about the security of its interests in the Gulf with ideas grander than the mere defense of oil wells. Iran remains the critical buffer between the Soviet Union and the Gulf, and U.S. policy must start with that fact in mind. It would be beneficial indeed if Iran were to return to a pro-Western orientation. But whatever Iran's policy, U.S. policy must aim to minimize the Soviet position in Iran and in particular to keep Iran free of Soviet forces.

This is preeminently a task for diplomacy. The Soviets must not be confused about Iran's overall importance to U.S. interests in the Gulf.[1] The United States must make clear to Moscow that Iran as a whole is critically important to the interests of the United States and that Moscow should not regard as irreversible any Iranian move toward the Soviet camp. The United States must also devise a diplomatic strategy that provides Iran with alternatives to greater reliance on the Soviet Union. If it is too soon for the United States and Iran to deal with one another, then U.S. allies should be encouraged to forge links to Tehran.

Diplomacy alone is likely to be empty, however, in the absence of a

---

1. At least one observer feels that such confusion already exists: "When newspapers report that the United States expects the Soviet Union to invade northern Iran if the United States attacks that country and ignorant discussions of the 1921 Treaty [between Iran and the Soviet Union] refer to a general Soviet right to intervene in Iran, then the Soviet Union may be excused for believing that Iran has been conceded as in its sphere of influence." See Shahram Chubin, "Gains for Soviet Policy in the Middle East," *International Security,* vol. 6 (Spring 1982), p. 141.

supporting military posture and strategy. Diplomacy alone may suffice under most conditions. But under extreme conditions military capabilities become relevant. And under such conditions, vaguely defined capabilities and an ambiguous military strategy will fail to protect U.S. interests. What if, after a long flirtation with Moscow, the Tehran regime seeks accommodation with the West?[2] What if revolutionary turbulence or xenophobia in Iran creates enough instability to raise Moscow's interest in military options? What if provinces like Kurdistan or Azerbaijan become sufficiently disaffected from Tehran that elements in these areas seek Moscow's help? In these circumstances diplomatic understandings may seem less important to Moscow than the capabilities of U.S. military forces.

The surest way of influencing Soviet calculations is to prepare to defend Iran at its border with the Soviet Union.[3] But the sheer impracticality of doing that without forsaking virtually all other U.S. military commitments suggests that the United States will have to be satisfied with something less than outright defense.[4] More important, it would be unwise to seek to defend Iran. The relatively low readiness of Soviet forces above Iran and the low priority of Southwest Asia in Soviet military planning currently work to the U.S. advantage by reducing the speed with which Moscow can mount a robust military threat to Iran. A

2. "What would the Soviet Union find unacceptable in Iran?" asks Chubin. "Certainly a pro-Western and probably an independent leftist regime." Ibid., p. 141.

3. As Zalmay Khalilzad put it, "The Soviet calculus for intervention [in Iran] is actually quite simple: the higher the Western stakes in Iran and *the greater the Western ability to retaliate against a Soviet threat,* the more likely it is that Moscow will avoid using massive direct means to bring about important changes in Iran." (Emphasis added.) See his "Islamic Iran: Soviet Dilemma," *Problems of Communism,* vol. 33 (January–February 1984), pp. 19–20.

4. Given time to mobilize, the Soviets could put nearly thirty divisions into the northern part of the country. In fiscal 1985, by contrast, the United States fielded thirty ground force divisions in its entire force posture, including mobilized reserve component divisions. Even allowing for the relatively larger size of U.S. divisions, it is difficult to imagine U.S. forces pushing the Soviets out of Iran. Planning to do so would clearly involve planning to forsake virtually all other defense commitments, notably Europe. Yet it is Europe that faces the more robust and ready Soviet threat, one U.S. policymakers would find it hard to ignore even as crisis loomed in the Gulf.

Current planning does envision a defense of southern Iran, with major tank battles at Esfahan and points south. Yet southern Iran is territory the Soviets probably do not want and surely do not need either to defend their southern flank or to extend their power over important parts of Iran and the northern Gulf. A defense of this area may be all the United States can reasonably muster. But it is not clear that the Soviets will cooperate by attacking.

U.S. military strategy that gratuitously prompted Moscow to increase the readiness of its forces to meet a substantially increased threat off the Soviet Union's southern flank would be counterproductive. Overreacting to the strategic situation created by the shah's downfall is likely to be as dangerous as not reacting at all.

The Requirements of Deterrence

Trip-wire strategies are more feasible and less potentially destabilizing than a strategy of outright defense but otherwise make little sense. A thin cordon of U.S. forces around Iran's oil fields probably would not be tripped. Even if Moscow sought to take the wells, it would have every incentive to take the northern half of Iran, stop, proclaim its defensive intentions and limited goals, and wait for domestic and international pressure to remove the U.S. presence. A U.S. trip-wire force inserted farther north in Iran might well confront the Soviets and in so doing might deter their action. But such a force could be quickly overwhelmed, leaving the United States with no option but to escalate. With only a trip wire at their disposal, U.S. policymakers might find surrender or inaction attractive in a crisis.

To the extent that Southwest Asia remains a secondary zone for Soviet military action, the middle ground between outright defense of Iran and the insertion of a trip-wire force makes sense. That middle ground is a strategy of conventional deterrence. Moscow is not planning to attack Iran. But Moscow may want to take advantage of opportunities that arise in Iran, or the Soviets may be drawn into the country for defensive purposes. Under these circumstances decisionmaking in Moscow will probably be contingent on military assessments of the difficulty of the operation and an analysis of the prospects for U.S. counteraction. U.S. forces should be capable of influencing those assessments. The Soviet leadership should know in advance that it cannot move, even quickly toward limited objectives, without facing a strong possibility that U.S. forces will be deployed in a way that will substantially increase the cost and risk of Soviet operations. U.S. policymakers should be able to deploy a force that could put up a serious conventional fight, buying them time and flexibility for negotiating with Moscow.

A conventional deterrence strategy would be based first on an air interdiction campaign that could be mounted quickly against key targets

in northern Iran. Air interdiction would promise the Soviets a confrontation with U.S. forces near their border with Iran. If the Soviets nonetheless attacked, an air interdiction campaign would curb the aggressive use
of Soviet airborne forces, encourage the Soviets to operate at night, and
make any movement difficult. The strategy would also involve ground
forces capable of engaging Soviet forces as far north in Iran as would be
practical, and in strength sufficient to disrupt Soviet operations and
increase casualties. Neither set of operations should be expected to
defeat Soviet forces in northern Iran. But such operations would certainly increase the cost and risk of Soviet actions in an area likely to
contain the key objectives of the Soviet attack.

Although the chief function of forces deployed in this way would be to
confront the Soviets near their border with Iran and promise them a stiff
series of conventional battles should they head south, this strategy would
unquestionably raise the risk of escalation. Any conventional forces
placed in advance of Soviet forces would constitute a trip-wire in this
sense. Yet it is difficult to see how using nuclear weapons would be in the
U.S. interest. An announced strategy of first use would probably alienate
local powers, and their actual use might alienate virtually all U.S. allies.
In a strictly military sense the use of nuclear weapons locally would
certainly increase the cost of Soviet operations in Iran. But it would also
greatly increase the risk of Soviet counter use, which would increase the
cost of U.S. operations as well. Significantly, Moscow would confront a
rich array of potential targets, all of them falling short of U.S. territory:
U.S. forces in Iran, bases in nearby states, carriers at sea, Diego Garcia,
and other places. The United States, by contrast, would be operating
against forces close to bases in the USSR and would face almost
immediately the tough choice of whether or not to attack Soviet territory.

Alternatively, the United States could threaten to escalate horizontally
by extending the conflict to Europe or to the world's oceans. But the first
step makes no sense; the Soviets enjoy the edge in the conventional
balance in Europe, and they also enjoy interior lines in supplying two
theaters. By contrast, the second step pits U.S. ships against a clearly
inferior Soviet navy. But it is hardly clear that a war at sea would be in
the interests of a nation that depends on ocean-going commerce a great
deal more than its adversary does. Nor is it clear that the Soviets would
allow the United States to make all the escalatory choices while they
watched their navy sink. To the extent that the Soviets were expected to

escalate on their own, U.S. decisionmakers might be reluctant to start a war at sea.

This is not to say that the United States should not plan for the use of nuclear weapons or for wars on more than one front. If the Soviets chose to use nuclear weapons, the United States might wish to respond at that level. At the very least, the U.S. ability to respond might deter the Soviets from escalating in the first place.

The Soviets might also escalate horizontally to the European theater, or at least mobilize their forces in Europe in an attempt to tie down U.S. forces otherwise useful for Gulf contingencies.[5] The United States must be capable of hedging on two fronts until it is clear where the attack is taking place; this would involve basic mobilization to support both theaters. But the United States cannot, within anything approaching reasonable fiscal constraints, fight a major war in both the Gulf and Europe. Should fighting break out in both theaters, the United States would have to decide where to focus its resources, and Europe seems clearly to be the more important theater. A win there would defeat the core components of the Soviet force posture, after which the United States could return to the Gulf. Conversely, if NATO were defeated in Europe, a U.S. win in the Gulf would be of little consequence.

If the conflict in the Gulf remained local and conventional, the Soviets should be expected to prevail at some cost, at least in northern Iran. Then the United States would have to define its secondary objectives. Clearly one objective would be to end the conflict as soon as possible, both to limit the Soviet advance and to reduce the likelihood of escalation. A second objective would be to restore the status quo ante, or barring that, to create a new regional accommodation that limits the damage of Soviet military action.

Forces structured to deter could not by themselves restore the status quo ante. Several points should be made, however. First, a contained conventional conflict has its own levels of escalation. The initial U.S.

---

5. Although the Soviets enjoy the advantage of interior lines between the Gulf and Europe, it is not clear that it would be in Moscow's interest to turn a small and potentially containable war in the Gulf into a large and very likely nuclear war in Europe. Nor is it clear that Soviet logistics are capable of taking advantage of interior lines. See, for example, Joshua M. Epstein, *Measuring Military Power: The Soviet Air Threat to Europe* (Princeton University Press, 1984), especially pp. 56–97, for a study of logistics problems that would hamper Soviet military action in Europe, where the Soviets have concentrated so much attention.

confrontation with Soviet forces would be an air interdiction campaign; U.S. ground forces would be inserted ahead of the Soviet advance after Soviet troops had progressed some distance. The confrontation of each superpower's conventional ground forces would probably be perceived as a new level of conflict and might in itself create the grounds for a cease-fire.

Second, the conventional advantage Soviet forces enjoy at their border with Iran would diminish as they advanced south, navigating Iran's harsh terrain. Thus U.S. forces, although structured to deter, nonetheless might be able to bring the Soviet advance to a halt, if only above Abadan.[6] Although a beachhead at Abadan would surround many of Iran's oil fields, the beachhead's value would stem from its status as a major U.S. military base strategically positioned at the head of the Gulf. Over the long haul it would help the United States to balance the new Soviet position in the Gulf. Or it could become a chip in negotiations aimed at eliminating the Soviet and U.S. presence in Iran.

But the third point is most important: behind the military confrontation would lie diplomatic maneuvering whose results would be crucial in determining the broad outcome of the conflict. A crisis in Southwest Asia would immerse the United States in intense negotiations both with its industrialized allies and its friends in the region. An emerging united front among these nations, which raised the prospect of a solid commitment to defense, would have a substantially deterring effect on Soviet leaders before, during, and after the conflict itself.[7] Fear of the long-term consequences of renewed resolve in the West, and a desire to erode that resolve through some kind of "peace offensive," might be the only considerations that would motivate the Soviets to vacate territory already won. Events on the battlefield might be decisively influenced by diplomacy.

The approach suggested here is not a strategy for all seasons. But insofar as Soviet military interest in its southern flank may grow in

6. As William W. Kaufmann notes, "The chances are better than even that the Soviet Union, under attack from the air, could not move (much less support) a large ground capability south of the Zagros Mountains. Only relatively modest U.S. ground forces might then be necessary to hold a beachhead along the upper reaches of the Persian Gulf—if that were the initial objective." See his *Defense in the 1980s* (Brookings Institution, 1981), p. 28. See also Joshua M. Epstein, "Soviet Vulnerabilities in Iran and the RDF Deterrent," *International Security,* vol. 6 (Fall 1981), pp. 126–58 (Brookings Reprint 401).

7. See Vernon V. Aspaturian, "Soviet Global Power and the Correlation of Forces," *Problems of Communism,* vol. 29 (May–June 1980), pp. 1–18.

reaction to a perceived U.S. buildup there, it is a strategy designed to avoid an unwelcome change of season. Still, even without a perceived U.S. military buildup, Soviet military planners might begin to show greater interest in Iran, and the readiness and power of Soviet units near the area would then increase commensurately. So would demands on U.S. forces. But those demands would call first for greater speed of deployment of forces rather than for more forces. The more effectively U.S. units met and stymied the Soviet advance, the more time they would buy for deployment of other units to the area. Thus if the approach taken here is not a strategy for all seasons, the forces and planning this strategy demands are the starting points for meeting possible future contingencies.

The Operational Problem

It is difficult to overestimate the difficulties inherent in trying to implement the deterrence strategy just described. The distances involved are enormous—not only is the Gulf about 8,000 air miles from the United States, but northern Iran is several hundred miles inland from the northern end of the Gulf. The operational environment, the rigors of which would complicate a Soviet attack, would also place special demands on U.S. forces. Finally, strategic withdrawal is among the most difficult of military operations. Yet that is precisely what forward-deployed U.S. divisions would be undertaking. Using U.S. Central Command (CENTCOM) forces and current access agreements as a baseline, this section examines the military problems connected with the strategy's two components, revealing the basic planning and procurement priorities that attend these military operations.[8]

The Air Interdiction Campaign

U.S. strike aircraft must be able to sustain an effective air interdiction campaign in the northern portion of Iran. The clear capability to mount

---

8. Northern Iran is not the only potential arena for a U.S.-Soviet clash near the Gulf, but it is the most likely and also the most challenging for U.S. military planners. The assumption here is that forces capable of engaging the Soviets in northern Iran could, with modest allowances for different terrain and basing access, be employed with still greater effect against a Soviet invasion of, for example, southern Pakistan or southeastern Iran.

such a campaign rapidly would affect Soviet planning at both the strategic level (do we attack?) and the operational level (*how* do we attack?). Interdiction cannot be expected to stop the Soviet advance, but the goal of a deterrent strategy is not to stop but rather to slow, confuse, and damage the Soviet advance should deterrence fail. The mountains awaiting Soviet forces in northern Iran constitute fairly good terrain for an interdiction campaign.[9] Given Iran's limited road network to the south of the Soviet border and the number of passes, bridges, and choke points that mark these mountains, air interdiction can be expected to exact a sizable toll on Soviet operations.[10] The continuing development of extremely accurate (smart) munitions should enhance interdiction effectiveness against point targets like bridges, supply points, or intersections. These increase the possibilities for successful interdiction, even at night.

What kind of problems do U.S. forces currently face in trying to fulfill this strategic requirement, and how can they best be resolved? Significantly, CENTCOM's current force posture, shown in table 3-1, compares favorably with the number of aircraft immediately available to Soviet commanders in the area.[11] Fighter aircraft contribute indirectly to the effectiveness of interdiction by protecting interdiction aircraft as well as bases. U.S. strike aircraft usually carry a limited air-to-air capability, though, and use of electronic warfare aircraft can help protect strike aircraft operating beyond fighter cover. Ultimately, it is the strike aircraft themselves that deliver munitions, and in this category CENTCOM's

---

9. For a suitably skeptical and well-informed view of the prospects for air interdiction, see Edmund Dews and Felix Kozaczka, *Air Interdiction: Lessons from Past Campaigns,* N-1743-PA&E (Santa Monica, Calif.: Rand Corp., 1981). The authors point out that in addition to terrain, new and accurate weapons may have increased the effectiveness of air interdiction—"*when* the operational situation is favorable and *if* the interdicting aircraft are not subject to unacceptable attrition or forced to adopt inefficient delivery profiles so as to enhance their survivability." (Emphasis in original.) (p. 13.)

10. For a more detailed look at the air interdiction problem in Iran, see Epstein, "Soviet Vulnerabilities in Iran and the RDF Deterrent," pp. 128–37.

11. The number of aircraft usually available to CENTCOM would vary, perhaps radically, with circumstances. If war began in the Gulf but the rest of the world remained quiet, CENTCOM might be able to obtain more than the seven tactical fighter wings normally associated with it for planning purposes. Conversely, if war seemed imminent in Europe as well as in the Gulf, CENTCOM would probably get fewer than seven, and also fewer of the aircraft carriers than the three allocated to it for planning. The figures in table 3-1 thus are approximate but still serve as a useful basis for discussion.

Table 3-1. *CENTCOM Air Forces*[a]

Units	Aircraft	Capability	Quantity
Six air force tactical fighter wings[b]			
1st	F-15	Fighter	72
27th	F-111	Strike	72
347th	F-4	Fighter/strike	72
354th	A-10	Strike	72
366th	F-111	Strike	72
121st[c]	A-7	Strike	72
Three navy carrier-based air wings			
6 squadrons	F-4, F-14	Fighter	72
6 squadrons	A-7, FA-18	Strike	72
3 squadrons	A-6	Strike	42
One marine air wing			
4 squadrons	F-4, FA-18	Fighter/strike	48
2-3 squadrons	A-4, AV-8A	Strike	38–57
1-2 squadrons	A-6	Strike	10–20

Sources: "United States Central Command" (MacDill Air Force Base, Florida: undated public relations document available from CENTCOM); *U.S. Department of Defense Annual Report to the Congress, Fiscal Year 1984*, pp. 162–63; Andrew J. Ambrose, "US Central Command: Revised Support Structure," *Jane's Defence Review*, vol. 4, no. 7 (1983), p. 625.

a. Table does not include electronic warfare, early warning, utility, or rotary-wing aircraft.

b. Air force assets include the equivalent of ten tactical fighter wings. Three of these are fillers, however, for the wings noted above. A seventh wing is included in CENTCOM's assets, but its composition has never been noted in publicly available literature.

c. Air National Guard.

roughly 400–500 aircraft is nearly the number of aircraft used with some success over North Korea during the Korean War.[12]

Obtaining basing in the region for these aircraft has been more problematical than obtaining the aircraft themselves. Besides its own aircraft carriers and distant Diego Garcia (2,500 miles from the Strait of Hormuz), the United States has no assured access to regional bases. It has acquired conditional access rights to several air bases in Oman as well as to Cairo West in Egypt. Egypt's unwillingness to clarify in writing the conditions of access to its base at Ras Banas has held up construction there, although further work on this base, which could be used as a staging area for troops as well as aircraft, remains a possibility. There has been no public discussion of access to bases in Saudi Arabia, but it is clear that the Saudis stock more air-delivered munitions, F-15 support equipment, and fuel than they alone are likely to need.[13]

12. See the case study by Dews and Kozaczka in *Air Interdiction*, pp. 43–62, especially table A-1 on p. 50.

13. Although its fleet of sixty F-15s constitutes about a wing, for example, the Royal Saudi Air Force has purchased enough F-15 maintenance equipment to support four wings. See *The Proposed AWACS/F-15 Enhancement Sale to Saudi Arabia*, prepared for

In the fall of 1982 Turkey agreed to allow the United States, acting under NATO auspices, to modernize ten of its air bases, including several in the eastern portion of the country.[14] The proximity of these bases to northern Iran gives them exceptional military value, and they have special deterrent value as well, since a Soviet decision to attack them would be a decision to attack NATO. But basing is a delicate issue for the Turks. It makes them a more likely target for Soviet attack in wartime and may damage their relations with Moscow in peacetime. It may also damage their relations with the Gulf states, who worry lest Turkey's bases be used to attack their oil fields rather than Soviet forces in Iran. Thus the Turks, like the Arabs, have been reluctant to grant the United States unconditional access and instead have insisted that their bases are for use only in NATO contingencies. The question of whether a Soviet threat to Iran constitutes a NATO contingency will be answered only when events demand an answer.[15]

Israel has been comparatively forthcoming on basing issues, searching as it is for still closer ties to the United States. Progress on base development in Israel has been hampered, however, by the U.S. need to balance its relations with Israel with its ties to Arab states. Arab states see U.S.-Israeli military cooperation as simply another sign of a U.S. pro-Israeli bias, and they fear that U.S. and Israeli military forces might someday attack their oil fields. Prepositioning of equipment has moved haltingly, though in the aftermath of the Israeli prime minister's visit to the United States in November 1983 progress is once again being made.[16] In any case, Israel's own arsenal of U.S. weaponry implicitly creates a logistics base there that could be useful in a crisis.

To compensate for basing uncertainties, the U.S. Air Force has sought

the Senate Committee on Foreign Relations, 97 Cong. 1 sess. (Government Printing Office, 1981), p. 13, where it is also noted that some U.S. Air Force officers "anticipate that the Saudis would go so far as to allow U.S. pilots to fly Saudi F-15s to meet a threat." On munitions, see *Proposed U.S. Arms Sales to Saudi Arabia,* Hearing before the Subcommittees on International Security and Scientific Affairs and on Europe and the Middle East of the House Committee on Foreign Affairs, 96 Cong. 1 sess. (GPO, 1980), p. 35.

14. See "U.S. to Pay for Upgrading Turkish Military Airfields," *New York Times,* October 16, 1982. The base at Konya began hosting U.S. AWACS aircraft in October 1983. See "Awacs Base Open in Turkey," *New York Times,* October 26, 1983.

15. For Turkey's reservations, see Metin Demirsar, "U.S. Upgrades Military Links to Turkey with Eye to Soviet Union and the Mideast," *Wall Street Journal,* January 12, 1983.

16. For a history of U.S.-Israeli efforts to cooperate and an assessment of current initiatives, see Christopher Madison, "Reagan Links Middle East Disputes to Global East-West Struggle," *National Journal,* vol. 16 (January 28, 1984), pp. 158–63.

to expand its inventory of bare-base equipment, that is, equipment that could be airlifted to relatively undeveloped air bases as they became available. Such equipment could be flown into eastern Turkey, for example; into Dhahran to enhance facilities already there; or into Iran itself should the Iranians ask for U.S. assistance, or if or when U.S. forces secure an airhead near Abadan. The flexibility of bare-base equipment is only partly real, however, since such bases would have to be supported and protected—not easy tasks. Still, bare-base equipment enables the United States to take advantage of military or political opportunities as they arise. In a region where political constraints limit basing access, such equipment is a worthwhile hedge.

BASING AND SORTIE RATE. The critical importance of basing to the success of the U.S. interdiction campaign becomes clear when it is recognized that air interdiction depends less on sheer numbers of aircraft available than on the number of munitions dropped accurately on targets in northern Iran over time. This in turn is a function, notably, of the load an aircraft can carry, the accuracy of its munitions, the aircraft's ability to fly in foul weather or at night, the time it can spend over target, and the range from bases to targets. For most of CENTCOM's aircraft all-weather capabilities can be assumed, and each aircraft can carry the full range of precision-guided munitions. Table 3-2 lists other important variables for several U.S. strike aircraft. It omits the B-52Hs since, even without refueling, these aircraft can reach targets throughout Iran from the U.S. base at Diego Garcia. Taking range figures for other strike aircraft from table 3-2, figures 3-1 through 3-5 show the effects of various assumptions concerning available basing on the number of useful aircraft at CENTCOM's disposal.

The full range of strike aircraft can cover northern Iran only from bases in eastern Turkey. From second-tier bases like Incirlik, Dhahran, and Israel, air force F-111s and B-52Hs (and, later, F-15Es) could threaten the Soviets near their border, as could U.S. Marine Corps A-6Es and U.S. Navy A-6Es relocated from carriers to land bases. All would have to fly outside fighter cover to reach Iran, however. Thus it is likely that missions flown from these bases would occur at night, which might affect targeting accuracy. None of these aircraft would be able to loiter over the target area: the F-111 and A-6E because they would be flying near maximum range; the B-52Hs because of their size, lack of maneuverability, and basic vulnerability. All aircraft save the B-52Hs would

Table 3-2. *Mission Radii, U.S. Tactical Aircraft*[a]

Aircraft[b] (weapons load)[c]	Without refueling	With refueling[d]
F-111D/E (6,000)	800	1,000
A-6E (6,000)	700	950
A-7D/E (4,000)	550	650
F-16 (3,000)	500	650
A-10 (3,000)	400	500
F-4E (4,000)	275	400
F-15E (8,000)[e]	750	950

Source: Derived from the performance section of aircraft technical orders for individual aircraft.

a. Radius for high-low-low-high flight profile, fifty nautical miles (n.m.) low altitude segment.

b. Aircraft are assumed to carry ECM, AAMs, gun ammunition, and external fuel tanks if stations are available and gross takeoff weight limits permit.

c. Weight in pounds for nominal bomb load; bomb load in most cases would be Maverick or smart bombs (GBU-10).

d. Tanks topped off at cruise altitude in a single aerial refueling.

e. Selected in February 1984 to "augment the F-111 in performing long-range, high-payload missions at night and in adverse weather." Some 392 F-15Es will be purchased, with first delivery scheduled for 1988. See Eugene Kozicharow, "USAF Selects F-15 as Dual Role Fighter," *Aviation Week & Space Technology*, vol. 120 (March 5, 1984), pp. 18–19.

require tanker support that would complicate operations and drain tankers from other uses in a crisis.[17]

Figure 3-5 illustrates the usefulness of the area around Abadan. Capturing that area would be an important part of the ground force campaign. Bases here would increase the operational effectiveness of A-7s and F-16s over northern Iran. But U.S. forces would probably have to construct a useful base in this area virtually from scratch. Their ability to do so would depend on the effectiveness of both the ground force campaign and attempts to establish air superiority over the northern edge of the Gulf.

With more distant land bases—Ras Banas, Cairo West, Masirah, and so forth—useful only for staging, maintenance, and other kinds of support, CENTCOM would have to rely on B-52Hs and carrier-based aircraft were it unable to obtain access to the bases just noted. Carrier-based A-6Es could cover targets in northern Iran from the eastern Mediterranean and also from the northern Persian Gulf. But few admirals would be anxious to move into the Gulf, where maneuver room is

17. The Saudis are nearing completion of King Khalid Military City (KKMC), an elaborate base near their border with Kuwait. When completed KKMC will include several airfields, making it another useful second-tier air base, closer than Dhahran to likely targets. Much of what is said here could be applied to KKMC as it becomes operational (if the Saudis are willing to discuss the issue). See Kingdom of Saudi Arabia, Ministry of Defense and Aviation, Directorate of Military Works, "King Khalid Military City" (n.d.). Bases in eastern Jordan would also be useful, but it is unlikely that the United States can substantially improve Jordan's bases, especially in ways that favor its own high-performance aircraft, in the absence of peace between Jordan and Israel.

Figure 3-1. *Air Interdiction, Basing in Eastern Turkey*

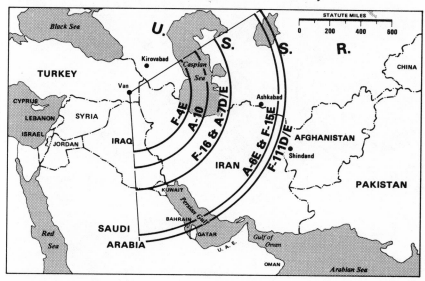

Figure 3-2. *Air Interdiction, Basing in Dhahran, Saudi Arabia*

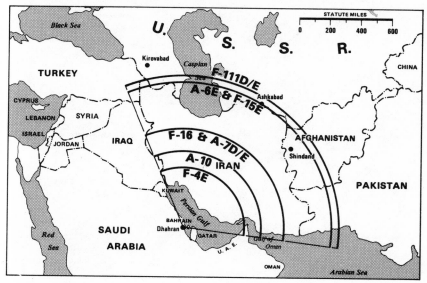

Figure 3-3. *Air Interdiction, Basing in Incirlik, Turkey*

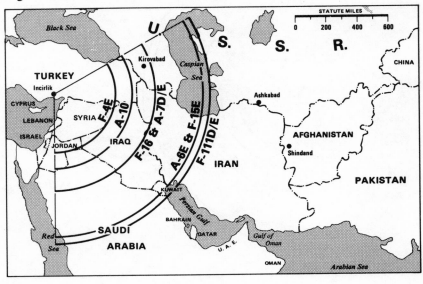

Figure 3-4. *Air Interdiction, Basing in Israel*

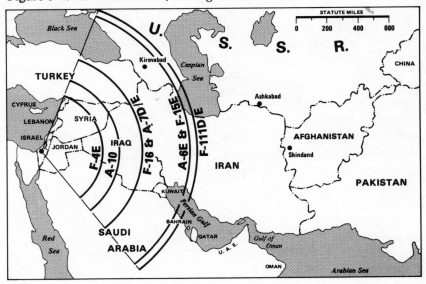

Figure 3-5. *Air Interdiction, Basing in Abadan*

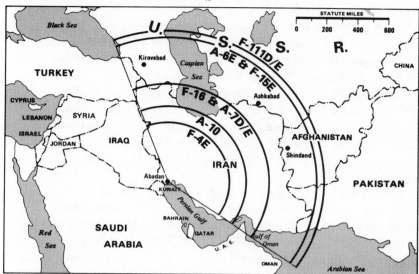

minimal and carriers could be threatened by local as well as Soviet aircraft. The eastern Mediterranean would hold out its own risks to carriers, especially if Soviet aircraft were able to use bases in Syria. Still, this is the more realistic alternative for carrier operations, making it likely that an air interdiction campaign shorn of any land basing in the region would involve B-52Hs flying from Diego Garcia and perhaps two carrier decks of A-6Es flying from the eastern Mediterranean.

Basing clearly makes a big difference to the kind of interdiction campaign CENTCOM can expect to mount, especially at the outset, before a base can be seized at Abadan. Even if CENTCOM were to be given full control of the aircraft listed in table 3-1, without basing in the region, only about fifty-six of these (twenty-eight B-52Hs and two carriers' worth of A-6Es) would be capable of reaching northern Iran. Conversely, under ideal conditions in which CENTCOM obtained access to bases in Turkey, Israel, and also the Gulf, 400–500 strike aircraft could be brought to bear over Soviet forces, and fighter aircraft could cover the full interdiction campaign.

Obvious incentives exist for CENTCOM to work closely with regional powers to clarify the conditions of U.S. access to local bases. And U.S. crisis diplomacy should aim to increase the chances for access. Still, CENTCOM cannot base its planning on the assumption of unfettered access throughout the area. Nor can CENTCOM assume that the valuable bases in eastern Turkey will survive Soviet strikes even if it obtains access to them. Thus there is a premium on being able to increase CENTCOM's access to long-range strike capabilities.

To do that, the U.S. services could buy more long-range strike aircraft. B-52Hs, F-111s, and A-7s are no longer in production. The navy is still purchasing small numbers of the A-6E, which is especially useful for these missions, but these numbers barely cover the costs of attrition. The A-6E line is open, though, and more could be purchased, even by the U.S. Air Force. The air force is also planning to purchase a longer-range version of the F-15 (the F-15E Strike Eagle), also useful in Southwest Asia.

CENTCOM could also increase the usefulness of navy A-6Es by planning to move these aircraft from carriers to land bases closer to northern Iran. At a minimum, carrier-based A-6Es could touch down at refueling sites at bases in the Gulf or Turkey and then return to their carriers. Or they could be refueled in the air by tankers based closer to northern Iran, rather than by carrier-based tankers. But the greatest increase in sortie rate could be achieved if the A-6Es and their associated carrier-based maintenance and support detachments were flown to land bases like those at Incirlik and Dhahran. No technical impediment precludes that option. But the usefulness of doing so could be enhanced by increasing the number of spares and support items on board carriers.

Finally, the United States could make available to CENTCOM the long-range strike aircraft in the inventory that are not currently assigned to CENTCOM. Total inventories of appropriate aircraft are shown in table 3-3. In a one-front situation, for example, the considerable number of F-111s assigned to European missions could be swung into the Gulf. A-6Es on carriers outside the Indian Ocean could be swung into the region, as could additional Marine Corps A-6Es. These would not have to be long-term redeployments, because at some point an air base at Abadan would become available, giving shorter-range strike aircraft access to valuable targets. A variety of available long-range strike aircraft thus could be surged into and out of the Gulf, adding significantly to CENTCOM's interdiction capabilities even without further purchases of long-range strike aircraft.

BASING, REDEPLOYMENT, AND SUPPORT. Redeployment of aircraft is critically a function of the ability of bases near the Gulf to receive large numbers of aircraft quickly, Fuel is available everywhere. Munitions are

Table 3-3. *Total Inventories, U.S. Long-range Strike Aircraft*

Aircraft	Number available (approximately)	Deployment
F-111A/D	140	Continental United States
F-111E/F	140	Europe
A-6E	120	Navy (carriers)
A-6E	50	Navy (pipeline)[a]
A-6E	50	Marine Corps air wings

Source: International Institute for Strategic Studies (IISS), *The Military Balance, 1983–1984* (London: IISS, 1983), p. 9; Graham Warwick, "F-111: Strike Fighter for the 1990s?" *Flight International*, vol. 121 (January 9, 1982), pp. 67–77; and *Jane's All the World's Aircraft, 1982–83* (London: Jane's Publishing Co., 1982), pp. 376–77.
a. Includes training and maintenance "float" aircraft.

largely interchangeable, and U.S. arms transfer policies have placed large numbers of them in Saudi Arabia, Turkey, and Israel. But spare parts generally are not interchangeable, and the long-range strike aircraft most useful for the interdiction campaign are not among those transferred to states in the region. Prestocking spare parts at essentially inactive bases like Dhahran risks losing them in case of political upheaval. Planning to deliver spares in a crisis would place more demands on transport assets likely to have other important uses. Perhaps the best solution to this dilemma is prepositioning additional spares on ships, or at a location near but not in the region, where intratheater lift could carry the major burden of delivery to those bases actually used in the interdiction campaign. In fact, some prepositioning of air force spares and supplies has already occurred.[18]

The more important support and prestocking issue in any event has to do with air defense. Bases must be protected before they can be used; any attempt to fly in interdiction aircraft, spares, and munitions, not to mention ground forces for the ground campaign, could occur only under air cover. Thus if resource constraints dictate a choice between what is prestocked and what is delivered quickly, priority of prestocking goes to air defense equipment. Significantly, U.S. arms transfers work advantageously in this area, with both Dhahran and Incirlik being reasonably well stocked to accept first-line U.S. fighter aircraft. Saudi Arabia has also purchased U.S. Improved-Hawk air defense missiles, and U.S.

18. As discussed more fully later in this chapter, eleven ships have been prepositioned at Diego Garcia with supplies for early-arriving air force and army units. The precise composition of these stocks is classified. See *U.S. Department of Defense Annual Report to the Congress, Fiscal Year 1985*, p. 183.

airborne warning and control system (AWACS) aircraft have been on station in that country since 1980.

Eastern Turkey presents the most severe problem. Bases there would be vulnerable to the whole range of Soviet tactical aircraft, as would the aircraft flying from them and the land supply routes leading to them. This might not detract from their deterrent value; aircraft based there would certainly promise Moscow a confrontation. But the confrontation might occur over Turkey rather than over northern Iran; it might involve many U.S. aircraft otherwise intended for interdiction missions; and it might be both short and unpleasant for the United States, not to mention Turkey. If bases in eastern Turkey are to be used at all they should be well developed and prestocked for air defense. Concrete shelters could increase the survivability of aircraft to all but nuclear attack. Antiaircraft missiles could free aircraft for interdiction missions and force the air battle back over northern Iran. Prestocking could alleviate the need for quick resupply.

The Ground Force Campaign

U.S. ground forces deployed to meet Soviet units advancing into Iran would raise both the cost and risk of Soviet operations. Better than strike aircraft, ground forces would be able to confront Soviet units, direct fire accurately, maneuver to defeat lead columns in detail, and withdraw, leaving uncertain the questions when and where they would strike next. More than air interdiction, a ground force campaign would represent the full commitment of U.S. conventional power to the confrontation, signaling greater resolve, higher stakes, and increased risk. The presence of U.S. ground forces in Iran would also probably enhance the prospects for a negotiated settlement that would remove the forces of both superpowers from that country.

The most difficult operation, that designed to deter a short Soviet jump into northern Iran, would unfold in two prongs. One would secure key ports and airfields along Iran's coast, with Bushere and the Abadan area the most prominent targets. This mission would fall initially to U.S. Marine Corps units whose equipment would be on station in the Indian Ocean and would involve later insertion of U.S. Army ground forces. The other prong would involve the air insertion of ground forces further north and east of Abadan, with the location determined by the direction and pace of the Soviet advance (as it has been affected by U.S. air strikes), the speed of the ground forces' response, and key terrain. This mission would fall to light army units capable of fighting away from the coast.

Even more than with the air interdiction campaign, the feasibility of the ground force campaign ultimately would depend on politics and diplomacy. Indeed, the ground force campaign could not go forward without proper air cover, making it partially dependent on prior diplomatic success in gaining access to air bases in the Gulf itself. Furthermore, Iranian opposition to the entry of U.S. ground forces would make it difficult indeed to deploy large American units to Iran's mountains, although small Ranger teams might be able to operate in the north, and U.S. units might still be able to take the Abadan-Bushere area. The deployment of ground forces to Iran would make sense only if a large portion of the population were either to acquiesce in or support the U.S. presence.

In strictly military terms, the feasibility of the ground force campaign would depend basically on the number of ground forces available to CENTCOM and the speed with which at least some of these units could be delivered. CENTCOM currently has access, for planning purposes, to the following ground force units:[19]

> 82d Airborne Division
> 101st Air Assault Division
> 24th Mechanized Infantry Division
> 7th Infantry Division[20]
> 9th High-Technology Motorized Division[21]
> 6th Combat Brigade, Air Cavalry
> One Marine Amphibious Division[22]
> One Marine Amphibious Regiment[23]

---

19. "United States Central Command" (MacDill Air Force Base, Florida: undated public relations document available from CENTCOM); Department of Army briefing on the Light Infantry Division; *U.S. Department of Defense Annual Report, Fiscal Year 1985,* p. 212.

20. The 7th Infantry Division will remain associated with CENTCOM through fiscal 1985, when it will be converted to the new Light Infantry Division.

21. The 9th High-Technology Motorized Division (HTMD) will join CENTCOM in fiscal 1986, replacing the 7th Infantry Division.

22. Part of a marine amphibious force that includes a marine air wing.

23. Part of a marine amphibious brigade that includes a marine air group.

Two of the army divisions are light units—the 82d Airborne Division and the 7th Infantry Division.[24] The 9th High-Technology Motorized Division is also considered a light unit. The 101st Air Assault is light in weight but possesses a helicopter component that complicates airlift.

In broad terms, the nation's current strategic lift assets can move a battalion of the 82d Airborne Division to a major airfield near the Gulf in forty-eight hours, about the time it takes to deliver a marine battalion if one is attached to naval forces in the area. The marine amphibious brigade, with equipment also prepositioned at Diego Garcia,[25] can close on the region in about a week, while amphibious lift can deliver the rest of the division in three to four weeks. The entire 82d Airborne Division can deploy by air in three weeks. Sealift can deliver another full division in thirty to thirty-five days.[26] Deliveries over time are roughly those depicted in figure 3-6.

New acquisition programs will improve this situation. Purchase of eight SL-7 fast deployment ships, which should be ready by 1986, will allow the army to deploy another division from the East Coast to the Gulf in roughly three to four weeks.[27] Prepositioning of the equipment and supplies for three marine brigades aboard maritime prepositioning ships (MPS), to be deployed by 1987, will make it possible to place ground equipment and thirty days' supplies for a full marine amphibi-

24. Light army units here refers to units like the 82d Airborne Division and the 7th Infantry Division as currently structured. As of this writing, the army is planning to field a five-division force of light units substantially smaller and lighter than existing units. These changes will not alter the thrust of the message here or the delivery rates depicted in figures 3-6 through 3-10, since the new, smaller light division would have to be augmented with mobility and antiarmor elements that would make it larger and heavier.

25. This equipment is on board seven ships of the Near-Term Prepositioned Force (NTPF), docked at Diego Garcia. The NTPF was created in July 1980 to speed Marine Corps deployments to the Gulf. Eleven more ships were added to the force in 1981–82, carrying ammunition and supplies for air force and army units. See *U.S. Department of Defense Annual Report, Fiscal Year 1985*, p. 183.

26. See Headquarters, Rapid Deployment Joint Task Force, Public Affairs Office, "Fact Sheet" (MacDill Air Force Base, Florida: January 1981), p. 5.

27. Steaming time for the SL-7s from the East Coast to the Gulf is roughly eleven days if the ships use the Suez Canal, nineteen days if they round the Cape of Good Hope. Assuming that army equipment is readily available at ports on the East Coast, loading will take five to six days, and unloading in the Gulf will take about a week. Thus complete deployment time from mobilization to unloading in the Gulf could take from twenty-three to thirty-two days. See Congressional Budget Office, *Rapid Deployment Forces: Policy and Budgetary Implications* (CBO, February 1983), p. 37; and *Department of Defense Appropriations for 1982*, Hearings before a Subcommittee of the Committee on Appropriations, 97 Cong. 1 sess. (GPO, 1981), pt. 2, pp. 630–35.

Figure 3-6. *Force Delivery, Fiscal 1984 Assets*

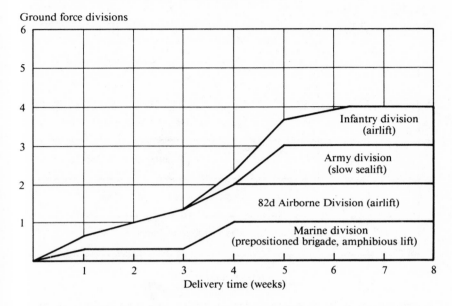

Ground force divisions

Infantry division
(airlift)

Army division
(slow sealift)

82d Airborne Division (airlift)

Marine division
(prepositioned brigade, amphibious lift)

Delivery time (weeks)

ous force (MAF) in the region in ten days or less.[28] Airlift will have only
to deliver personnel to man the equipment. Purchase by 1988 of fifty
C-5Bs will increase by more than 60 percent the size of the U.S. Air Force
fleet of outsize cargo aircraft, allowing delivery of the 82d Airborne
Division in two weeks. When these programs are all completed, the
United States should be able to deploy all four of the divisions currently
available in roughly thirty days (figure 3-7), assuming that all lift assets
are set in motion simultaneously and that other contingencies do not rob
CENTCOM of lift assets. But much of the buildup would come after the
third week and would be confined principally to positions near the
Gulf's shore.

28. The precise number of ships in the NTPF varies as equipment is cycled through
maintenance and ships of varied capacity are leased for the fleet. Present plans call for one
brigade of the Maritime Prepositioning Ships (MPS) Division to replace the Marine Corps
component of the NTPF in fiscal 1986. Depot ships carrying supplies for army and air
force units (roughly eleven ships) will remain in place at Diego Garcia. The other two MPS
brigades will be stationed outside the Indian Ocean area, but their response time for Gulf
contingencies is expected to be ten days or less, depending on warning. *U.S. Department of
Defense Annual Report, Fiscal Year 1985*, p. 183; *U.S. Department of Defense Annual
Report, Fiscal Year 1982*, pp. 205–06; and CBO, *Rapid Deployment Forces*, pp. 38–39.

Figure 3-7. *Force Delivery, Fiscal 1988 Assets*

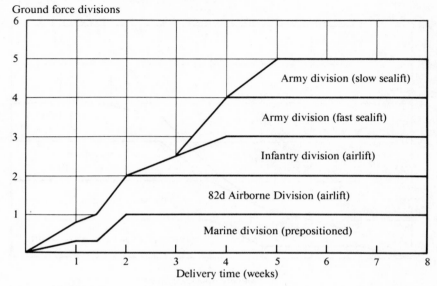

Ground force divisions

None of these numbers includes the time required to deploy units to Iran's mountains, which is a matter of intratheater rather than intertheater or strategic lift. The principal vehicle for intratheater lift is the C-130, the only aircraft capable of delivering light equipment to undeveloped and relatively short forward airfields.[29] The time needed to deliver two divisions to Iran's mountains would vary according to the number of C-130s available and the distance between deployment points in the Zagros and bases of entry further south. For the moment, it is reasonable to assume that intratheater delivery of CENTCOM's two forward divisions will require ten to fourteen days beyond the time required to deliver those units to the region itself.

Significantly, commonly offered delivery rates for U.S. lift include only modest supplies. Prepositioned equipment with the Maritime Prepositioning Fleet (MPF) will include thirty days' supplies for Marine Corps units, and the Near-Term Prepositioned Force (NTPF) includes

29. Trucks could ease the intratheater lift problem, though only after routes from Abadan to forward areas had been secured. Light units like the 82d Airborne Division have few large trucks, however. Borrowing trucks from other CENTCOM divisions or prepositioning additional trucks near the region would be necessary if this form of intratheater lift is to make a great contribution to supplying forward units.

eleven depot ships that carry ammunition, supplies, and hospital equipment for air force and army units. But CENTCOM's army units would be delivered to the region with about three days' worth of supplies and ammunition. Getting prepositioned supplies to forward-deployed units and getting more supplies to the region would be imperative. The dimensions of these logistical problems will be discussed later. For the moment, it is sufficient to recognize that bringing supplies to CENTCOM's forces presents challenges beyond those connected with delivering the forces themselves.

CENTCOM capabilities are a useful point of departure for fielding a force capable of implementing the strategy under discussion, but key failings in force size, lift, and support remain to be addressed. These issues are closely related; the size and kind of force being delivered obviously affect the usefulness of available lift, as do support requirements for deployed divisions. This discussion starts by considering the appropriate force structure before moving on to the issues of lift and support.

FORCE SIZE, STRUCTURE, AND TRAINING. Virtually all major army and Marine Corps units are earmarked for NATO, and the six divisions associated with CENTCOM (one MAF, the 82d, 101st, 7th, 24th, and 9th Divisions, and the 6th Combat Brigade, Air Cavalry [CBAC]) are no exception. Yet it is not clear what role CENTCOM's lighter units would play in the European theater, where armor-heavy Soviet units pose a serious challenge even to heavy NATO forces.[30] Only the 24th Mechanized Division and the 6th CBAC (because of its tank-killing helicopter assets) would seem to be useful in both theaters. Thus for single-theater operations CENTCOM should be able to count on getting six divisions, while even in potential two-front situations CENTCOM should be able to depend on getting five. Deploying these units to the Gulf would provide the United States with a hedge against the possibility that war would break out there rather than in Europe. And if war finally did break out in Europe, units deployed to the Gulf as a hedge would not seriously undermine NATO's ability to prosecute the war there, especially in its crucial early stages.

---

30. It is often argued that infantry forces would be useful for fighting in European cities as well as forested areas. Yet Soviet forces are not structured to fight in these areas, and Soviet doctrine calls for rapid advances that would only be bogged down by entering cities. At the very least it can be said that light units will have little or no use early in the fighting.

It can be argued that with five or six divisions CENTCOM could hold a perimeter around Abadan even against a Soviet attack.[31] Abadan may not be Moscow's objective, however, and the more important question concerns how many of CENTCOM's divisions should be deployed well north in Iran's mountains to complicate a Soviet advance against more limited objectives. Insofar as these units are not required to push the Soviets back toward their border, the maximum size of CENTCOM's forward element is less important than the minimum size—this must be a force that the Soviets cannot easily sweep aside. Given Iran's terrain and limited road network, and, finally, given an effective air interdiction campaign, two U.S. divisions and smaller Ranger units lodged along the northern rim of the Zagros Mountains should be quite adequate—if they are structured and trained to do the job.

The forward operation favors light divisions capable of breaking down into small, highly mobile units able to engage Soviet armor in a strategic withdrawal. (Moving heavy tanks in for this operation would only tie U.S. forces to main roads, giving them the same liabilities that the Soviets have.) The army already has light, infantry-carried forms of antitank firepower in its TOW and Dragon missiles, and the 9th Division has adapted these to light, open vehicles in a way that increases their mobility. Still, there is a need for light, armored, tank-killing vehicles that provide more firepower and crew protection without unduly complicating airlift. Prototypes of such vehicles have been available for some years, though the army has yet to begin a formal development program for them.[32] Until it does so, the army's only light tank will be the aging Sheridan, a battalion of which is now part of the 82d Airborne Division.[33]

Training must be in mountain tactics emphasizing maneuver, stealth, and hit-and-run tactics. Although some analysts have argued that proper tactics would allow the United States to defeat Soviet forces in detail in

31. See, for example, Epstein, "Soviet Vulnerabilities in Iran and the RDF Deterrent," pp. 141–52.

32. See Richard M Ogorkiewicz, "The U.S. Armoured Combat Vehicle Technology Program—a Closer Look," *International Defense Review,* vol. 12, no. 5 (1979), pp. 811–15.

33. As of this writing the army is considering transferring its remaining Sheridans to the 9th Division. In the process the basic vehicle may be upgraded with the addition of a new, low-recoil 105mm gun. See "Army Ponders Sheridan Revival," *Defense Week,* vol. 5 (November 19, 1984), p. 3.

the Zagros, such success is unprovable.[34] But units not properly trained are likely to have little effect or longevity in these mountains.

Obvious candidates for the forward prong of the operation are the Ranger units, the light army divisions (the 82d, 7th, or 9th), the 101st Air Assault Division, and the 6th CBAC. The 82d Airborne Division and the infantry division are rapidly deployable, while the 101st and the 6th CBAC have helicopter components that would increase mobility and antiarmor firepower of strictly ground units. Indeed, attack helicopters represent perhaps the single most mobile and lethal tank-killing asset available.

But helicopters represent a mixed blessing for the forward operation, undermining the wisdom of their early deployment. Because they constitute low-density cargo, helicopters complicate the strategic lift problem. Moreover, helicopters are major fuel and ammunition consumers whose relatively short combat radius (about 140 miles for an AH-1 Cobra gunship) requires that full support be available in the Zagros, not at bases to the rear. Thus opportunity costs are linked with trying to move helicopter and helicopter-supported units early, and serious questions arise about whether such units would be useful until secure bases were available to them—whether forward or to the rear.

These considerations suggest that more efficient use of airlift could be made if two light divisions were deployed forward initially, and helicopter assets were delivered in later waves, after basing had been secured. Besides the 82d Airborne Division, the 7th or the 9th Division could be deployed forward, with the 101st and the 6th CBAC coming in later, through Abadan, and working their way forward from there. SL-7 sealift normally allocated to moving the 24th Mechanized Division might then be allocated to the 101st and 6th first, since time constraints would not be so pressing. Slower sealift would deliver the 24th Mechanized Division within thirty-five days in any case. These deployments are shown in figure 3-8.

A six-division force structured in this way would be sufficiently balanced to act as a deterrent to other possible Soviet actions around the Gulf. Only two of the six divisions would be both light and trained extensively for operations in Iran's rugged mountains. Although three of

34. For suggestions on such tactics, see Steven L. Canby, "The Iranian Military: Political Symbolism Versus Military Usefulness," in Hossein Amirsadeghi, ed., *The Security of the Persian Gulf* (St. Martin's, 1981), pp. 100–30, especially pp. 111–30.

Figure 3-8. *U.S. Ground Force Deployments to Iran*

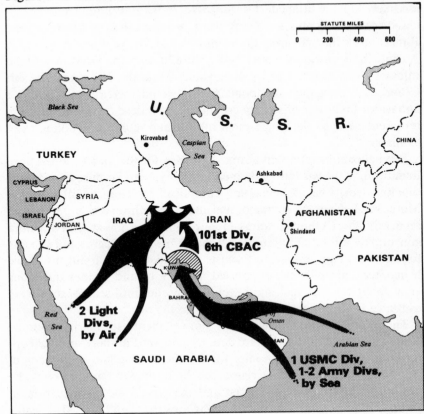

the remaining four divisions would hardly be called heavy by comparison, they would have substantially greater antitank assets, and two (the
24th Mechanized Division and the Marine Amphibious Division)
would contain a reasonably large armor contingent. There would be
enough strength here to engage Soviet forces in southern Iran or Pakistan. Moreover, because these actions would unfold closer to the rim of
the Indian Ocean, the lift problem, as well as the problem of supporting
helicopters, would be simplified considerably.

THE STRATEGIC LIFT PROBLEM. Forces available or potentially available
to CENTCOM might be adequate for deterrence, but could they be
positioned in time to meet the Soviet attack? To conduct operations the
United States would want to deploy its forward divisions to Iran's

mountains in advance of the arrival of Soviet forces, with time to set up bases and deploy tactically. Heavier rearward divisions would be inserted soon thereafter. Could U.S. strategic and tactical lift assets deliver units to the Gulf to meet these operational requirements?

There is no clear answer to that question. Instead, the answer depends on three major uncertainties. First, would the United States have and be able to exploit warning time? Second, how quickly would Soviet forces move south, given Iran's terrain, possible local resistance, and U.S. air strikes? Third, would a near-simultaneous crisis in Europe drain lift assets away from CENTCOM?

Consider, first, uncertainty about warning time. Programmed lift assets would be capable of delivering four U.S. divisions to the Gulf region in about thirty days under ideal conditions. Tactical lift would be able to deploy two light divisions forward in about two weeks. If it took the Soviets thirty days to mobilize, even for a short hop into northern Iran, and if the United States mobilized alongside the Soviets, then U.S. forces could be in the region within days after the Soviets crossed the border, and the bulk of one light division would be in the mountains soon thereafter. Under these assumptions there appears to be no lift inadequacy.

Yet sanguine assumptions about warning may not be realistic. As Richard K. Betts has pointed out, countries that set out to surprise their enemies have usually succeeded, at least at the tactical level.[35] Even if U.S. policymakers were to pick up signs of an impending Soviet attack, they would not want to respond precipitously. With the kind of murky events likely to draw the Soviets into Iran, the ability of the United States to gain allies and access in a crisis may depend on Moscow's being perceived as the clear aggressor. If there were some doubt about Soviet intentions, U.S. policymakers might be reluctant to dispatch airborne forces to the region for fear of provoking a Soviet attack that might otherwise have been avoided. Although air-delivered units could be mobilized at their home bases, none might fly to the region until Soviet units actually crossed the border with Iran.

Sealift may be seen as inherently less provocative. SL-7s and slower sealift vessels could be loaded and set to sail without immediately changing the military situation in the Gulf region itself. Figure 3-9

---

35. *Surprise Attack: Lessons for Defense Planning* (Brookings Institution, 1982), chaps. 4 and 5.

Figure 3-9. *Force Delivery, Sealift Mobilized Two Weeks Early*[a]

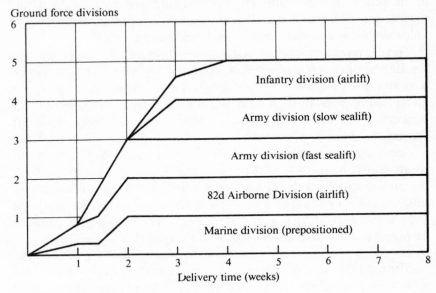

Ground force divisions

a. Assumes purchase of all currently programmed assets.

illustrates the effect on force delivery of doing so two weeks in advance of the Soviet attack. Although mobilizing airlift this way has no effect on the delivery of light units to Iran's mountains, it does ensure that all supporting divisions reach the Gulf region in about four weeks. Still, fast sealift is more efficient in carrying heavier or bulkier units like the 101st Air Assault Division or the 24th Mechanized Division, both of which would be loaded from ports on the East Coast or the Gulf of Mexico. If sealift were to carry the additional light division, it would have to be loaded on the West Coast. Unless CENTCOM planned to do so in advance, loading SL-7s early would have no effect on the delivery of light units to Iran's mountains.

Prudent assumptions about warning thus do little to change the most critical portion of the ground force campaign: currently programmed assets would take roughly six weeks to place the bulk of two divisions forward in Iran. CENTCOM might be willing to begin operations with less than two full divisions; the method of Soviet operations might make it impossible to avoid doing so. But reasonable concerns about the friction likely to be connected with the introduction of light troops into

Iran's mountains suggest that a six-week delivery rate remains a minimum below which no commander would want to go.

Whether six weeks is indeed an adequate delivery rate for U.S. forces depends on how rapidly Soviet forces advance, which is the second uncertainty connected with the strategic lift problem. The strategy calls for the insertion of U.S. ground forces ahead of the Soviet advance, but if the goal were to engage Soviet forces as far north as possible, the Soviets should not be allowed to travel more than about 250 miles into Iran (to a line running east-west through Tehran) before U.S. forces are in place. Whether or not it would take Soviet forces six weeks to move 250 miles is impossible to say. Iran's terrain makes the use of armor advance rates from past campaigns misleading at best, and uncertainties about the effectiveness of the U.S. air interdiction campaign introduce still more uncertainty. Possibly, the Soviets could be bogged down to a crawl of less than six miles a day. But CENTCOM might be understandably reluctant to plan on so slow an advance rate. To the extent that this is the case, currently programmed lift assets must be considered inadequate.

The third uncertainty about the strategic lift problem concerns the effects of possible simultaneous crises in Europe and the Persian Gulf. The lift inadequacies just described would grow substantially if a crisis in Europe were to absorb U.S. lift assets, or if U.S. policymakers sought to hedge against the possibility of such a crisis by withholding some lift assets from CENTCOM. The brigade-sized portion of the MPS fleet that is to be prepositioned at Diego Garcia would probably remain available for Gulf operations, but CENTCOM's access to the rest of the MPS fleet would be uncertain. Although there is no clear policy on the use of SL-7s in this situation, CENTCOM might retain this asset as well. There might be enough slow sealift to deliver a division to the Gulf, but on the whole seaborne support to CENTCOM would be cut drastically to favor Europe. And airlift assets would be entirely absorbed by the European reinforcement for roughly ten days, to conform to the announced U.S. policy of moving ten divisions to Europe in that period.[36] Thus the sequence of these two crises is important; thirty days' lag between crises in Europe and the Gulf, for example, would greatly reduce the lift shortfall.

---

36. This assumes that the United States continues its program of placing six division sets of equipment in Europe. As of this writing only four sets are in place, and construction has begun on the other two sites. See *U.S. Department of Defense Annual Report, Fiscal Year 1985*, pp. 182–83.

Figure 3-10. *Force Delivery, Simultaneous Two-theater Crisis*[a]

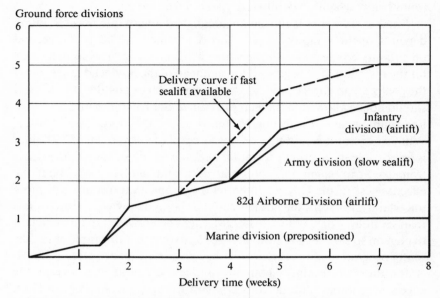

Ground force divisions

Delivery curve if fast
sealift available

Infantry
division (airlift)

Army division (slow sealift)

82d Airborne Division (airlift)

Marine division (prepositioned)

Delivery time (weeks)

a. Assumes purchase of all currently programmed assets; European deployment occurs first.

In regard to units required for deterrence in the Gulf, European lift requirements would undermine CENTCOM's critical ability to airlift light units to the Gulf, with the size of the problem dependent on the timing of the crises. If both crises escalated at about the same time, the Gulf would have to wait. Airlift to the Gulf would begin at least ten days later than expected and would move at a slower pace, because of both residual airlift requirements for Europe and simple wear and tear on aircraft. The effects of simultaneity on CENTCOM's delivery rate are shown in figure 3-10. If the United States reinforced Europe early, or if the European crisis were to lag that in the Gulf by thirty days, the United States might still be able to devote a substantial portion of its airlift to CENTCOM's requirements as soon as Soviet forces cross Iran's border. This best case approximates the one-front scenario outlined in figure 3-7.

This analysis merely confirms the validity of the long-standing contention that U.S. forces lack adequate strategic mobility. But it also focuses attention on the critical specific requirement to deploy one light infantry division to the Gulf more quickly. There are three general solutions to the problem of mobility: prepositioning, fast sealift, and airlift. Of these,

Table 3-4. *Cost of Moving a Mechanized Division to Southwest Asia*
Costs in billions of fiscal 1984 dollars

Mode	Twenty-year life cycle costs
Airlift (10 days)	49–65
Prepositioning plus airlift (10 days)	6.5–9.0
Fast sealift (22–27 days)	1.3–1.5

Source: U.S. Department of Defense, Office of Program Analysis and Evaluation.

fast sealift is not useful in the specific case of a light infantry division; sealift is more efficient in carrying heavier units, and in this case both light divisions would have to be loaded on the West Coast, raising the distance and time factors associated with delivery to the Gulf. Of the two remaining alternatives, the prepositioning/airlift option is by far the less expensive; Department of Defense (DoD) estimates for alternative ways of moving a mechanized division, shown in table 3-4, give some idea of the size of the cost differences (no DoD estimates for light divisions are available). Either method would place two full light divisions into the Gulf region in less than two weeks, as shown in figure 3-11, making it possible to deploy forward units from the United States to Iran's mountains in less than four weeks. If the United States exploited two weeks' warning to mobilize its sealift assets, as shown in figure 3-11, it could move and deploy a five-division force to Iran in about four weeks.

Fast sealift is included in table 3-4 to suggest that for approximately 20 percent more money than the prepositioning/airlift option alone the United States could purchase the ability to secure at least one division's worth of sealift assets for use during a two-front scenario, and two divisions' worth under one-front assumptions. That would give CENTCOM additional assets to account for friction and uncertainty as well as the possibility of a two-front crisis. Force delivery rate for the simultaneous two-front case is shown in figure 3-12. Total life cycle cost of buying both fast-deployment modes would come to roughly $10 billion (in 1984 dollars).

Logistics and Strategic Lift

With the comparatively limited outlays suggested previously, CENTCOM could substantially increase the speed with which it could deliver a five- or six-division force to the Gulf. But could CENTCOM also deliver to the region the supplies these units would need once they

Figure 3-11. *Force Delivery, Light Division Prepositioned*[a]

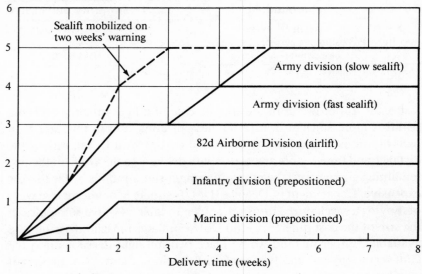

a. Assumes purchase of all currently programmed assets.

Figure 3-12. *Force Delivery, Additional Prepositioning and Fast Sealift*[a]

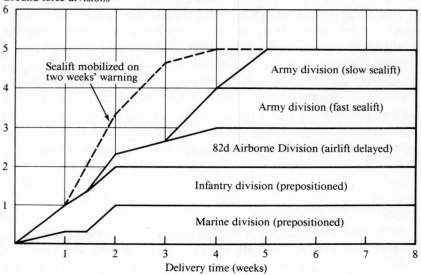

a. Assumes purchase of all currently programmed assets; simultaneous delivery to Europe and the Gulf.

arrive? The marine division would present no major problem, since it would carry supplies for thirty days' operations and would probably not face major combat around Abadan at the outset. But army units carry only three days' worth of supplies, and it is army units, particularly the two light divisions deployed to Iran's mountains, that would probably see combat early in the campaign. Besides food and water, these units would need fuel, ammunition, and medical supplies.

Reasonable assumptions can be used to bound this problem. Slow sealift would begin to deliver large quantities of supplies to the region after day 35, at which point the strategic lift problem would ease substantially. Conversely, even if CENTCOM owned an additional prepositioned division, as suggested previously, neither that unit nor the 82d Airborne Division would begin to assume positions in Iran's mountains until day 7. These units would need no resupply for three days, so new supplies would not have to reach lead elements until day 10. Thus the principal logistical problem would occupy a window reaching from day 10 to day 35.

Gauging the magnitude of this logistical problem is difficult. First, it is not clear that lead units would engage the Soviets immediately. More important, it is not clear how much ammunition would be consumed when the battle did begin. These units would be attempting to pursue a hit-and-run campaign designed less to win or to regain territory than to confuse Soviet operations, slow the advance, and increase Soviet casualties. Consumption of ammunition and fuel would probably be lower in Iran than in high-intensity combat in Europe. Army planning documents specify that in high-intensity warfare each soldier requires roughly 130 pounds (0.065 tons) of all kinds of supplies (food, tentage, construction equipment, ammunition, and fuel among other things) a day.[37] Although this figure may be too high for the kind of operations envisioned here, it can serve as a conservative planning estimate.

At full strength, the 82d Airborne Division contains roughly 16,000 soldiers, while a standard infantry division contains about 18,000 troops. Thus a total of 34,000 soldiers would have to be supported for twenty-five days. At 0.065 tons per soldier per day, total deliverable tonnage comes to 55,250 tons. Significantly, the eleven supply ships already prepositioned at Diego Garcia carry about 5,000 tons each,

---

37. U.S. Department of the Army, *Staff Officers' Field Manual: Organizational, Technical and Logistic Data*, FM 101-10-1 (Dept. of the Army, 1976), pp. 3–4.

meaning that 55,000 tons of supplies "for early arriving Air Force and Army units" are already available in the region.[38] The precise composition of these supplies is classified, but if it is assumed that half (27,500 tons) of these supplies are destined for army units, then an additional 27,750 tons would remain to be delivered to the region. This amount represents the capacity of three SL-7 ships, and since timing would not be crucial, given the presence of prepositioned supplies, fast sealift could make this delivery. Thus the strategic lift purchases suggested previously are more than adequate to cover support as well as force delivery.

Intratheater Lift and the Transshipment Problem

Solving CENTCOM's strategic lift problem does not automatically place the command in a position to implement a strategy of conventional deterrence. C-130s must ferry supplies and soldiers to Iran's mountains. There were 518 of these aircraft in the U.S. inventory in fiscal 1985 (excluding maintenance float aircraft); 216 were in the active air force, and 302 were in the U.S. Air Force Reserve and National Guard.[39] Although early models of the C-130 are now thirty years old, with modification programs early in the 1980s, "the entire C-130 force will be able to remain in service through the end of the century."[40] Because the aircraft are allocated to various commands, however, the number that could be made available to CENTCOM is uncertain.

As important as the number of C-130s available is the sortie rate CENTCOM is able to squeeze out of these aircraft. Loaded to its capacity of 20 tons, the C-130 has a combat radius of roughly 1,000 miles, and it flies at a speed of about 300 knots. The aircraft's normal operational day is eight hours, although it can be surged to twelve hours per day for short periods before it requires major maintenance. If army units are delivered to airports comparatively far from deployment points in Iran's mountains—Jiddah, Tel Aviv, or Ras Banas, for example—CENTCOM is likely to get an average of little more than 1 sortie per day per aircraft. Flying shorter missions from bases like Dhahran or King Khalid Military City in Saudi Arabia, by contrast, the average sortie rate may run as high as 1.8 or 2 per aircraft per day. In effect, basing

38. *U.S. Department of Defense Annual Report, Fiscal Year 1985*, p. 183.
39. Ibid., p. 288.
40. Ibid., p. 180.

arrangements can nearly double the usefulness of CENTCOM's C-130 fleet, whatever its size.

The task confronting CENTCOM involves two components. First, two divisions and additional supplies for them must be delivered to Iran's mountains as quickly as possible. Second, a continuous flow of supplies must be maintained as those units engage Soviet forces. The second of these components is not especially demanding. Two army divisions, or a total of 34,000 soldiers, would require 2,210 tons of supplies per day (34,000 × 0.065 tons per soldier per day). Assuming that supplies can be loaded aboard C-130s fairly efficiently, such that each aircraft can carry 20 tons, then 110 C-130s could handle this mission flying just 1 sortie per day. This is well within range of the C-130 fleet that CENTCOM can expect to have available to it.

Moving troops and supplies simultaneously into positions in Iran's mountains would be considerably more demanding. In contrast to supplies, divisions cannot be loaded on board C-130s very efficiently, owing to the size and density of divisional equipment. Although the total weight of the 82d Airborne Division is only 15,000 tons, it requires 1,709 C-130 sorties to carry the division administratively. If the division is loaded tactically, such that each aircraft load is configured to fight and support future incoming units, loading rates fall still further; the 82d Airborne Division requires 2,100 sorties for tactical delivery.[41] A standard infantry division weighs considerably more than the 82d Airborne Division and requires about 2,158 sorties for administrative delivery.[42] Using the administrative to tactical ratio of the 82d Airborne Division, it can be assumed that a standard infantry division would require roughly 2,650 C-130 sorties for tactical delivery. Thus a total of 4,750 sorties would be required to deliver both units to Iran's mountains.

Supplies must also be delivered to these units to keep them functional as the supplies they carry run out. The total lift burden implied here is a function of the speed with which the two divisions (a total of 34,000

41. Taken from unclassified loading documents for the division.

42. Information provided by U.S. Department of the Army, Office of the Deputy Chief of Staff for Operations and Plans. Note that in fiscal 1986 the 9th High-Technology Motorized Division will replace the infantry division on CENTCOM's force list. Because the 9th HTMD is lighter and more easily carried than a standard infantry division, the calculations offered here are conservative in relation to CENTCOM's future forces. See F. Clifton Berry, Jr., "The US Army's 9th Infantry Division," *International Defense Review,* vol. 17, no. 9 (1984), especially pp. 1227–28.

soldiers) are delivered to the mountains. If a linear buildup of troop strength that takes n days is assumed, then the average number of soldiers that must be supplied is $n/2 \times 34,000$ or $17,000n$, and the additional tonnage of supplies these units will need as they are being delivered will be:

$$(17,000n \times 0.065) - (3 \times 34,000 \times 0.065)$$
$$\text{or}$$
$$1,105n - 6,630,$$

where 6,630 is the three days' supplies the units carry with them. Assuming that each C-130 carries 20 tons of supplies per sortie, the total C-130 sorties required for supplying these units is

$$\frac{1,105n - 6,630}{20}.$$

To this must be added the 4,750 sorties required to deliver the divisions themselves. Dividing by n produces a formula for relating n to sorties per day:

$$S(\text{sorties per day}) = \frac{4,750}{n} + \frac{1,105n - 6,630}{20n}.$$

Table 3-5 solves this equation for various ns and shows the number of C-130s required at sortie rates of 1 and 2 per day.

The intratheater lift problem is demanding but not beyond the reach of available resources (table 3-5), especially if CENTCOM can operate its C-130s at fairly high sortie rates from nearby bases like that at Dhahran. The number of C-130s available to CENTCOM is crucial. Note that CENTCOM's major challenge is a surge problem, not a continuing one; after day n, when both units have been positioned in the mountains, the resupply problem shrinks to more manageable proportions. Consequently, a premium exists on doing here what was suggested earlier for the air interdiction campaign—surging the U.S. inventory of C-130s and surging each aircraft beyond its normal operational day to meet a demanding but short-term problem. If CENTCOM could gain even temporary control of C-130s usually allocated to various other U.S. commands, or if it could gain access to Saudi Arabia's fleet of more than 50 C-130s, it could manage its intratheater delivery problem.

Table 3-5. *C-130 Aircraft Required for Intratheater Delivery of Two Divisions and Supplies*

Days required for delivery (n)	C-130s required (one sortie per day)	C-130s required (two sorties per day)
7	686	343
10	497	249
14	371	185

One further challenge remains—transferring cargo from strategic lift to C-130s—the so-called transshipment problem. The chief constraint here stems from the facts of base geography (so-called ramp space): How many runways are available? How much room is available for turning aircraft around? How many aircraft can be parked at one time? Furthermore, forklifts, cranes, and people must be available to coordinate the cargo transfer. These mundane items are rarely discussed. Yet basing requirements would be more demanding, in size and number of bases available, than those involved in the air interdiction campaign. Perhaps the only consolation is that airports in the Gulf area are numerous and very large, thanks to oil revenues over the past decade.

Although the U.S. Air Force's proposed C-17 aircraft, now being developed, would add to its overall outsize airlift assets, the aircraft's real value would lie in its ability to sidestep the transshipment issue. Assuming that initial requirements for the aircraft are met, the C-17 will be able to land at roughly the kind of airfield now open only to C-130s, while carrying the full range of military cargo. With proper tanker support it could fly directly from the United States to Iran's mountains, eliminating both the need for transshipment in the region and the time consumed by the C-130 leg of current delivery methods. The C-17 would speed the delivery of light units and perhaps lessen political problems linked with taking over a number of airports in the Gulf region.

Even if it is acquired on schedule, however, the C-17 will not be available in force until the mid-1990s. In the meantime, CENTCOM must try to handle the transshipment problem with the assets available to it. Significantly, much of the equipment and people needed to transfer cargo are located in the U.S. Army Reserves, though in portions of the reserves earmarked for especially rapid mobilization. The urgency of the transshipment requirement, which must begin about day 7 of the overall operation, makes this arrangement questionable. For CENTCOM, a basic quota of the equipment and personnel needed to handle transshipment should be part of the active force and should be exercised frequently.

The complexities and possible shortcomings of the support operations implied in this discussion could be elaborated endlessly. How many C-130s would be shot down over the Zagros Mountains? Would enough stevedores and air traffic controllers be available to handle the transshipment problem? How would CENTCOM handle the enormous communications and coordination challenges implied by the airlift operation—while simultaneously managing the air interdiction campaign? Military operations are more complicated in practice than they are on paper, and logistics operations may be the most complex of all.

The calculations offered are not meant to suggest that supporting two divisions in north-central Iran would be a simple task. They merely assess whether the task is feasible in the broadest sense and where major shortfalls are likely to appear. The fact is that, using very conservative assumptions, delivering two light divisions to the Zagros Mountains and supporting them once they are there are not overwhelming problems. Furthermore, the support of those divisions would not require enormous additional expenditures. It can be handled within existing resource levels if some flexibility is permitted among U.S. forces.

Conclusions

Although current acquisition programs will not produce a force structure fully adequate to deter Soviet forces from entering Iran, they are neither inappropriate to that mission nor far from being adequate. Marginal additional purchases of lift and prepositioning assets in particular would provide CENTCOM with delivery and support capabilities that would be very robust under one-front assumptions. Those assets would be adequate to hedge against the possibility of war in Europe as well as (or instead of) in the Gulf. The major requirements are (1) to preposition the equipment for a light infantry division near the Gulf; and (2) to purchase an additional eight SL-7 fast sealift vessels. Total cost would be roughly $10 billion (in 1984 dollars) over several years, or less than $2 billion in any single year. That figure is not high considering that the United States would be protecting interests likely to be vital for years to come.

Yet clearly it makes little sense to discuss the adequacy of U.S.

military capabilities without recognizing that the exercise of these capabilities rests largely on a political foundation. Without air bases in Turkey and the interior Gulf, CENTCOM's air interdiction campaign would have to rely on B-52Hs and carrier-based A-6Es. These could certainly promise the Soviets a confrontation, and they might also help deter long-range Soviet airborne operations or an attack out of southern Afghanistan. But the ability of these aircraft alone to sustain an interdiction campaign against Soviet forces in northern Iran is questionable.

Without bases in the interior Gulf and the neutrality or active support of Iranians themselves, it would be impossible for CENTCOM to put any but small, highly trained units into northern Iran, and the operation might look disturbingly like a suicide mission. The United States might also consider simply taking the area around Abadan and accepting a fight with the Iranians as well as a possible fight with the Soviet Union. Facing no appreciable U.S. resistance to the north, the Soviets would be able to consolidate a position in northern Iran, leaving the country split. But U.S. forces would be at the end of a much longer supply line than Soviet forces, leaving the United States in a weaker bargaining position than the Soviet Union so far as negotiations about the future of Iran are concerned. Faced with this prospect, the United States might not want to engage in ground force action at all.

An examination of the operational problems that attend U.S. efforts to meet Soviet forces in Iran only emphasizes the basing problem and the political and diplomatic challenges it imposes. The need to transship U.S. ground forces confronts planners with the need to mount an elaborate staging operation rapidly, possibly from a wide network of bases. Some of those bases might also be supporting the air interdiction campaign. Meanwhile, the advantages that flow from exploiting warning time place a high premium on gaining access to basing early. This in turn imposes a need to work with local elites in an effort to generate a common understanding of the nature of likely Soviet military activity, how it affects their interests, and the requirements for a timely U.S. military response.

The uncertainties inherent in doing these things often lead U.S. policymakers to turn to Israel as the one reliable U.S. regional ally. Whether or not Israel is the only reliable ally in the area, it should be clear that Israel alone simply cannot support useful military operations aimed at deterring the Soviet military threat to the region. Israel could play a limited role in such operations, and if a Soviet military threat were indeed to materialize, Arab and Iranian rulers, normally critical of Israel and U.S. ties to it, might be willing to accept some Israeli involvement in their own defense. But the United States should not rely solely on Israel, nor should U.S.-Israeli ties be allowed to undermine constructive relations with the Gulf states themselves.

Even from the rather narrow perspective of balancing Soviet power in the Gulf, there is no escaping the need to deal constructively with key Gulf states. Iran is a special problem; at the moment perhaps all the United States can do is avoid needlessly closing off the possibility of constructive dialogue. The principal focus of concern falls on Saudi Arabia, Oman, and, to a lesser extent, the smaller oil sheikhdoms that line the Gulf's southern shores. Part of the relationship that the United States maintains with these states must include the development of their role in balancing Soviet power in the Gulf.

The fact is, of course, that the Soviet threat is not the principal concern in these states, any more than handling the Soviet threat is the sole or even principal rationale for U.S. ties to the Gulf. Indeed, discussions about basing, prepositioning, and the like fold into a host of other topics for discussion with rulers in these states. Seeking to meet the Soviet threat in the Gulf meshes with the problem of dealing practically with the array of local and regional threats that the Arabian Peninsula must confront. How the United States can successfully play its role in this complicated picture is the subject of part 2 of this book.

PART TWO

The United States
and Peninsular Security

THE NEED to balance Soviet power in the Gulf is only one concern encouraging the United States to seek closer security ties to the oil-rich kingdoms of the Arabian Peninsula. The larger concern stems from the enormous influence these states, especially Saudi Arabia, are likely to wield over oil markets for years to come. Clearly a need exists for greater cooperation between the oil kingdoms and oil consumers. And in this volatile region a clear role also exists for the instruments of security—arms, assistance, and possibly U.S. forces—within the context of a broader U.S. policy of support to the peninsular regimes.

Yet, the seeming indecisiveness and unreliability of the Gulf's traditional rulers; their unwillingness to host a U.S. military presence; and questions about the stability of their rule complicate the U.S. role. Some analysts would avoid facing these issues by eschewing U.S. military involvement in local affairs. Instead, they would simply plan to seize the oil fields.[1] Yet such a policy runs counter to the security assistance that the United States and its allies now extend to the peninsular oil states, much of which purports to improve their ability to defend oil wells. Moreover, reducing the supportive elements of U.S. security policy toward the Gulf in favor of planning to seize oil wells would reduce U.S. influence in all but the extreme case in which seizing oil wells seemed absolutely necessary.

But embracing the peninsular rulers as President Reagan did when he suggested that the United States would not allow the Saudis to succumb to the kind of internal problems that toppled the shah may not be the

1. As suggested by Kenneth N. Waltz, "A Strategy for the Rapid Deployment Force," *International Security,* vol. 5 (Spring 1981), pp. 49–73, especially pp. 61–62.

wisest route to a supportive security policy.[2] No president can promise to keep such a commitment. Nor would the American public or peninsular rulers find that policy comforting. On the Peninsula, as in many other parts of the world, the United States faces conflicting pressures favoring commitment and detachment. On the Arabian Peninsula the interests are critical enough, the regimes seemingly vulnerable enough, to give these issues a special urgency.

Official U.S. policy has long been committed to stability and peaceful change. But if the United States accepts stability and peaceful change as useful goals, how can they be translated into operational U.S. security policy? Although U.S. military planners might not wish to abjure planning for the use of U.S. forces against local states, under current conditions the only useful approach is to understand the local security situation in its full complexity. What are the components of the local and regional security problem? What forces have shaped the security policies of local states, in particular Saudi Arabia, whose size and oil resources make it exceptionally important to U.S. and allied interests? How has the United States fit into this situation in the past? Can it find ways, despite its enduring ties to Israel and the new conditions created by Iran's revolution, to buttress the forces that favor stability and to protect what chances remain for peaceful change?

Part 2 of this book addresses these questions. The focus is on the six peninsular oil states: Saudi Arabia, Kuwait, Bahrain, Qatar, the United Arab Emirates (UAE), and Oman. Among them, these states hold roughly 55 percent of the world's known oil reserves. Saudi Arabia dominates the group in every sense; it is by far the largest in both population and land mass, has the largest military forces, and holds three times more oil reserves than any other country in the world. Saudi Arabia also has the closest relationship of any of the Gulf states with the United States. Yet the six states are joined by their position on the Arabian Peninsula, by their common and very traditional political systems, and by increasing efforts in recent years to cooperate in security matters. Although Saudi Arabia should be given special attention, all six states deserve to be treated as a unit.

Chapter 4 considers the overall peninsular security situation, looking at internal and external threats as well as their interaction. This chapter may be seen as an analysis of threats in an area where threat assessment

---

2. See Bernard Gwertzman, "Reagan Asserts U.S. Is Committed to Security of Some in Middle East," *New York Times,* October 27, 1981.

is far more complex than the kind of division counts and terrain analysis that planners apply to the Soviet threat to Iran. Chapter 5 turns to local responses to these threats. It focuses on Saudi Arabia and the associated oil states and seeks to explain the pressures that shape the peculiar security strategy these states have adopted. Chapter 6 takes up the U.S. security roles suggested by this analysis and addresses how the United States can help the local states, how it should deal with likely changes in the security environment, and how the United States should plan to use its own forces should the quest for stability and peaceful change be overtaken by events.

CHAPTER FOUR

The Components
of Peninsular Security

U.S. POLICYMAKERS who toured the Gulf area after 1979 looking for bases to help the United States deter Soviet aggression were confronted by rulers on the Arabian Peninsula who had different priorities. These rulers seemed unmoved by talk of a Soviet invasion, or even Soviet-sponsored subversion. In fact, they were more concerned with the internal and regional implications of Iran's revolution (and, later, of the Iran-Iraq war); with the corrosive internal effects of the Palestinian issue; and with the problems posed by their burgeoning oil revenues. Even their resistance to U.S. basing requests seemed motivated in part by the potential effects that a permanent U.S. presence might have on their legitimacy.

Events since 1979 tend to confirm their view of the local security problem. The Soviets have not invaded Iran. But Saudi Arabia, Bahrain, and Kuwait have experienced violence related at least partly to Iran's revolution. War between Iran and Iraq has led to sporadic Iranian attacks on Kuwait. More important, that war has raised the possibility of threats to Gulf oil exports or even of an Iranian invasion of the Arabian Peninsula. Meanwhile, a slumping oil market has forced these rulers to manage a substantial contraction of their economies after nearly a decade of rapid growth—a task no national leader would be anxious to face.

The best way to understand the security problems facing the peninsular oil states is to work from the inside out. Consequently, this chapter looks first at the internal component of the overall security situation that these states confront, briefly examining internal security in each of the six peninsular oil states. Then it discusses the peninsular component of

91

their security—the threats posed by conflict among them and the other states that occupy the Arabian Peninsula. And finally, the problem of external attack from the surrounding region is examined. Clear and distinguishable problems within each of these three components characterize the issue of peninsular security. More important, however, significant interactions occur between components. Events in the region around the Peninsula can produce repercussions within the peninsular states, for example, while turbulence within these states can invite outside intervention.

Indeed, this chapter highlights the complexity and ambiguity of the peninsular security situation. These rulers must deal with rapid socioeconomic change that alone could generate social forces capable of bringing them down. They must manage this problem in a regional context in which events within their borders can be linked to events across the Middle East as a whole. Meanwhile, the tools available to preserve their security—military forces, oil revenues, traditional sources of legitimacy, and so forth—also have the potential to work against them. Thus their situation is murky and ill-defined. Small-scale violence may be an ominous warning of larger threats to come, and rulers can never be certain that they are in control of, or even fully understand, the situation. This breeds an understandable cautiousness in their policies, a cautiousness that must be appreciated if the United States is to help these rulers with their security instead of posing yet another threat to them.

The Internal Component

Before turning to each one of the six peninsular oil states, it is useful to highlight common problems that all six face. Each set of rulers must deal, first, with the residue of old conflicts that go unresolved. Tribal loyalties run deep in some areas and are only slightly in the background in others. Other conflicts draw on the various regions of the Peninsula (figure 4-1); the vast conquests of Abd al-Aziz ibn Abd al-Rahman Al Saud have given Saudi Arabia a special regional problem in this regard. Finally, racial and religious differences among peoples of the Peninsula, often the product of population flows centuries ago, have created dissident pockets within individual states.

The presence of Arab and Persian Shi'a Muslims along the Peninsula's eastern coast is a special case in point. Sunni and Shi'a Muslims differ on

Figure 4-1. *States and Regions of the Arabian Peninsula*

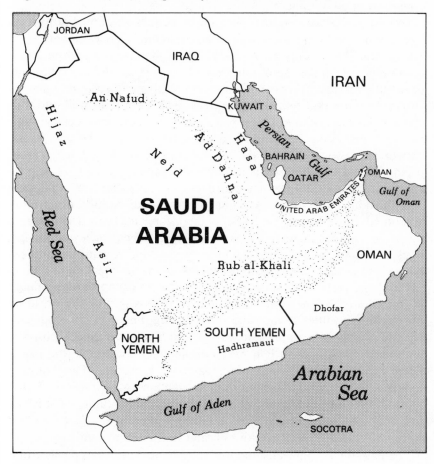

fundamental questions concerning the succession to the prophet Mohammed, the relationship of the state to God, and the relationship of
rulers to ruled. Shi'as make up the vast majority in Iran, but Shi'a tribes
have also lived along the Peninsula's eastern edge for centuries. In more
recent times Persian traders have also moved to the peninsular sheikhdoms. For the Peninsula's Sunni rulers the problem with Iran's Shi'a
revolution thus is not simply the vivid image of a genuinely Muslim
revolution that it presents to all Muslims, although this in itself is
worrisome. These rulers must also worry about the effects of Iran's

revolutionary proselytizing on their own Shi'as, many of whom feel oppressed in predominantly Sunni states.[1]

Second, each state must deal with the consequences of oil wealth. The wealth is new; oil was discovered in Kuwait in the 1930s, exploitation on a large scale began only after World War II, and large oil revenues to rulers themselves are the product mostly of the last decade. Thus the peninsular oil states have experienced incredibly rapid economic growth amidst societies that retained their traditional form until well into this century. This has created a class problem, with traditional social groups having to make way for rising technocratic and bourgeois groups. Rapid growth has also exhausted the limited supply of skilled indigenous personnel and thus has produced enormous inflows of foreign labor. In Kuwait, the UAE, and Qatar, expatriates outnumber the native population. Although this is not yet the case in Saudi Arabia, expatriates accounted for 43 percent of the Saudi labor force in the mid-1970s, and the percentage has increased in the years since.[2] The presence of foreign workers complicates domestic politics by causing resentment and by tying events inside the oil states to events the world over.

Third and perhaps most important, the process of coping with change is complicated by the continuing salience in this part of the world of overarching loyalties to race and religion. Legitimacy in the Arab and Islamic worlds is in important ways a function of the ruler's position with respect to trends in Pan-Arab and Islamic thought.[3] In the 1960s Egypt's Gamal Abdel Nasser manipulated the symbols of Pan-Arabism to attack the conservative peninsular monarchies. More recently, Iran's Ayatollah Khomeini has employed the symbols of fundamentalist Islam to attack the same states from a different direction. Again, on the Arabian Peninsula, external powers can cause internal conflict.

The Palestinian issue falls into this category and draws its power from both Arab and Islamic forces. Peninsular rulers must worry about

1. See the excellent discussion in James A. Bill, "Resurgent Islam in the Persian Gulf," *Foreign Affairs,* vol. 63 (Fall 1984), pp. 108–127.

2. See Saad Eddin Ibrahim, *The New Arab Social Order: A Study of the Social Impact of Oil Wealth* (Boulder, Colo.: Westview Press, 1982), p. 95. For a breakdown of Saudi Arabia's expatriates in nationality and skill level, see Naiem A. Sherbiny and Ismail Serageldin, "Expatriate Labor and Economic Growth: Saudi Demand for Egyptian Labor," in Malcolm H. Kerr and El Sayed Yassin, eds., *Rich and Poor States in the Middle East: Egypt and the New Arab Order* (Boulder, Colo.: Westview Press, 1982), pp. 225–57.

3. See Michael C. Hudson, *Arab Politics: The Search for Legitimacy* (Yale University Press, 1977), p. 54.

Palestinian terrorism. King Abdullah of Transjordan was assassinated in 1951 by a Palestinian, allegedly for dealing too openly with Israel. Rulers must also worry about the loyalties of the well-educated diaspora Palestinians, many of whom hold important positions in governments all around the Peninsula. But the more insidious problem is the gradual erosion of legitimacy resulting from the failure of Arab and Islamic regimes to deliver either a military victory or an acceptable peace with Israel. The Palestinian issue is intertwined with the legitimacy of Arab regimes, operating so subtly that even peninsular rulers themselves are probably uncertain about its effects. That uncertainty conditions their actions, however.

Mention of Palestinian terrorism raises the final internal problem common to these states—the violence that others export to them. The Ayatollah Khomeini can seek to provoke internal violence in Saudi Arabia, for example, by proselytizing among that country's small Shi'a population. But he can also send terrorists of his own, or from other countries, to cause violence. Open coastlines and long, desolate borders among countries on the Peninsula make infiltration—by boat, for example—fairly easy. And targets are plentiful, especially among the oil facilities along the Peninsula's eastern coast. Thus far Kuwait, in particular, has experienced this problem: in December 1983 a string of bombings was attributed to members of the Islamic Al Dawaa party, a Shi'a group with close ties to Iran.[4] But the Saudis must worry that an escalation of the Iran-Iraq war could bring Iranian terrorism to them as well.

These problems manifest themselves in different ways and to different degrees in each of the six oil kingdoms, depending on the history, geography, and social circumstances of each. This section makes no attempt to capture the full range of internal threats in individual states. Rather, the chapter summarizes the kinds of internal problems likely to exert the most influence over the security situation each state faces. Because Saudi Arabia is the dominant peninsular state, the survey begins with it and dwells on its problems in somewhat greater detail.

---

4. Iran in fact denied complicity in these bombings, which were aimed at the U.S. and French embassies, as well as at some Kuwaiti oil facilities. However, the conspirators were predominantly Lebanese and Iraqi Shia's, not native Kuwaitis. See "Kuwait Bombings: 10 Arrested," *Middle East Economic Digest,* vol. 27 (December 23–29, 1983), p. 3. (Hereafter *MEED.*)

Saudi Arabia

Captured in the rapid expansion of Saudi power early in this century was a diverse set of regions, tribes, and religious groups. On this potpourri King Abd al-Aziz sought to impose his conservative "Wahhabi" brand of Islam. Over this region, the Saudis have tended to rule as "tribal overlords,"[5] an approach many feel has perpetuated traditional loyalties. The persistence of traditional loyalties is difficult for outsiders to judge. Yet occasional outbreaks of violence suggest that such loyalties remain potent and complicate the ruling family's operations. Four such problems deserve special mention.

THE SHI'AS OF HASA PROVINCE. Saudi Arabia's Shi'as today number from a quarter to half a million, most of whom live in the oil-rich eastern Hasa province, where they comprise about half of the labor force of the Arab American Oil Company (ARAMCO). Little love has been lost between these Shi'as and the Saudi royal family. As one observer put it, Saudi Arabia's Shi'as

will not soon forget the Wahhabi fanaticism which has oppressed them for two centuries, nor their religious attachment which has frequently cost them their lives. This stimulates them to maintain strong ties with the Shi'i centers, such as An-Najaf in southern Iraq, Qum in Iran, or Bahrain, where their coreligionists make up the majority of the population.[6]

Rioting among the Shi'as in November 1979 and February 1980 suggests that they remain disaffected and enjoy little of the wealth or political access many Saudis enjoy. Believed to have been sparked by taped messages from the Ayatollah Khomeini, the riots also attest to the links these Shi'as forge between events inside and outside of Saudi Arabia.[7]

THE HIJAZIS. Along the mountainous western coast of the Arabian Peninsula lies the Hijaz, an area that includes the Muslim holy cities of Mecca and Medina. Long association with Muslims coming from all directions to visit Islam's holy shrines at Mecca and Medina gave the Hijazis a cosmopolitan and commercial outlook at odds with that of the Wahhabi fanatics who conquered them in 1925–26. The Hijazis tend to retain a distinct identity within the Saudi state. Talk of Hijazi separat-

---

5. Adeed Dawisha, *Saudi Arabia's Search for Security,* Adelphi Paper 158 (London: International Institute for Strategic Studies, 1979), p. 13.

6. Ghassane Salameh, "Political Power and the Saudi State," *MERIP Reports* (Middle East Research and Information Project), no. 91 (October 1980), p. 14.

7. See Arnold Hottinger, "Who Held the Grand Mosque Hostage?" *New York Review of Books,* March 6, 1980, p. 36.

ism, frequently heard into the 1960s, has abated as increasing oil revenues generated on the other side of the Arabian Peninsula have given the Hijazis good reason to remain part of Saudi Arabia. Completion of a pipeline linking the eastern fields with the Hijazi port at Yanbu symbolizes the connection between these two parts of the Saudi state, but questions remain about the loyalty of Hijazis to the Al Saud (literally, the family of Saud).

THE TRIBES OF THE ASIR. Just above North Yemen lie tribes that were formerly part of the Yemeni Imamate. They were taken under Saudi control between 1920 and 1934. Tribal ties to the Yemen appear to remain strong, and there is constant travel across the Saudi-Yemeni border.[8] Because this border is a matter of broad security concern to the Saudis, the loyalty of these tribes is of special importance in Riyadh.

ISLAMIC FUNDAMENTALISTS. Because their family's legitimacy rests partly on its long-standing affiliation with Wahhabism, often called a puritanical branch of Islam, today's Saudi rulers must tread an especially arduous course as they seek to modernize their country. King Abd al-Aziz himself occasionally found it difficult to control the fanaticism of his Wahhabi followers, the more extreme of whom opposed the introduction of the automobile, the telephone, or any other modern device. Abd al-Aziz finally crushed the more rebellious of these dissidents in the battle of Sibila in 1929. But his descendants must still contend with the possibility of outbursts of religious conservatism. The most recent and well known of these occurred in November 1979, when a group of religious fanatics upset by, among other things, what they saw as corruption in the Saudi state, occupied the Grand Mosque at Mecca. Saudi police and ground forces, working with French help, slowly cleared the mosque room by room, but only after the king had obtained the support of the country's Ulama, or religious leadership, to do so.[9]

---

8. See Christopher S. Wren, "Saudi-Yemen Frontier: Skirmishes in the Desert," *New York Times*, May 8, 1980. Note also John E. Peterson's remarks on the Asir: "Many Yemenis have yet to fully reconcile themselves to the loss of Asir province, the port of Jizan and the oasis of Najran, which they feel are legitimate parts of greater Yemen. As is the case elsewhere in the Middle East, national boundaries cut across tribal lines and Saudi interference in what Yemenis consider to be internal disputes has not improved the popular image of Saudis south of their border." See his *Conflict in the Yemens and Superpower Involvement*, Occasional Paper Series (Georgetown University, Center for Contemporary Arab Studies, 1982), pp. 9–10.

9. For a brief description of the Mecca Mosque incident, see William B. Quandt, *Saudi Arabia in the 1980s: Foreign Policy, Security, and Oil* (Brookings Institution, 1981), pp. 93–96.

To these traditional social cleavages, rapid economic growth has added a new set of distinctions. It has begun to produce a "bourgeoisie" whose members are said to chafe at the power of the conservative Ulama in ruling councils, resent the lack of civil liberties in Saudi society, and in general find Saudi rule oppressive.[10] Rapid growth has also vastly enlarged the country's foreign population. Most foreigners are blue-collar laborers, the most numerous by far being Yemenis, who number close to a million, and whom for various historical reasons the Saudis regard with suspicion.[11]

Partly because of the size and diversity of their country, the Saudis have a special problem with their armed forces. They have seen military coups topple a number of regimes in the region. They have experienced a modest amount of turbulence and plotting within their own military, especially the air force. And they can remember the problems Abd al-Aziz himself had with dissident sheikhs in command of disloyal forces in 1929–30.[12] Their armed forces today are too large to be a family-dominated praetorian guard. The services recruit from various regions of the state, giving them a touch of the heterogeneity that marks Saudi society as a whole. Thus the ruling family today is no more willing than Abd al-Aziz was to take the loyalty of the armed forces for granted. As is detailed in chapter 5, their suspicions lead them to take steps that seriously limit the capability of their armed forces to provide for the nation's defense.

The last problem worth discussing in connection with stability and conflict within Saudi Arabia is that of schisms within the Al Saud itself. King Abd al-Aziz made adroit use of marriage to help win the loyalty of tribes within his expanding domain. He fathered 400 children, most of whom have varying degrees of status within the ruling families. Key members of these families reportedly disagree on crucial issues—the pace of modernization, policy toward the United States, position on the Palestinian issue, and so forth. Thus far the Saudis have been at pains to

10. See, for example, Michael Field, "The Balancing Act Facing the House of Saud,"*Financial Times* (London), August 12, 1982.

11. For much broader treatments, see J. E. Peterson, *Yemen: The Search for a Modern State* (Johns Hopkins University Press, 1982), pp. 17–19; and Robert G. Darius and Robert H. Pelletreau, *Possible Scenarios for Iran and Saudi Arabia in the 1980s* (Carlisle Barracks, Pa.: U.S. Army War College, Strategic Studies Institute, October 25, 1982), p. 19.

12. On the "Ikhwan Revolt" see Christine Moss Helms, *The Cohesion of Saudi Arabia: Evolution of Political Identity* (London: Croom Helm, 1981), pp. 250–74.

hide signs of interfamilial strife. Such strife has occasionally broken into the open, however, and might do so again.

The Coastal Sheikhdoms

Saudi Arabia's neighboring sheikhdoms share many of the internal problems that plague the Saudis, but several factors set them apart. In contrast to Saudi Arabia, most of the littoral sheikhdoms have substantial Iranian minorities. All have experienced greater popular demands for political participation than the Saudis, and all have experimented with political institutions that at least grant the appearance of public participation. Where the Saudis face an enormous internal control problem, internal security concerns in the coastal sheikhdoms are concentrated in the cities that contain most of their population. This feature eases the problem of political control but also provides insurgents and political dissidents with a single geographic focus for their activities. On balance, size would appear to make these states more vulnerable than Saudi Arabia to internal pressure for change. Conversely, the small size of these sheikhdoms appears to ease their fears of their own militaries. Military forces in the sheikhdoms are much smaller than those of Saudi Arabia and tend to be dominated by the ruling family. Thus for these states the military's domestic threat appears to be more of a potential problem, one that might accompany significant future expansion of their armed forces.

KUWAIT. Kuwait's relatively long experience with substantial oil revenues has brought to it an expatriate population that outnumbers native Kuwaitis. A substantial portion of Kuwait's population of approximately a million is Iranian or Arab Shi'a—and more than a fifth are Palestinian, leaving the ruling Al Sabah open to buffeting from virtually every political current in the region.[13] A series of terrorist incidents by the Palestinian Liberation Organization and the Popular Front for the Liberation of Palestine between 1972 and 1975,[14] for example, height-

---

13. The 1975 census showed native Kuwaitis to comprise 47.5 percent of Kuwait's population. Other major groups were Palestinians and Jordanians (20.5 percent), Egyptians (6.1 percent), Iraqis (4.1 percent), Iranians (4.1 percent), and Syrians (4.1 percent). "Foreign Workers Essential to the Economy," *Financial Times*, Survey, February 23, 1983.

14. See Richard F. Nyrop and others, *Area Handbook for the Persian Gulf States* (Government Printing Office, 1977), p. 202.

ened Kuwait's sense of threat from the Palestinians, while political ferment among Persian and Arab Shi'as in the aftermath of Iran's revolution exposed Kuwait's vulnerability on that front.

Having used its oil revenues to create the most advanced system of social welfare (for native Kuwaitis) among the Gulf sheikhdoms, the Al Sabah now confronts a fairly well-educated native population that, combined with sophisticated elements among resident expatriates, has pressed hard for political reform. Kuwaitis elected their first National Assembly in 1963, but because that body opposed the Al Sabah on a variety of issues it was dissolved in 1976.[15] The assembly was reinstituted in 1981.[16] It is difficult to know where these experiments will take Kuwait. But it is almost certain that the pressure that gave rise to the experiments will not disappear.

BAHRAIN. Bahrain's population of less than half a million is split between Shi'a and Sunni Muslims, with Shi'as a slight majority. Although some Shi'a families have been successful economically and Shi'as are represented in Bahrain's cabinet, the ruling Al Khalifah and important merchant families are Sunnis, while members of the working class and small farmers tend to be Shi'as. This aligns religious with class differences.

The potential for domestic turbulence in this situation and the crucial linkage between the Peninsula's Shi'as and the Iranian revolution were manifest in December 1981, when the Bahraini police uncovered a coup plot involving Shi'a Muslims from Saudi Arabia as well as Bahrain itself. The plot apparently was conceived and sponsored by Iran's "Gulf Affairs Section," headed by Hojatolislam Hadi Modarresi, an Iranian Shi'a clergyman exiled to Bahrain in the 1970s, who returned to Iran in 1979. Iran is said to have provided the plotters with small arms and replicas of the Bahraini police uniform. Some argue that Iran had also assembled its fleet of hovercraft to support the coup if it succeeded initially. In fact, the plot was uncovered a few weeks before the coup

15. Significantly, the assembly's dissolution was precipitated by vocal elements among Kuwait's Palestinian population who opposed the government's failure to condemn Syrian intervention in Lebanon. Ibid., p. 203.

16. Never terribly representative, the 1981 assembly resulted from a vote involving only 3 percent of Kuwait's population. The vote apparently "was preceded by some careful redrawing of the constituency boundaries which successfully watered down the Shi'a vote. The result was the return of safe and loyal conservatives." Kathleen Evans, "Kuwait: Challenges Ahead for Revived Democracy," *Financial Times,* Survey, February 23, 1983.

attempt was to be made. Seventy-three conspirators were convicted and given jail sentences ranging from seven years to life.[17]

Although its oil resources are now small and declining, Bahrain was one of the first states to experience the rush of oil wealth. This has given it a comparatively sophisticated population with a wide range of political views. Like the Al Sabah in Kuwait, the Al Khalifah has been pressed to experiment with representative institutions. As in Kuwait, however, Bahrain's experiment was short-lived, in large part because debate in the National Assembly tended to be polarized and highly ideological and revealed strong open hostility to the ruling family. The assembly was dissolved in 1975 and has not been reconvened.[18]

If Kuwait's special tie to the Palestinian issue stems from its fairly large Palestinian expatriate community, Bahrain's lies in the presence of a U.S. naval administrative support unit and five-ship fleet (MIDEASTFOR) at a leased base at Jufair, just outside the capital city of Manama. The status of this lease became especially controversial just after the 1973 Arab-Israeli war, when Bahrain's rulers, embarrassed by the visible tie to Israel's principal ally, threatened to cancel it. The lease ultimately remained in effect, albeit in modified form, but it could become a target for domestic dissent in the wider context of unhappiness with the Arab-Israeli situation. Under those circumstances the Al Khalifah's willingness to host U.S. forces would certainly not add to its popularity or legitimacy.

QATAR. Although Iranians may constitute as much as 20 percent of Qatar's population, that population is otherwise relatively homogeneous and shares with Saudi Arabia the puritanical Wahhabi faith. This may help account for Qatar's relative lack of social development in comparison with Kuwait or Bahrain. Qatar's people are considered less sophisticated, for example, and its trade unions have a somewhat shorter history than those in Kuwait or Bahrain. In addition, through intermarriage the ruling al-Thani family has apparently spread itself widely through the population. Qatar has experienced little political unrest, and the persis-

17. See "65 Arabs Arrested in Sabotage Plot," *New York Times,* December 17, 1981; "Iran: Again Trying to Export Revolution?" *Defense & Foreign Affairs Daily,* vol. 11 (January 7, 1982), p. 2; "Bahrain: Did Iran Plan Invasion?" *Defense & Foreign Affairs Daily,* vol. 11 (January 15, 1982), p. 2; and John Vinocur, "1981 Plot in Bahrain Linked to Iranians," *New York Times,* July 25, 1982.

18. Emile Nakleh, "Why the Unrelenting Focussing on Democracy in the Gulf and not in the Rest of the Arab World?" *Middle East* (London), no. 70 (August 1980), pp. 32–35.

tence of traditional tribally based political institutions has produced little visible pressure on the Al Thani for wider participation.[19] Qatar's internal troubles thus tend to involve traditional tribal and dynastic squabbles of limited significance to the Peninsula as a whole.[20]

THE UNITED ARAB EMIRATES. The UAE was created by the British in 1971 from seven small sheikhdoms. Dynastic squabbles within ruling families thus are overlaid with feuds among the UAE's seven ruling families. These feuds are exacerbated by wide disparities in the distribution of oil wealth among the seven constituent sheikhdoms, and by the long-standing close relationship between Iran and Dubai, the second most powerful of the seven emirates (Abu Dhabi is by far the largest of the seven and its ruler, Sheikh Zayed, is also president of the UAE). This relationship, born of trade and the presence of a large Iranian contingent among Dubai's population, is especially important from the perspective of security. In the recent past Iran has sided consistently with Dubai in its attempts to maintain relative independence within the federation, effectively encouraging separatist tendencies within the UAE and weakening the federation.[21]

Fairly strong internal pressure exists in the UAE for the establishment of some form of democracy. A "Joint Memorandum" written early in 1979 by members of the Federal National Council called for the replacement of the UAE's federal structure by real, centralizing, democratic institutions.[22] Nothing came of the memo, and although the council still

19. Ibid.

20. In particular, there is some suggestion of a dynastic problem in Qatar. The current ruler took the throne in 1972 in a bloodless coup precipitated, reportedly, by his predecessor's indifference to government affairs and rumors that he planned to put his son on the throne in violation of the existing family consensus. More recently, one observer has suggested that the ruler's younger brother is seeking to assert a claim to the throne over the ruler's son, who currently commands Qatar's armed forces. Information on this subject is scant, however. Gwynne Dyer, "Qatar," in John Keegan, ed., *World Armies* (New York: Facts on File, 1979), p. 586; and Nyrop and others, *Area Handbook for the Persian Gulf States,* pp. 256–58.

21. Oman has usually sided with Dubai in these cases, pitting itself with Iran and Dubai against Abu Dhabi, which has been backed by Saudi Arabia. Internecine strife in the UAE thus has implications for wider cooperation on the Arabian Peninsula. John Duke Anthony, "The Persian Gulf in Regional and International Politics: The Arab Side of the Gulf," in Hossein Amirsadeghi, ed., *The Security of the Persian Gulf* (St. Martin's, 1981), pp. 189–90.

22. See Ann Fyfe, "Of All the Quasi-Parliamentary Bodies of the Gulf, the UAE National Assembly Alone Has Never Been Dissolved," *Middle East* (London), no. 68 (June 1980), pp. 29–33.

exists, its powers are overshadowed by those of the principal emirates, Dubai and Abu Dhabi. Nonetheless, there appears to be pressure for liberalization here as well as in Bahrain and Kuwait.

Oman

Oman's geography, history, and political structure distinguish it from the Gulf sheikhdoms.[23] Perched on the eastern edge of the Arabian Peninsula, Oman's historic domain was primarily the Indian Ocean and the littoral regions of India and East Africa. Oman's tie to the Peninsula extended only to the lower Gulf states, which it occasionally controlled in the nineteenth century. Reflecting this history, Oman's expatriate population tends to be low on Palestinians and other Arabs and high on Indians, Sri Lankans, and Pakistanis.

More important than its various expatriates, however, is Oman's heterogeneous native population, the product of the country's varied geography (figure 4-2). Earlier in the present century the central internal conflict in Oman pitted the sultan in Muscat against the Imamate of the interior.[24] More recently the Dhofar has been the focus of internal strife. Neglected and alienated under the fiercely traditional rule of Sultan Said bin Taimur Al Bu Said, the Dhofaris rebelled beginning in 1964. Over the next six years the rebellion grew in intensity and scope as the Dhofaris acquired—or were infiltrated by—outside supporters, mostly Yemeni Marxists but also some Iraqis, who broadened the rebellion's ideological themes. Largely because of his father's failure to deal with the rebellion, Sultan Said's son, Qabus, deposed him in 1970 and initiated sweeping economic and military reforms. With British, Jordanian, and Iranian help, Qabus brought the rebellion under control and promised to integrate the Dhofar more fully into Omani national life. Although a few rebels remain scattered around the Dhofar, their rebellion effectively ended by 1976.[25]

Since 1970 Sultan Qabus has used Oman's comparatively small but significant oil revenues to introduce enormous change to Oman, much

23. Much of this and the Yemeni section is taken from interviews with Omani and Yemeni defense officials as well as some of their U.S. and British advisors.

24. See J. E. Peterson, *Oman in the Twentieth Century: Political Foundations of an Emerging State* (London: Croom Helm, 1978), pp. 163–87. On the Dhofar rebellion, see ibid., pp. 187–21.

25. Nyrop and others, *Area Handbook for the Persian Gulf States*, pp. 385–99.

Figure 4-2. *Oman*

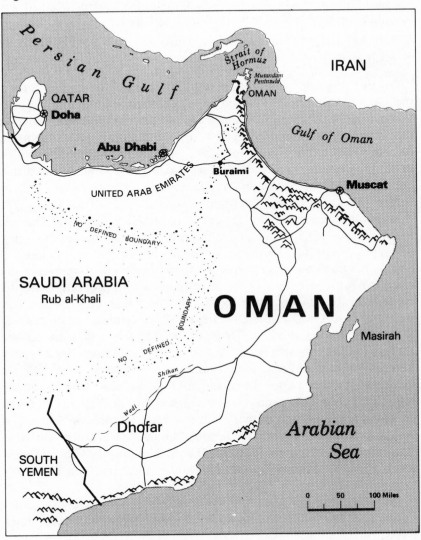

of it designed to link outlying regions physically and economically with
Muscat.[26] Evidence on the success of this effort is scanty and mixed. The
Dhofar is better off economically today than ever before, yet tribal life-

26. Oman's oil exports, which account for 90 percent of government revenues, peaked
at 390,000 barrels a day (b/d) in 1976, fell to 270,000 b/d in 1980, and rose in 1984 to more
than 400,000 b/d. Oil experts say Oman has enough reserves to export about 330,000 b/d

styles and economic patterns remain strong. Thus the prospect of renewed internal strife remains open, particularly if sharp declines in oil revenues should occur. Should internal strife pick up once again, Oman's location on the Arabian Peninsula and also at the entrance to the Persian Gulf may invite outside intervention, just as it did during the Dhofar rebellion.

Oman also faces a dynastic problem. Qabus has yet to produce an heir, and the retinue of potential successors in the larger royal family is quite limited. Given the singular importance of Qabus in bringing Oman to its present position, his death might seriously affect the country's internal stability.

Internal Threats and Regional Stability

On the Arabian Peninsula as elsewhere in the world, socioeconomic change heightens the prospect for internal violence. But here perhaps more than elsewhere, domestic tranquillity is linked with regional tranquillity. The diverse array of ethnic and religious groups in the peninsular states, the power of competing regional ideologies, and, in the case of the Arab-Israeli conflict, repeated demonstrations of Arab impotence are among the things that tie events on the Peninsula to events beyond it. It is easy to see why peninsular rulers like the Saudis wish to see stability around them, w'.y events like the coup in Egypt in 1952, the fall of the Hashemites in Iraq in 1958, or the shah's fall in 1979 frighten them. They have enough problems managing the changes wrought by their oil revenues.

Still, although there is a certain amount of violence in these states, much of it has been small in scale. It is impossible to know whether it will continue in this vein. Saudi Arabia's population is small and dispersed. The marital prowess of the country's founder has given it a large ruling family that is also spread across the country. Under these circumstances the revolutionary social violence that toppled the shah is not a useful model for Saudi Arabia. Changes in relationships within the Al Saud are more likely than social revolution. Such changes may in fact cause fairly significant changes in the complexion of the ruling group.

---

through the end of the century, although actual levels will of course be affected by world oil demand. See "Oil," *Oman: A MEED Special Report*, November 18, 1980, p. 13, and "Introduction," *Oman: A MEED Special Report*, December 1984, p. 2.

The littoral sheikhdoms may be more vulnerable. They have progressed further along the curve of social change, while relatively large blocs of foreigners in Kuwait, Bahrain, and the UAE create especially strong ties between domestic events in these states and events in the surrounding region. While the example of Iran's fundamentalist revolution may pose a threat to all six peninsular monarchies, large Persian and Arab Shi'a communities in these states give Iran special leverage there.

Significantly, the prospects for communist-inspired subversion are fairly low. More likely would be shifts to the right (toward more conservative Islamic institutions), toward the center (a coup based on middle-class technocrats), or toward a military regime likely to have ties to the West. Equally likely in these societies of many social, ethnic, and regional groups, however, would be initial violence leading to chaos with no clear outcome for some time. Such violence no doubt would invite outside intervention, possibly from the Soviet Union as well as the United States and regional powers. Indeed, outside powers seeking to intervene in peninsular affairs have every incentive to manipulate politics on the Peninsula. And the links between peninsular and regional stability often enable them to do so.

The Peninsular Component

Ruling families in the six peninsular oil states were engaged in internecine dynastic conflict with one another well into this century. The residual conflicts born of the Peninsula's earlier evolution remain with it today, albeit in attenuated form. Bahrain and Qatar still contest possession of the Hawar Islands, from which the Al Khalifah of Bahrain was ejected two centuries ago. Oman and Ras al-Khaimah deployed small military units to their disputed border as recently as 1977. Conflicting Saudi and UAE claims to territory around the Buraimi oasis were finally settled in 1974. The sheikhdoms have been reluctant to provoke disputes by seeking to draw borders through offshore oil fields, thus contributing to laggard exploitation in some offshore areas.[27]

27. Will D. Swearingen, "Sources of Conflict Over Oil in the Persian/Arabian Gulf," *Middle East Journal.* vol. 35 (Summer 1981), pp. 315–30. For a reasonably current discussion of the status of boundaries in the Gulf itself, see Robert Litwak, *Security in the Persian Gulf: Sources of Inter-State Conflict* (Montclair, N.J.: Allanheld, Osmun for the International Institute for Strategic Studies, 1981). pp. 66–71.

None of these border conflicts caused extensive bloodshed in the postwar era. Bedouin warfare has not as a rule been terribly bloody but rather has tended to involve small and loosely organized battles in which booty and glory have been more sought after than enemy lives. The Saudi "force" that occupied Buraimi in 1952, for example, consisted of about forty lightly armed Bedouin transported in ARAMCO trucks.[28] The lack of bloodshed is also symptomatic of the decline of traditional animosities. Since the discovery of oil, but more importantly since 1971, when Great Britain relinquished what remained of its position in the Gulf, the peninsular sheikhdoms have had more important things to worry about than bickering among themselves. Nevertheless, old jealousies and antagonisms will probably continue to place limits on how much these states will be able to coordinate policies, especially in the security realm. But overt conflict has been smothered in an effort to present a united front to the rest of the region and the world.

While traditional rivalries among the oil states have abated, another set of conflicts and threats has risen in importance. These involve the Yemens, the two non-oil-producing states of the Peninsula. Problems and conflicts between the oil states and the Yemens are not new. Although the Saudis have fought brief border battles with South Yemeni forces in the postwar era, for example, the really large battles were fought between 1930 and 1934. During that period the forces of Abd al-Aziz wrested the Peninsula's Asir region (see again figure 4-1) from the Yemeni Imam.

Yet in recent years the Yemens have acquired an importance seemingly out of proportion to the kind of threat these poor, inward-turned states are likely to produce. The Saudis deploy a substantial portion of their military forces to two bases near their borders with both Yemens, suggesting considerable worry in Riyadh about the Yemeni threat. Omanis place conflict with South Yemen at the top of their list of planning scenarios. Noting South Yemen's large inventory of Soviet tanks and the presence of Cubans both there and in nearby Ethiopia, one American analyst has suggested the possibility of a grand Soviet–South Yemeni design on the Peninsula's eastern corner:

With a revived Dhorfar movement providing the political camouflage of an

---

28. David Holden and Richard Johns, *The House of Saud: The Rise and Rule of the Most Powerful Dynasty in the Arab World* (Holt, Rinehart and Winston, 1981), p.147.

internal revolt, and the chronically aggressive South Yemen government mounting a military attack in the guise of an intra-Arab fight, the Cubans could inject the *coup de grace* of an armored threat which the small Omani army could not possibly resist.[29]

The peninsular security problem is in fact largely the Yemeni problem. But it is not a problem that can be fully understood in strictly military terms, although military threats remain a possibility. To understand the threats these two states pose, and to lay the groundwork for an assessment of their military potential, it is necessary to understand both the countries themselves and their past relations with oil-rich neighbors.

The Yemen Arab Republic (YAR)—North Yemen

North Yemen is perhaps the largest of the peninsular states in population. It is also one of the most traditional peninsular states, despite its "republican" form of government. Most of North Yemen's population lives along the mountain spine that runs parallel to the Red Sea coast, both the coastal and eastern plains being too arid to support much population. The ruggedness of the mountains and the difficulty of farming in them have dispersed and fragmented the Yemenis into small, isolated communities that are intensely traditional. The Imams who governed all or parts of the Yemen through most of its history played little more than a mediating role between tribes.

Overarching the tribal and geographic fragmentation of North Yemen is a major religious cleavage.[30] In the northern half of the country live tribes of the Zaydi sect of Islam, a branch of Shi'ism fairly close to Sunnism in faith and practice. In the southern half live members of the Shafi'i sect, a branch of Sunni Islam. The Yemeni Imams were Zaydis whose control over the southern Shafi'is varied but tended to be oppressive when in force. Although the civil war that rocked this country between 1962 and 1969 did not pit Zaydi against Shafi'i, the Shafi'is provided the republican faction with some of its more radical members.

That civil war began in September 1962 with a coup that drove the ruling Zaydi Imam into the northern mountains. Strong Egyptian military support to the Yemeni republicans could not overcome conser-

29. Edward N. Luttwak, "Cubans in Arabia? Or, The Meaning of Strategy," *Commentary*, vol. 68 (December 1979), p. 65.

30. See the discussion in Peterson, *Yemen*, pp. 12–16.

vative tribal forces lodged in the mountains; the tribes were supported by Saudi Arabia. Thus the civil war ran its course through 1969 but never ended definitively. Rather, competing factions were more or less reconciled under a republican regime that had to contend with continuing tensions between conservative and radical, Zaydi and Shafi'i factions within the same state.

Governing North Yemen since the civil war has not differed fundamentally from governing it before 1962. Although forces are working to broaden tribal horizons, strong tribal institutions and loyalties still hamper the imposition of centralized rule. To the extent that since the civil war the Saudis have meddled in Yemeni politics primarily through subsidies to Zaydi tribes, the religious distinction may be even more important today than it was in the past. Saudis and Zaydis alike have been suspicious of Shafi'i influence in Sana'a, North Yemen's capital, while Shafi'i alienation ebbs and flows with the dominance of Zaydis in the government.

Under these circumstances, there has been a continuing problem with insurgency in the south. Radical Shafi'is belonging to the National Democratic Front (NDF) conduct a low-level insurgency from bases in, and using arms provided by, the Marxist-ruled People's Democratic Republic of Yemen (PDRY). This gives North Yemen the appearance of being two countries, a conservative Zaydi region in the north with ties to Saudi Arabia, and a more radical Shafi'i region in the south with variable ties to the PDRY. Significantly, in the spring and summer of 1982 North Yemen's president, acting more decisively than usual and bringing Zaydi units down from the north, soundly defeated NDF forces that had moved, once again, into the south. He has since appointed Shafi'is to a modest number of key governmental positions. Whether this represents progress, or simply an upswing in the sinusoidal pattern of Yemeni politics, remains to be seen.

Unlike the peninsular oil states, the YAR maintains long-standing ties to the Soviet Union. Partly this results from Soviet support, through Egypt, to the Yemeni republicans. But it is also necessary as part of the balancing act by which President Saleh (and probably any other YAR ruler) seeks to maintain his position. Whatever the reason, Soviet advisors help train the YAR's military forces (occasionally operating within sight of their U.S. counterparts). Yemenis are frequently offered scholarships for advanced study in the Soviet Union, and much of the YAR's military equipment is of Soviet make.

The People's Democratic Republic of Yemen (PDRY)—South Yemen

If North Yemen's politics are marked by persistent conflict between the central government and outlying tribes, South Yemeni politics are marked by internecine political conflict among factions of the country's Marxist-Leninist regime. Such conflict marked the PDRY's birth as an independent state in 1967, after more than a century of British domination. Two radical groups, the Front for the Liberation of Occupied South Yemen (FLOSY) and the National Liberation Front (NLF), warred against each other as well as the British in their efforts to achieve independence and dominate the new state. The more radical of these two, the NLF, consolidated its grip on the country soon after the British left.[31] Since 1967 conflict has occurred within the NLF itself, with radical Abdul Fattah Ismail replacing the first president, Rubayi Ali, in 1978, only to be replaced himself in 1980 by the slightly more moderate Ali Nasser Muhammad. These conflicts have changed the orientation of the PDRY toward its neighbors in small but noticeable ways. But such conflicts have not changed the basic pro-Soviet attitude of the regime.

Relations between Aden and the interior of the PDRY have been considerably less conflictual than those between Sana'a and its interior tribes, for several reasons. The PDRY's terrain lacks the stark ruggedness of North Yemen, leaving tribes in the south less isolated. Under British rule power was centralized, and modernizing influences reached out from Aden to the eastern and western protectorates in a way unheard of in the north. Finally, the radical movements that ejected the British in 1967 came from the countryside. In the Hadhramaut region east of Aden, for example, the tribal rulers sustained under British rule were quickly replaced by leaders from the NLF. The NLF had strong bases among the tribes to the north and west of Aden as well. Thus while there has been some conflict between Aden and the interior (especially the Hadhramaut), it has never dominated the PDRY's internal scene as has been the case in North Yemen.

The PDRY's initial ties to the People's Republic of China were supplanted in the early 1970s by strong and continuing ties to the Soviet

---

31. This prompted the Front for the Liberation of Occupied South Yemen (FLOSY) members to flee to surrounding states, including Saudi Arabia, which tried for a time and without much success to use these disaffected Yemenis to harass the new regime.

Union. Although the PDRY has given Moscow no permanent bases on its territory, the Soviets have been able to use Aden harbor as a dry dock and submarine facility and have access as well to various Yemeni air bases. Soviets, Cubans, and East Germans train various elements of the PDRY's security forces, in which Soviet equipment dominates. Alone on the Peninsula (and nearly alone in the Arab world as a whole), the PDRY strongly supported the Dergue in Ethiopia, allowing the Soviets to stage their support to the Dergue from Aden's bases, and contributing soldiers and pilots to Ethiopia's efforts to subdue the Eritreans. Its foreign policy thus has been as radical as its domestic policy.

Peninsular Conflict and the Yemens

The Yemens engage most persistently in conflict with one another. The Zaydi-based regime in Sana'a is ideologically at odds with the Marxist regime in Aden, and also at odds with many of the Shafi'i groups of the southern YAR that formed the NDF after the Yemeni civil war ended. NDF insurgents base themselves on PDRY territory and are often supplied by the PDRY. In 1972 and 1979 this situation produced conflict between the two Yemens themselves. In neither case was combat very serious from a military viewpoint, and YAR terrain makes a serious PDRY assault on Sana'a virtually impossible. In both cases cease-fires arranged by other Arab states returned conditions to essentially the status quo ante. Renewed conflict remains possible in the periodic ups and downs of Yemeni relations, but unifying the Yemens by force or diplomacy remains an unlikely prospect. So long as they remain separate states, the two Yemens will pose essentially separate threats to the oil states they border, as they have in the past.

PDRY-OMANI CONFLICT. Although Oman's Dhofar rebellion originated in internal Omani political and social conditions, the rebels were supported by Iraq and the PDRY. PDRY support began soon after the British left Aden in the hands of the NLF in 1967. The PDRY provided a sanctuary just across the Omani border and supplies from both the People's Republic of China and the Soviet Union. The "Popular Front for the Liberation of the Occupied Arab Gulf" (PFLOAG) had headquarters in Aden, and the Voice of Oman radio station was established there as well. Effective PDRY support to the rebellion ended with the rebellion itself, although it had begun to fall off as early as 1974, as economic conditions forced the Adeni regime to turn inward to its own problems.[32] Nonetheless, the PDRY has kept three understrength brigades posted on the Omani border (though these may serve internal security functions for Aden, which may wish to keep an eye on the PDRY's eastern tribes), and the Voice of Oman continued to broadcast pro-Soviet and anti–Sultan Qabus propaganda through 1982.[33]

In recent years PDRY relations with Oman have improved, partly as a result of the ascendancy of Ali Nasser Muhammad in Aden, which brought a less strident ideological tone to the PDRY's relations with other peninsular states. In 1982 Omani and South Yemeni foreign ministers met to discuss a formal end to their latent hostility. This produced an agreement in October 1982 and the establishment of diplomatic ties in October 1983,[34] promising more friendly relations. Still, some Omanis see this as a move by the PDRY to obtain financial help from the richer Gulf states. These Omanis fear that such help ultimately would strengthen the PDRY's ability to threaten them.

SAUDI-PDRY CONFLICT. The PDRY's Marxist rhetoric, the presence of Soviet, Cuban, and East German advisors in Aden, and periodic talk of unity with North Yemen under a radical banner are the bases for long-term political conflict between the PDRY and Riyadh. The Saudis have tried to employ the usual carrots and sticks in this relationship, offering aid in times of economic hardship and reportedly subverting some of the tribes of the Hadhramaut area of South Yemen in an effort to destabilize the Adeni regime. But Saudi levers are far less effective here than in North Yemen.

This underlying conflict broke into open warfare in November 1969, when PDRY infantry and armored car units attacked the tiny, under-manned Saudi outpost at El Wadieh. Although the Saudis responded quickly (with the help of British and Pakistani pilots), PDRY forces held the outpost for ten days before being driven back behind their own border. This was the most notable conflict between the two states in the past two decades. Aden's somewhat conciliatory posture since 1980 may lessen chances for conflict in the future. But the basis for political conflict between the two is built into the nature of the two governments.

SAUDI-YAR CONFLICT. The Saudis have many reasons to worry about

---

32. Nyrop and others, *Area Handbook for the Persian Gulf States,* pp. 390–96.

33. It apparently stopped broadcasting late in 1982, as PDRY-Omani talks moved these countries toward normalized relations. See Foreign Broadcast Information Service, *Daily Report: Middle East and Africa,* November 9, 1982, p. ii.

34. See *Oman: A MEED Special Report,* November 1983, p. 2.

North Yemen: the subversive potential of Yemeni laborers in Saudi Arabia; the questionable loyalties of tribes in the Asir; the enmity engendered by the Saudi conquest of the Asir in 1934; the sheer size and penury of Yemen's population; and the willingness of the Sana'a regime to deal with the Soviet Union. There have been no conflicts along the Saudi border with the YAR since 1934, yet a large base at Khamis Mushayt testifies to Saudi concern for that possibility, as well as concern for the course of future conflict between the two Yemens. Even a small YAR victory over Saudi forces might be deeply embarrassing and potentially harmful politically, given the history of Saudi-Yemeni relations and the ambiguous loyalties of tribes living in the Asir.

The Military Dimension of the Yemeni Threat

Do real military threats to the oil states lurk in the Yemens? The data shown in table 4-1 convey very little about Yemeni capabilities, for two reasons. First, domestic resources and political constraints limit the projection of Yemeni military forces, especially those of the YAR. In both Yemens, for example, the number of air force personnel—far smaller than the Saudi total—gives a truer picture of air force capabilities than numbers of aircraft. North Yemen had only twelve trained pilots in 1979; most of its aircraft remain grounded. South Yemen has become a warehouse for Soviet aircraft whose number far exceeds indigenous support capabilities. North Yemen's six "brigades" contain about 1,200 soldiers each; armor brigades contain about twenty-one tanks. YAR President Saleh's fear of the threat these forces pose to his rule leads him to undermine their effectiveness. The residual military power here is directed primarily toward the PDRY-supported insurgency threat in the south and toward trying to contain the centrifugal forces within the YAR. The PDRY army, by some accounts better organized and trained than YAR forces,[35] is also understrength.

Second, terrain limits force projection capabilities (figure 4-3). South Yemen's forces are buffered from Saudi Arabia's interior by the Empty Quarter. The border incursions of recent years have been fairly easy military operations, but they also constitute the worst these forces can do on their own. The ability of PDRY forces to move beyond the lower

35. Peterson argues that when serious fighting occurred between YAR and PDRY forces in February 1979, "the better trained, organised and equipped PDRY forces were quickly able to establish their superiority." *Yemen*, p. 125.

Figure 4-3. *The Yemens*

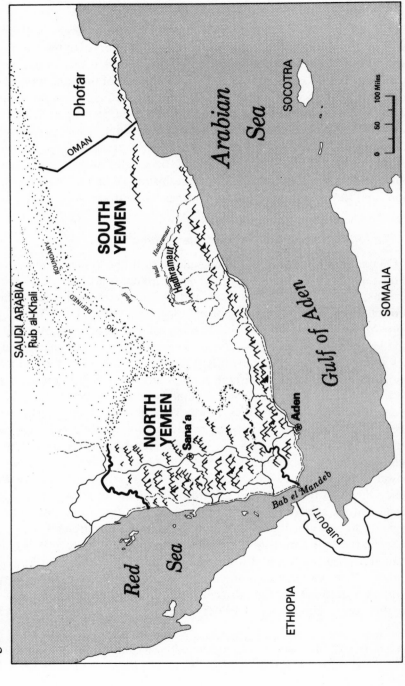

Table 4-1. *Military Dimensions of the Yemeni Problem*

Military elements	North Yemen	South Yemen	Saudi Arabia	Oman
Size of armed forces	21,550	25,500	51,500	23,550[a]
Size of army	20,000	22,000	35,000	19,550
Main battle tanks	714	450	450	12
Size of air force	1,000	2,500	14,000	2,000
Combat aircraft	75	113	170	37
Paramilitary forces[b]	20,000	30,000	25,000	3,500

Source: International Institute for Strategic Studies (IISS), *The Military Balance, 1983–1984* (London: IISS, 1983), pp. 60–62, 64–65.
a. Includes about 3,700 foreign personnel.
b. Paramilitary forces are drawn from tribal levies in North Yemen; popular militia in South Yemen; the National Guard in Saudi Arabia; and Firqats in Oman.

reaches of North Yemen is blocked by mountainous terrain, as well as by the fierce independence of the YAR's Zaydi tribesmen. These two factors frustrated the Egyptians, who sought to bring North Yemen under control in the 1960s. Egypt's experience suggests that nothing short of a major Soviet military commitment to Yemeni unity could promise significant changes in the situation.

The PDRY's military potential against Oman is limited by its own terrain as well as that of southern Oman. As of this writing, the PDRY stations three understrength brigades on its border with Oman. Major attack thus would require a substantial logistics buildup in this area, more likely to come by air and sea than by road, given the limitations on South Yemen's road network through the Hadhramaut. The Dhofar area of Oman is mountainous and heavily vegetated, more hospitable to insurgents than to armored units. An armored thrust north and then east around the Dhofar toward Thumarit, the major Omani base in the Dhofar, would similarly be channelized by the wadis of this inland area, which in any case run away from, rather than toward, central Oman. This suggests PDRY military action is likely to come in the form of support to a renewed Dhofar insurgency rather than as outright aggression.

Significantly, Cuban reinforcement of the PDRY military would change this situation only slightly. Cubans will have no better luck than PDRY soldiers themselves in finding suitable military objectives in the Rub al-Khali, while Soviet support to Egyptian soldiers in North Yemen in the 1960s did little to ease their plight in that conflict. Oman might make a better target for such a reinforced attack. Still, leaving aside for now the question of Oman's defense capabilities, it seems clear that the attack itself, based on the PDRY's inventory of about two understrength divisions of Soviet tanks, would occur in very inhospitable terrain. Long distances would separate the attack from its support bases and from useful military objectives. Thus the notion of a Cuban tank threat to Oman is difficult to visualize.

The YAR does face an array of useful military objectives in the densely populated area of the southern Asir. As suggested earlier, given the history of this area and of YAR-Saudi relations, even small Yemeni military forays might be politically dangerous to the Saudis and thus might be seen in Sana'a as a way to coerce Riyadh. But given the size of the YAR's armed forces, the domestic role they play, and Saudi power among the northern tribes, border harassment may be all the YAR could do unless and until national integration has progressed far beyond its present stage.

The Yemens and the Kingdoms

The fact that conflicts between the Yemens and the peninsular oil states are unlikely to involve large military battles does little to diminish the sense of threat that the Yemens produce elsewhere on the Peninsula. In part, the problem stems from ideological and institutional differences. The mere existence of "revolutionary" regimes in the Yemens, let alone their ability to threaten the other peninsular states, must remind rulers in the oil kingdoms that traditional regimes need not last forever. In part, the problem stems from a history of animosity. The Saudis dominated the Yemens earlier in this century, and today's Saudi rulers must worry that even a minor defeat by Yemeni forces might raise broader questions about their fitness as rulers. In part, the problem stems from sheer contiguity; tribes along the border are of questionable loyalty, while age-old smuggling routes make it easy for subversive elements to infiltrate Saudi Arabia, in particular, from North Yemen.

Indeed, contiguity defines perhaps the most salient feature of the Yemeni problem. As a rule, internal security in the oil kingdoms is affected by events beyond their borders. This holds true for events in the Yemens as well as elsewhere in the Middle East. But the rest of the Middle East is buffered from the Peninsula by water and desert. The Yemens, by contrast, lie on rather than off the Peninsula, giving them a common history, claims to common territory, and sheer physical access to the oil states that other Middle Eastern states lack. That the Yemens lie within the peninsular domain yet are otherwise so different from the oil kingdoms makes them a special security problem.

Table 4-2. *Population and Military Power in the Middle East*

State	Population (1)	Size of armed forces (2)	Military participation ratio (1 ÷ 2)
Egypt	46,000,000	447,000	0.010
Iran[a]	41,500,000	2,000,000	0.048
Iraq[a]	14,300,000	517,250	0.036
Syria	9,200,000	222,500	0.024
Israel	4,100,000	172,000[b]	0.042
Jordan	2,469,500	72,800	0.029
Peninsular oil states			
Saudi Arabia	8–12,000,000[c]	51,500	0.004
Kuwait	1,450,000	12,400	0.009
Bahrain	400,000	2,700	0.007
Qatar	260,000	6,000	0.023
United Arab Emirates	1,130,000	49,000	0.043
Oman	970,000	23,550	0.024

Source: IISS, *The Military Balance, 1983–1984*, pp. 52–57, 60–62, 64.

a. Figures for Iran and Iraq are uncertain due to Iran-Iraq war. Pre-war figures for these countries were: Iran—39,330,000/415,000/0.011; Iraq—12,730,000/222,000/0.017. IISS, *The Military Balance, 1979–1980* (London: IISS, 1979), pp. 39–40.

b. Mobilized strength (48 hours) for Israeli armed forces is 500,000, giving it a participation ratio of 0.122.

c. *Military Balance* figures for Saudi Arabia's population tend to be high; a more common figure is 5,000,000, giving a participation ratio of 0.01.

The External Component

If the Peninsula's internal scene is complicated by conflict and tension, the scene facing outward toward external threats is simpler. To be sure, the peninsular states are dwarfed, in military terms, by the major states around them (see table 4-2). Although Israel vividly demonstrates that small states need not be militarily weak, the states on the Arabian Peninsula are in a more difficult situation. They lack technical sophistication, and they are fearful of the domestic threat that a large military organization could pose. Consequently, these states cannot generate the large ratio of military participation that underwrites Israel's impressive force posture.

The Peninsula as a whole, however, is protected from the full weight of potential adversaries by geography. Water on three sides of the Peninsula separates it completely from Egypt and Iran, the two largest powers around it, and thus limits the threat of overland invasion from these two powers. The arid An Nafud buffers the Peninsula's northern edge. Even Iraq, which shares a long border with Kuwait and Saudi Arabia, is constrained from attacking through all but a fairly narrow corridor next to the Gulf coast by the harshness of the interior desert and by the lack of military support facilities there.

The Peninsula is also protected because its more powerful neighbors focus most of their martial energies on one another. Historically, for example, the long-standing border dispute between Iraq and Iran has drawn Iraq's attention primarily to the major invasion routes from the east.[36] Iraqi-Syrian relations have blown hot and cold, but they have never been warm enough to free Iraq from planning to meet a Syrian military threat from the northwest toward Kirkuk. Meanwhile, Iraq's Kurds have drawn Iraqi forces to the north and provided them with their primary source of military experience until the recent war with Iran.[37] Before that war began, only two of Iraq's twelve divisions were stationed in the south at Basra. Any attack toward the Peninsula would have been seriously constrained by the need to protect borders to the west, north, and east.[38]

The logic applies to other states as well. Iran's military forces historically have been deployed along the Iraqi border, where they are now engaged. Any serious Iranian attempt to invade the Peninsula would present an exposed flank through the southern portion of Iraq. Until recently, much of Egypt's military energy went into preparations for war with Israel, and any move across the northern portion of the Red Sea basin would have to violate Israeli as well as Jordanian territory and expose a flank to both powers. The larger and more powerful states around the Peninsula thus tend to distract one another, reinforcing the Peninsula's favorable geography in reducing military threats to the peninsular states.

If geography tends to channelize overland attack to narrow routes at

36. Anthony H. Cordesman, "Lessons of the Iran-Iraq War: The First Round, " *Armed Forces Journal International,* vol. 119 (April 1982), p. 44. See also Gwynne Dyer, "Iraq," in Keegan, *World Armies,* p. 344.

37. According to Alvin Cottrell, at the height of the Kurdish rebellion (circa 1974), 80 percent of Iraq's armed forces were involved in meeting the Kurdish threat. See Cottrell, Robert J. Hanks, and Frank T. Bray, "Military Affairs in the Persian Gulf," in Alvin J. Cottrell and others, eds., *The Persian Gulf States: A General Survey* (Johns Hopkins University Press, 1980), p. 149. Dyer holds that about half the Iraqi army has been stationed in the Kurdish region over the past twenty years. "Iraq," *World Armies,* p. 343.

38. Significantly, Iraq's 1961 threat to absorb Kuwait was not, in the opinion of the British forces called in to meet it, backed up by real Iraqi force deployments. Elizabeth Monroe, "Kuwayt and Aden: A Contrast in British Policies," *Middle East Journal,* vol. 18 (Winter 1964), p. 66.

each of the Peninsula's northern corners, political factors limit the size of such attacks to those forces available to potential attackers after other commitments have been met. These factors virtually rule out overland attack from the northwest. By contrast, air and seaborne attack are relatively unrestricted, both because such attacks can overcome geographic barriers and because they are inherently more flexible. Thus geographic and political facts narrow the range of external military threats to the Peninsula to a few special categories.

Air and Sea Bombardment

Water and desert around the Peninsula encourage potential attackers to approach by air or sea. Such attacks could involve bombardment of oil or military targets, or the delivery of forces. Three kinds of attack seem plausible.

THE HARASSING THREAT. Clearly there are many valuable oil-related targets on the Peninsula, especially along its Gulf coast. These could be threatened by air and sea bombardment, or by the delivery of commando teams to destroy key facilities. The limited data available on the efficacy of such attacks suggest that eliminating oil production capabilities is fairly difficult, even under sustained bombardment. But temporarily disrupting the flow of oil, either by bombardment or by disrupting tanker traffic, forcing insurance rates up, and intimidating tanker crews, is fairly easy.[39] Given the importance of Gulf oil facilities to the world's economy, any such attack risks world condemnation. Thus the pure bombardment threat is more likely to consist of harassing attacks aimed less at damaging facilities than at embarrassing, intimidating, and coercing the relatively weak governments of the peninsular oil states.

---

39. In its war with Iran, Iraq attacked oil tankers and other ships along Iran's coast throughout 1984, using Exocet antiship missiles supplied by France. Although persistent attacks on tankers near Iran's oil terminal at Kharg Island briefly disrupted Iran's oil exports in May, generally the Iraqi air campaign did little to slow the movement of tankers through the Gulf. Gulf shipping would be far less resilient, however, in the face of attacks by more powerful and reliable missiles than the Exocet, whose small (200 kg) warhead did little damage to tankers on those few occasions when it actually exploded. The U.S. Harpoon or Soviet-made AS-4s and AS6s (both reportedly delivered to Iraq late in 1984) all carry warheads that could seriously damage or sink tankers. Were such attacks to occur when demand for oil was high, the world might be less willing to let events take their course than it was in 1984, when an oil glut greatly reduced the possibility that modest disruptions in the Gulf's oil exports would produce a serious oil crisis. See *War in the Gulf,* prepared for the Senate Committee on Foreign Relations, 98 Cong. 2 sess. (GPO, 1984).

The most obvious source for such attacks at the moment is Iran, although over the long term Iraq's position north of the Peninsula's oil fields gives it relatively easy access by air, less so by sea. Iran is likely to remain the worst case by virtue of its sheer size and a long coast that gives its air and naval forces easy access along the Peninsula's eastern shore. Almost any forces are capable of mild harassment, even those as debilitated as Iran's air force after three years of war. But the size and sophistication of the Iranian threat will increase as it returns, along some unpredictable route, from its present size to something approaching its size before the Iran-Iraq war began.

THE PREEMPTIVE STRIKE ON MILITARY TARGETS. Preemptive strikes might come in the context of overland attack from Iraq or Iran. By itself, preemptive strike is most likely to come from Israel, which has expressed growing concern with Saudi air capabilities as the Saudis have acquired F-15s and conformal fuel tanks to increase their range.[40] Such a preemptive attack would most likely come in the context of a major Arab-Israeli confrontation that included Egypt, a situation in which enough Arab pressure might be brought to bear on Saudi Arabia to force it to use its F-15s against Israel. Under such circumstances, the Israelis would seek to eliminate bases from which Saudi F-15s might become engaged in the conflict; at the very least the several bases around Tabuq, in the northwest, would be targeted. Such attacks would also warn the Saudis of the dangers of subsidizing Arab parties to the conflict and might threaten internal stability in Saudi Arabia by embarrassing the regime.

AIR OR SEABORNE DELIVERY OF FORCES. For most of the surrounding states, these would be easier than overland invasion, but follow-up support for such landings would be vulnerable to interdiction. In any case, air and sea transport capabilities of countries around the Peninsula are not well developed, limiting potential attacks in both size and sophistication. Under these circumstances, adversaries may await an invitation arising from domestic turbulence in one of the peninsular states, as was the case with Egypt in the Yemen in 1962, Iraq in the Dhofar in the late 1960s, and Iran in the Bahraini coup attempt in December 1981.

---

40. For a discussion, see Col. Andrew Duncan, "The Military Threat to Israel," *Survival,* vol. 24 (May/June 1982), pp. 100–01.

The Overland Attack Threat

Overland attack must come from the north. To the extent that overland attacks are constrained by the balance of forces around the Peninsula, they are likely to emanate from changes in these balances. By far the most likely threat would come from the area just above Kuwait and would stem from a fundamental change in the balance of power between Iran and Iraq. War between these two countries has focused world attention on this source of a potentially serious military threat to the Peninsula. Iraq's decisive defeat by Iran might be followed, in the worst case, by the collapse of the Baghdad regime and the emergence in southern Iraq of a Shi'a state aligned with Iran.[41] Iranian forces, their revolutionary elan piqued by victory, would spill into the area above Kuwait, posing an armed threat to the Peninsula unchecked by Iraq's army.

A scenario that seemed more plausible in 1980 would involve a weakened Iran. Had Iraq's attack on Iran in September 1980 actually splintered Iran's ethnically diverse population, leading to the dissolution of Iran's army as a coherent fighting force, Iraq would have become the most powerful state on the Gulf. It is not surprising that the peninsular states prefer that no clear winner emerge from the Iran-Iraq war. Their security lies in preserving the balance between them.

From a military perspective,[42] the threat is likely to be considerably smaller than the total armed forces either Iran or Iraq fields. Some portion of either state's forces would remain committed to the Iran-Iraq front.[43] Internal functions—the need to deal with dissident Kurds and other subnational ethnic groups—would probably continue to tax the victor's military resources. Even in peacetime, it should be remembered, various military requirements pulled the bulk of Iraq's forces away from

41. For a still worse case, suggesting the possibility of an alliance tying Iran to Iraq and Syria, see William Sullivan, "Frightening Realignment in the Persian Gulf?" *Los Angeles Times,* December 22, 1982.

42. This is not to suggest that a threat emanating from changing conditions between Iran and Iraq would be principally military in nature. A victory by Khomeini's forces in the Iran-Iraq war, for example, would first of all have loosed unsettling political forces on the Peninsula. There would also be a military threat, however, that would be difficult to ignore.

43. In this sense, the key issue in the war is less who wins it than the conditions of victory: how many forces are freed by victory to turn southward toward the Peninsula? In fact, it is difficult to imagine conditions of victory that would allow either power to shift the central thrust of its military activity toward the Peninsula.

the Peninsula. It seems reasonable to think in terms of a percentage—
say, 30 percent—of the ground forces of either power being freed for
action against the Peninsula.

Ground force attack would be accompanied by air and possibly coastal
strikes, making this a clear worst case with the potential to envelop the
entire Gulf in conflict. The conduct of the Iran-Iraq war does not suggest
that this conflict need involve sophisticated use of the sophisticated
weapons available to the participants. Neither Iran nor Iraq has provided its ground forces with effective close air support, for example. And
neither power's air strikes have been very accurate or effective, although
in the war's early stages Iran was more skillful than Iraq in selecting and
hitting targets. Still, even unskilled forces of the size Iran or Iraq could
field would be dangerous to the peninsular states, whose forces are tiny
indeed, and whose political systems may not be capable of bearing the
strain of attack.

At least one observer has suggested oil as a likely objective of such
attacks.[44] Even limited attacks into Kuwait, for example, would encoun-
ter the large underground deposits just south of the Iraqi border. The
Saudi fields lie perhaps 300 miles farther south, along a reasonably well-
developed coastal road. The validity of seeking oil fields as objectives is
at least questionable, however, given the presence of large reserves in all
states along the Gulf. A more plausible motive might be Iraq's desire to
acquire a longer strategic coastline by absorbing Kuwait. Equally plausible at the present time is an Iranian attack motivated primarily by
religious hostility. Finally, the threat of external attack may be used as a
means of coercion, aimed at securing loans, altering oil market shares, or
changing foreign policy positions.

Two-stage Attacks

Because geography shields the Peninsula as a whole from the surrounding states, it encourages what might be called two-stage attacks in
which external antagonists acquire a position anywhere on the Peninsula
and then seek to exploit it unhampered by geographic barriers to attack.
Nasser understood the importance of such a position when his forces
entered Sana'a in 1962; from a position in North Yemen Nasser could

---

44. Frank Fukuyama, "Iraq and Kuwait: Past Policies and Future Options" (Marina del
Ray, Calif.: Pan Heuristics, February 1980), pp. 6–13.

have engaged in a wide range of political and military activities threatening, in this case, to the Saudis. The Soviet position in Aden may likewise be seen as a stepping stone to other areas, although Aden is as politically and geographically isolated as any state on the Peninsula. In these cases the objective is simply a position on the Peninsula. Having achieved this objective, external powers are likely to find other objectives—coercing the Saudis on oil policy, for example, or creating instability in "heretical" and conservative monarchies—that much easier to achieve.

Given the geographic barriers to the use of force against the Peninsula, two-stage attacks are more likely to have political than military origins. Egyptian forces entered North Yemen in support of a coup. Iran's revolutionary regime seems to have taken the same approach in supporting the December 1981 coup attempt in Bahrain. Iraq was able to take advantage of local turbulence in coming to the aid of Oman's Dhofari rebels. Similarly, the Soviet position in Aden was the fortuitous result of political developments in South Yemen following the departure of British forces in 1968. Political vulnerabilities within the peninsular states are important not only in their own right but as potential points of leverage and entry to external powers.

Conflict among as well as within states on the Peninsula can be an excuse for outside intervention. Iran, in particular, has involved itself in border disputes on the Peninsula itself. As John Duke Anthony notes

Oman advanced a claim (in late 1977) to part of Ra's al-Khaimah . . . soon after reports that Ra's al-Khaimah had discovered oil offshore. This territorial dispute between two resource-poor states might well have been resolved with despatch and a measure of equity by the parties most directly concerned but for Iran's private assertion of support for Oman.[45]

In this sense the Peninsula can be seen as a whole, with conflict within or among the states that lie on it essentially internal, but internal conflict is dangerous to the extent that it attracts outside interference.

A discussion of the external security situation confronting the peninsular states thus comes back full circle to where the chapter started—with internal problems on the Peninsula itself. Internal events on the Peninsula have the potential to invite outside intervention—the two-stage attack. Conversely, the geographic and political buffers to external attack encourage outside powers to employ the levers they have over domestic events on the Peninsula—the power of ideas, or of ethnic and religious groups dissatisfied with traditional regimes. In both cases,

45. "The Persian Gulf in Regional and International Politics," p. 191.

external threats are intimately bound up with internal events on the Peninsula itself.

Finally, it is important to return to the Peninsula's internal scene because few external military attacks are likely to come without ideological clothing that gives them a domestic component as well. It is difficult, for example, to untangle Saudi Arabia's fear of Egyptian aircraft and soldiers in North Yemen from the fear of subversion invoked by the occasional defection of Saudi officers to Cairo throughout the 1960s. Likewise Iran's victory over Iraq might be feared as much for the example it would pose of a resurgent Iranian revolution as for the armored divisions it might free for action against Saudi Arabia and Kuwait. Popular responses on the Peninsula to external attack will probably vary with the circumstances and will be difficult to predict in advance. Attack might even increase national solidarity in the peninsular states. Still, for the peninsular sheikhdoms in particular, the worst case external attack would be one that involved fighting on both domestic and international fronts. Under these conditions traditional regimes might begin to unravel. Counting up tanks and aircraft or examining avenues of approach—however essential this may be—is unlikely to capture the full extent of the threat these forces pose to the peninsular states.

Conclusions

Americans tend to think about threats to their security in linear terms: the chief source of threat is the Soviet Union, and the chief manifestations of the Soviet threat are nuclear missiles aimed at the United States, large conventional forces in Eastern Europe, and so forth. Rulers among the peninsular oil kingdoms might long for such an unambigious situation. Instead they face a much more complex situation in which security is a matter of delicate balances and two-edged swords.

Internally, in seeking to pacify technocrats and entrepreneurs who favor more economic development, these rulers risk alienating traditional and religious social groups. In seeking to develop military forces to protect their borders, they risk creating a well-armed internal threat to their rule. In seeking to build political institutions that satisfy liberal and radical elements in their societies, they risk establishing a political alternative to their own rule. In seeking for various reasons to support the Palestinian cause, they fund a brand of political radicalism that might ultimately turn on them. They do not lack for threats. Indeed, the problem is that the threats they face come from all directions, leaving them with limited room for maneuver.

Looking outward from the Peninsula, these rulers see the same combination of balances and two-edged swords. External threats have been held in check mainly by regional power balances. Yet this means that enemies can also be friends, often at the same time. In 1961 Nasser sent troops to Kuwait to counter Iraqi threats. Yet at the same time he attacked the peninsular monarchies rhetorically, and only months later he sent troops to North Yemen, indirectly to threaten Saudi Arabia. Between 1961 and 1976 Iraq threatened Kuwait several times. Yet since 1982 Iraq has protected the Peninsula from the forces of revolutionary Iran. Israel would seem to pose a clear threat. Yet even the "Zionist entity" indirectly and inadvertently helps protect the Peninsula, a fact most evident in 1967 when Israel's attack on Egypt forced Nasser to retreat from North Yemen. There is little beyond the Peninsula's borders that is unambiguously threatening, or unambiguously helpful.

Adding a final element of complexity to peninsular security is the connection between internal and external events. To the extent that events beyond the Peninsula's borders—revolution in Iran, another Arab defeat by Israel—can send ripples through the Peninsula's domestic scene, peninsular rulers can never feel completely in control of their security, even its internal dimension. To the extent that countries beyond their borders have every incentive to meddle in the Peninsula's internal affairs, and often possess the tools to do so, peninsular rulers can never assume that even minor internal violence will be easily contained.

They have in fact survived thus far, despite the complexity of their situation. Geographic buffers have no doubt helped them. Although external adversaries may manipulate internal events on the Peninsula, peninsular elites can probably deal with internal threats better than they could handle a genuine invasion. Beyond this it is difficult to know what sustains them. Perhaps oil wealth provides a partial cure for its own disease of socioeconomic change. Perhaps the power of Islam, so threatening in the hands of a ruler like Khomeini, provides these rulers with special legitimacy. Perhaps kinship ties that bind Saudi Arabia's huge ruling family are sources of strength and resilience.

But it should not be too difficult for Americans to understand that these rulers attribute their longevity in part to the careful and conservative manner in which they have conducted themselves. They are not likely to become risk-takers. If the United States is to help them deal with the security issues described in this chapter, it is going to have to come to terms with the way in which these states have sought to defend themselves. That is the subject of the next chapter.

CHAPTER FIVE

The Local Approach
to Military Security

HOW DO the rich but vulnerable states of the Arabian Peninsula approach the quandary of military security? Very delicately indeed. These rulers remain carefully attuned to the Arab consensus. They seek economic development while reaffirming their allegiance to Islamic values. They use their oil revenues to support regional allies but also to attract and encourage moderation among regional adversaries. They try to preserve stability across the Middle East because regional stability helps control events within their own borders.

Much of the diplomatic maneuvering of the peninsular oil states is designed to prevent military confrontation by heading off violent threats before they arise. Yet precisely because these states cannot reach out aggressively to control their environment, they cannot discount the possibility that external threats will confront them despite their best diplomacy. They came close to facing a threat from Iran, for example, in early 1984, when Iran massed troops along the southern portion of its border with Iraq and sought—but fortunately failed—to break through Iraq's defenses. Meanwhile, the possibilities for internal violence, emanating from within these states or from infiltrators sent by external adversaries, are legion. The Gulf rulers have dealt successfully with internal violence in the past. But because even limited outbursts of violence may portend larger threats, these rulers cannot afford to be complacent.

Not surprisingly, the peninsular rulers have used their oil wealth to build up their defenses. Some of the world's most sophisticated weapons are found in Dhahran, Kuwait City, and Abu Dhabi. Faced with an array of potential threats emanating from the Iran-Iraq war, but also unconstrained by any interference from these two large warring states, the six peninsular oil kingdoms joined in May 1981 to form the Gulf Cooperation Council (GCC). Ambitious plans for security cooperation are attached to the council. GCC defense ministers have spoken optimistically of cooperative air defense, perhaps even the purchase of a standardized GCC fighter aircraft. Elements of their ground forces have already gathered for joint maneuvers, and intelligence sharing among the six has been enhanced.

What can the United States expect these states to do for themselves in the area of military security? How are they likely to deal with violence when diplomacy or domestic political maneuvering fails to prevent it? This chapter examines how the Gulf rulers handle the three components of their security: internal threats, peninsular conflict, and external threats.

The Approach to Internal Security

Internal security poses three broad challenges to these regimes. First, there is a challenge to each state's intelligence capabilities, especially posed by the problem of infiltration. Second, there is a challenge to each state's security forces, which must pursue intelligence quickly, head off violence before it explodes, and deal with violence when it does occur. Third, the state must protect likely targets from violence. Although little is known about the full scope or effectiveness of internal security instruments in the six oil states, this section will shed some light on how, and how well, they meet these challenges.

The Intelligence Challenge

Intelligence capabilities are usually visible only when they fail or almost fail—when religious fanatics take over the Mecca Mosque, or when Shi'a conspirators almost succeed in staging a coup in Bahrain. Successes go unreported for obvious reasons. Thus much that can be said about GCC intelligence mechanisms is at least partly speculative.

Nonetheless, most observers agree that these rulers have well-developed sources of intelligence on events and groups in their own societies. Saudi Arabia's Shi'as have been a problem for decades, even centuries; one would suspect that most Shi'a organizations have been well infiltrated by Saudi agents, and interviews suggest that this is true. It is probably also true with most of the long-standing sources of internal threat these rulers face—Hijazis or other tribal or regional factions in Saudi Arabia, Dhofaris in Oman, Shi'as in Bahrain, and Palestinians in Kuwait. Many of the basic intelligence-gathering techniques of the regimes are as old as the regimes themselves. There is no reason to think that traditional approaches to intelligence collection are any less useful now than in the past.

Infiltration poses a more difficult challenge. Smugglers have crossed GCC coastlines, and Yemenis have infiltrated both Saudi Arabia and Oman, for years. But the rising importance of oil in the postwar era has introduced a new set of targets, many of them close to the Gulf coast. And Iran's revolution raises the prospect of a new wave of infiltration, agitation, and terrorism in the present era. The key instruments of intelligence and police action in these cases are one and the same: coast guards, border patrols, and airport police. It is impossible to know how well these instruments are working, but it would be unrealistic to expect them to be foolproof. To take coastal infiltration alone as an example, the dhow (small boat) traffic on the Gulf is too large and heterogeneous to be tracked with full success. At best, coast guards and other types of border police can hope to catch an occasional infiltrator, thereby posing a deterrent to others.

Ultimately, intelligence cannot be expected to cope fully with the problem of internal security. Surprise is possible even when conspirators or agitators are known. That was true with the leaders of the Mecca Mosque incident and the Bahraini coup incident. The borders of these states are long and porous, and the openings to outsiders too numerous to allow effective tracking of all or perhaps even most infiltration. Intelligence mechanisms can be improved, but they cannot be expected to stop all threats. Consequently, the use of force and protective mechanisms inevitably figures importantly in the GCC approach to internal security.

Internal Security Forces

Internal security forces in the six GCC states usually come under the Ministry of Interior. In Saudi Arabia these forces number about 20,000. The Saudis began to modernize these forces and expand their power after the takeover of the Mecca Mosque. Borders are guarded by a

Frontier Force and Coast Guard totaling roughly 8,500 in strength, and the Coast Guard deploys nearly 500 coastal patrol craft. Finally, the Saudi Arabian National Guard (SANG), totaling perhaps 25,000 active personnel, plays primarily an internal security role from positions in every Saudi city.[1] Forces and numbers for the other five members of the GCC states are difficult to find. But in these countries even the external security forces could and probably do concentrate on internal security, giving the bulk of their force posture an internal security mission.

All six states rely on regional and international expertise for help. The Saudis drew on French and Jordanian advisors to deal with the take-over of the Mecca Mosque and in its aftermath signed a long-term contract with France for training internal security police.[2] Until recently, British, Jordanian, and Pakistani expatriates occupied most senior positions in the police forces of Bahrain, Qatar, and the UAE.[3] Presumably the use of foreign advisors afforded rulers additional technical expertise, but it also enhanced their control of such forces, since foreigners are likely to remain loyal to their paymasters and are less tempted to engage in internal affairs. Over the past decade there have been pressures in all states to move nationals into key police positions. Although this has been occurring, foreigners remain as advisors.[4]

Internal security forces, like intelligence capabilities, seem weakest in the oil fields. Although these rulers wrested control of the fields from the major oil firms over the 1970s, apparently they have been slow in moving forces in to protect the fields. For internal political reasons, for example, responsibility for the oil areas in Saudi Arabia falls exclusively to the Saudi Arabian National Guard; there are no Saudi army units stationed in the oil-rich Hasa province. Yet SANG modernization only

1. See Richard F. Nyrop and others, *Area Handbook for Saudi Arabia* (Government Printing Office, 1977), p. 340; and International Institute for Strategic Studies (IISS), *The Military Balance, 1983–1984* (London: IISS, 1983), p. 62.

2. See U.S. Library of Congress, Congressional Research Service, *Saudi Arabia and the United States: The New Context in an Evolving "Special Relationship,"* prepared for the Subcommittee on Europe and the Middle East of the House Committee on Foreign Affairs, 97 Cong. 1 sess. (GPO, 1981), pp. 23–24, 52 (Hereafter U.S. LOC, CRS, *Saudi Arabia and the United States*); and William B. Quandt, *Saudi Arabia in the 1980s: Foreign Policy, Security, and Oil* (Brookings Institution, 1981), pp. 83, 93–96. Interviews suggest, however, that as of this writing little has been done to implement the French contract.

3. John Duke Anthony, *Arab States of the Lower Gulf: People, Politics, Petroleum* (Washington, D.C.: Middle East Institute, 1975), pp. 59, 67, 79; and Richard F. Nyrop and others, *Area Handbook for the Persian Gulf States* (GPO, 1977), pp. 232, 269.

4. See, for example, Nyrop and others, *Area Handbook for the Persian Gulf States*, p. 269.

began in 1972, and SANG forces were stationed permanently in Hasa only after the Iran-Iraq war began.[5] Today no more than a large battalion of the SANG and various smaller irregular units are stationed in Hasa.

Protecting Targets

All six states deploy Royal Guards units, composed either of loyal Bedouins or mercenary Baluch or British, to protect members of the ruling families. In the wake of the Mecca Mosque take-over it seems likely that the Saudis also added to the protection of their religious shrines. But provisions for the protection of oil fields have apparently changed little since 1979. There are no additional barriers, no hardening of key technologies or port facilities, and no electronic surveillance technologies to scan for intruders. Indeed, U.S. personnel knowledgeable about the oil fields suggest that rigs, pumping stations, and other equipment have deteriorated somewhat since 1973 and that the fields lie fairly open to attack.

Internal Security and the Gulf Cooperation Council

Concern for internal security played an important role in the GCC's deliberations from the start. But this is a delicate matter; greater cooperation smacks of legitimizing Saudi interference in the internal affairs of its neighbors. Thus movement within the GCC toward greater cooperation in internal security affairs seems to have resulted less from the council's creation than in response to the Bahraini coup attempt of December 1981.

That the coup conspirators, using GCC passports, had been able to pass rather easily among the GCC states suggested that tighter airport and infiltration controls were necessary.[6] That Bahrain's rulers were apparently alerted to the coup by a tip from airport officials in Dubai suggested the benefits of greater cooperation and intelligence sharing.[7] In the months immediately after the attempt, Saudi Arabia signed bilateral

---

5. See Gwynne Dyer, "Saudi Arabia," in John Keegan, ed., *World Armies* (New York: Facts on File, 1979), p. 608; Adeed Dawisha, *Saudi Arabia's Search for Security,* Adelphi Paper 158 (London: IISS, 1979), p. 16; and Quandt, *Saudi Arabia in the 1980s,* p. 109, n. 2.

6. Foreign Broadcast Information Service, *Daily Report: Middle East and Africa,* December 21, 1981, p. C1. (Hereafter FBIS, *Daily Report: MEA.)*

7. Michael Sterner (U.S. Ambassador to the United Arab Emirates [UAE], 1972–75), "Perceptions and Policies of the Gulf States toward Regional Security and the Superpower Rivalry," n.d., p. 35.

internal security agreements with four of its five GCC compatriots. Only Kuwait refrained from signing.[8] Intelligence sharing, based partly on computer files housed in Saudi Arabia, has apparently become a priority.

Within a month after the coup attempt was foiled, Bahraini officials called for the formation of a GCC rapid deployment force.[9] This produced some interest in a joint military command for the GCC states, and joint ground force maneuvers took place in October 1983.[10] The timing of Bahraini interest coupled with the small size of GCC ground forces in comparison with those around them suggests strongly that such a force, if formed, will have internal security as its principal focus. To the extent that Iran lay behind the Bahraini coup attempt, the GCC rapid deployment force may represent the most expeditious and realistic approach that these states can take to deal with the threat that Khomeini's regime poses.

Saudi Arabia and Peninsular Security

Egypt's involvement in Yemen's civil war, in particular, made the Saudis aware of the linkage between peninsular conflict and the potential for attack or coercion by outside powers. The Saudis recognize that they would be the ultimate target of a two-stage attack, and that such attacks might emanate from the coastal sheikhdoms as well as from the Yemens. They also recognize that defending the Peninsula as a whole is likely to be easier, given the presence of geographic buffers, than defending their own borders. Thus, although Saudi Arabia's domineering attitude toward its peninsular neighbors is rooted partly in history and tradition, it is supported as well by sound military and political reasoning. In important ways Saudi Arabia's security is peninsular security.

Handling peninsular security involves the Saudis in two very different tasks. They must seek to preserve that which is similar (the other five oil states) while they attempt to control that which is bothersome and politically foreign (the Yemens). Although the Yemens could conceiv-

8. Kuwait appears to have objected most strenuously to the extradition clause of the proposed agreement, which violates its constitution. It also objected to a clause that would allow forces of one country to pursue suspects up to twenty kilometers inside the territory of another. "Defence," *Middle East Economic Digest,* vol. 27 (December 2, 1983), p. 6. (Hereafter *MEED.*)

9. See, for example, FBIS, *Daily Report: MEA,* December 23, 1981, p. C1.

10. On operation "Desert Shield," see "GCC Activity Increases," *MEED,* vol. 27 (October 21, 1983), p. 3.

ably mount small military threats to Saudi Arabia, neither of Saudi Arabia's peninsular security tasks is principally a military problem. Rather, the Saudis handle both tasks using predominantly traditional political techniques.

The Saudis interfere in North Yemen's politics with an aggressiveness absent from their relations with other peninsular states. Economic aid to Sana'a allows Saudi Arabia to influence the YAR's policies,[11] while subsidies to various Zaydi tribes of northern YAR enable the Saudis to indirectly pressure the North Yemeni regime. So deep is Saudi involvement in North Yemen's politics that when the popular YAR president Ibrahim al-Hamdi was assassinated in October 1977, many Yemenis assumed that the Saudis had killed Hamdi because he had tried to steer an independent course between Riyadh and Aden.[12]

The Saudis are less aggressive in their dealings with South Yemen, perhaps because they are less able to intrude there. Although the Saudis have supported dissident tribes in South Yemen, for example, Aden's control of the PDRY hinterland makes that tactic less effective than it is in the north. The Saudis have also tried to use economic aid to influence Aden, coming to Aden's aid, for instance, after serious flooding in the spring of 1982 had ruined a large portion of the country's agricultural production. Mainly, however, the Saudis seek simply to buffer themselves from the PDRY by attempting to dominate the YAR and by supporting Oman.

Significantly, Kuwait has been more open and aggressive in dealing with Aden. Kuwait's aid to the PDRY dates back to 1969. Kuwait has maintained diplomatic relations with Aden consistently since then, whereas the Saudis broke ties to that country in 1977, when the PDRY supported Soviet involvement in Ethiopia. Recently, Kuwait tried to help forge a rapprochement between the PDRY and Oman.[13]

11. "Saudi Arabia has little difficulty getting its way by tightening the purse strings. Concerned that President Saleh was becoming too cozy with Moscow and its client regime in Aden, Riyadh stopped its budget subsidies to Sana last December and January [1979–80] and many government employees went without pay." Christopher S. Wren, "Saudi-Yemen Frontier: Skirmishes in the Desert," *New York Times,* May 8, 1980.

12. Quandt, *Saudi Arabia in the 1980s,* p. 27. The assassination came on the eve of Hamdi's planned visit to Aden, which would have been the first ever by a YAR president. See J. E. Peterson, *Conflict in the Yemens and Superpower Involvement,* Occasional Paper Series (Georgetown University, Center for Contemporary Arab Studies, 1981), pp. 17, 37, n. 13.

13. For more on Kuwait's relations with the Yemens, see Robin Bidwell, *The Two Yemens* (Boulder, Colo.: Longman-Westview Press, 1983), p. 243.

Although rulers in the coastal sheikhdoms have never been immune to pressure or interference from Riyadh, the Saudis have been more positive in their approach to the other peninsular oil states than they have been with the Yemens. Indeed, as their oil incomes and their international importance have grown, all six peninsular oil states have sought to overcome petty jealousies and to cooperate on defense as well as other issues. Well before the creation of the GCC Saudi Arabia and Kuwait subsidized air defense expenditures among the two poorer oil states, Bahrain and Oman.[14] And throughout the 1970s all six states showed an increased willingness to settle, or at least to ameliorate, lingering border disputes that once attracted the attention of outside powers.[15]

Today many of these initiatives go forward under GCC auspices. It is the GCC, for example, rather than Saudi Arabia or Kuwait, that helps Bahrain and Oman with defense subsidies.[16] Although cooperation preceded the formation of the GCC, the council is the most tangible and recent demonstration of a growing spirit of cooperation among the Gulf states. The Arabian Peninsula's peculiar geographic and political circumstances reinforce that spirit.

The Problem of External Defense

Meeting external threats is far more difficult than meeting internal threats. Most internal threats are fairly small, and local forces can handle them. By contrast, although external threats would be reduced by geographic buffers, the worst of them would still be too large even for well-developed GCC ground or air forces. More important, internal security rests on a traditional foundation; it involves doing things that

14. Dyer, "Saudi Arabia," p. 614.

15. Most notably, Saudi Arabia and the UAE reached agreement on their borders near the Buraimi Oasis in 1974, in part because the Saudis saw "little point in trying to defend the area against external 'aggression' or internal 'alien' ideologies and influences, if frontier disputes continued to impede cooperation among the states of the region." See Dawisha, *Saudi Arabia's Search for Security,* p. 19.

16. In November 1982, for example, the GCC pledged $1 billion for upgrading Bahrain's air defenses. See *Bahrain: A MEED Special Report,* September 1983, p. 4. And in July 1983 the GCC approved a twelve-year grant of $1.8 billion for Oman's defense spending. See *Oman: A MEED Special Report,* November 1983, p. 2.

these rulers have done well for some time. By contrast, external defense propels these rulers into an entirely new enterprise, the development of modern military forces.

The cost of the enterprise is not prohibitive, given large oil revenues, although fluctuations in oil incomes have occasionally made it difficult for GCC rulers to finance ambitious defense schemes. Usually, however, these rulers are able to afford whatever weaponry is available. Their rationale for acquiring sophisticated Western arms—to increase the effectiveness and firepower of a limited number of skilled personnel— seems logical enough. It is the same rationale that the U.S. military employs to justify high-technology weaponry for use against the numerically larger Soviet threat. Yet buying these weapons may be the only aspect of developing modern military forces that comes easily. Beyond this the enterprise is both inherently difficult and potentially dangerous. Significantly, the steps that GCC rulers take to manage the problems inherent in building their forces place severe limits on the effectiveness of these forces.

The Newness of the Enterprise

Most of the weaponry entering peninsular arsenals is quite new. Saudi Arabia was the first member of the council to begin to modernize its military, having been prompted by Egypt's intervention in the Yemens in 1962. Even so, most of Saudi Arabia's military equipment arrived in the latter half of the 1970s, and some of the more prominent components of the Saudi armed forces—AWACS and F-15s, for example—were still being delivered as of this writing. Kuwait and Oman both began to modernize early in the 1970s, Kuwait in response to the 1973 border crisis with Iraq, Oman in response to the Dhofar rebellion. Bahrain and Qatar began serious purchases of external defense equipment only in the 1980s. Even Western militaries accustomed to high-technology weaponry cannot adapt to new equipment overnight. On the Peninsula, however, two additional problems hamper the development of effective forces.

The first is the sheer novelty of modern warfare, which demands martial skills quite at odds with those employed in the Bedouin warfare practiced on the Peninsula until quite recently. "In Bedouin raids," David Howarth notes, it was not the custom for very much blood to be drawn. Usually the attack was so sudden that the camp or the caravan had no time to do anything but surrender; but if it put up a defense which promised to be hard to overcome, the raiders drew off and searched for other victims.[17]

This is not the disciplined form of warfare demanded in modern military organizations. In Bedouin warfare commanders usually lost control of their men when the raid began, after which many raiders would disappear into the desert, apparently with enough booty to satisfy themselves. Even King Abd al-Aziz, whose charisma and military exploits were impressive indeed, could not always control his forces once they were committed.

Modern military forces also demand modern technical skills. Yet GCC populations are small, and skilled populations are tiny indeed. Hence the second problem constraining the development of these forces is manpower. To quote a study by the Senate Committee on Foreign Relations, manpower is "Saudi Arabia's largest economic development problem":

It is estimated that of the current working force of about 2.5 million people in Saudi Arabia, more than half are non-Saudis. Saudi literacy rates are low (20–30 percent) and those inclined to study generally prefer liberal arts to technical schools. In 1978, for example, only 38 percent of the 17,000 places available for technical training in Saudi Arabia were filled.[18]

The Saudis have the money to buy training programs, yet those who participate in technical training tend to learn slowly. A Rand Corporation study of military modernization in the Middle East noted that cultural inhibitions to training seemed "most severe" in Saudi Arabia and went on to state that

it may require twice as long to produce a Saudi pilot, mechanic, or supply clerk with U.S. proficiency standards. In the other countries where the U.S. trains military personnel—Iran, Jordan, Turkey—the training period exceeds U.S. specifications but by lesser amounts.[19]

Two factors aggravate the effects of these manpower problems on the defense sector. First, Saudi Arabia's enormous wealth and consequent modernization in civilian sectors present those trained in the military

17. *The Desert King: Ibn Saud and His Arabia* (McGraw-Hill, 1964), p. 15.
18. *The Proposed AWACS/F-15 Enhancement Sale to Saudi Arabia,* prepared for the Senate Committee on Foreign Relations, 97 Cong. 1 sess. (GPO, 1981), p. 54.
19. Anthony Pascal and others, *Men and Arms in the Middle East: The Human Factor in Military Modernization,* R-2460-NA, prepared for the Director of Net Assessment, Office of the Secretary of Defense (Santa Monica, Calif.: Rand Corp., 1979), p. 46.

with high-paying alternatives in the civilian sector of the economy. The Rand study notes that this "brain drain" has been especially severe in Saudi Arabia.[20] Second, a culturally based aversion to manual labor makes many Saudis reluctant to do the work that enables military organizations to function. Saudi Arabia's ground forces in particular suffer from this constraint. Their support involves work that few Saudis want or need to do, the kind of work they normally hire others to do.[21]

In the past members of the GCC compensated for their deficiencies by purchasing whole military capabilities. For example, Abd al-Aziz purchased four light aircraft and hired British pilots to fly them when he suppressed the Ikhwan rebellion in 1929–30. As recently as 1969, British and Pakistani expatriates piloted Saudi aircraft into the confrontation with PDRY forces along the country's southern border.[22] Even today, the UAE and Pakistan jointly own more than seventy French Mirage 3s, purchased by the UAE but flown and maintained, apparently, by Pakistanis.[23]

Increasingly, however, military modernization programs have yielded skilled operators and limited numbers of support personnel. With the new weaponry has come a large and growing polyglot community of foreigners to support the weapons as well as to develop infrastructure around them. Thousands of foreign "contract hire" laborers—Filipinos, Sri Lankans, South Koreans, and Pakistani civilians, for example—work in the defense sectors of GCC states. Reportedly about 6,000 Americans work in this capacity in Saudi Arabia alone. Military officers from a variety of states serve on contract in the GCC area. Pakistanis seem to dominate in virtually every country—1,500 serve in Saudi Arabia alone—while Jordanians also appear in great numbers. Finally, official military advisors often introduce newly purchased weapons. For example, U.S. Air Force officers introduced the Saudis to the F-15 and AWACS, and French pilots accompanied Mirage F-1s to Kuwait and

20. Ibid.
21. See Abdul Kasim Mansur (pseud.), "The Military Balance in the Persian Gulf: Who Will Guard the Gulf States From Their Guardians?" *Armed Forces Journal International,* vol. 118 (November 1980), p. 50.
22. David Holden and Richard Johns, *The House of Saud: The Rise and Rule of the Most Powerful Dynasty in the Arab World* (Holt, Rinehart and Winston, 1981), p. 281.
23. Alvin J. Cottrell, Robert J. Hanks, and Frank T. Bray, "Military Affairs in the Persian Gulf," in Alvin J. Cottrell and others, eds., *The Persian Gulf States: A General Survey* (Johns Hopkins University Press, 1980), p. 164; and Paul Beaver, "Gulf Air Power in Profile," *Islamic World Defence,* vol. 2 (April–June 1983), p. 21.

Qatar. The U.S. Military Training Mission (USMTM) in Saudi Arabia comprises about 650 uniformed service members.[24]

Foreigners would be involved with almost any kind of military modernization in these states. For example, Saudi Arabia has taken a decade to absorb the F-5, an aircraft designed with ease of maintenance in mind, yet even today foreign personnel perform most high-level maintenance. But concentration on simpler weapons would not bring foreigners in quite the quantities present in these states today. Nor would it ensure the presence of foreigners through the end of this century.[25] Significantly, the faster these states modernize, the faster they diminish the usefulness of their native skilled support personnel, the best of whom are switched to newer weapons entering the inventory. That of course only increases the importance of foreigners.

Costs as well as benefits are linked to the presence of foreign support. Without it these states would be unable to field modern military forces, at least in the short- and mid-term. Official foreign advisors also symbolize commitment. And foreign support personnel may enhance government control over the armed forces. Yet large foreign—and especially Western—support and assistance groups can spawn resentment among native populations. Official American support is especially problematical given the U.S. commitment to Israel. Too many foreigners from a single supplier state can create the appearance, and perhaps the reality, of dependence. GCC rulers try to solve some of these problems by diversifying suppliers, a procedure difficult to justify on military grounds because of the problems in logistics and coordination that accompany mixed inventories. Thus efforts to minimize the political cost of military expansion undermine the military rationale for expanding in the first place.

Large foreign support establishments behind GCC militaries also raise questions about the effectiveness of these forces. Post-revolutionary Iran

24. See the excellent discussion of expatriates in Saudi Arabia in Ghassane Salameh, "Political Power and the Saudi State," *MERIP Reports* (Middle East Research and Information Project), no. 91 (October 1980), p. 10.

25. Foreign support requirements of the Royal Saudi Air Force (RSAF), for example, will peak in 1986, according to official estimates, under the weight of both the F-15 and AWACS deliveries, will taper off through 1993, but will hold steady then through the year 2000 at about 15 percent of RSAF strength. See the chart in *The Proposed AWACS/F-15 Enhancement Sale to Saudi Arabia,* p. 56. As an official estimate, this may be fairly optimistic. It will certainly be optimistic if Saudi Arabia implements its plan, announced in the spring of 1984, to buy Tornado interdiction bombers from Great Britain. See "Tornado Sale," *Aviation Week & Space Technology,* vol. 120 (May 28, 1984), p. 15.

surprised most observers with its ability to keep sophisticated equipment working, at least during the first year of its war with Iraq. But the shah had sought much more consistently than have the GCC rulers to develop a class of military technicians—the homofars.[26] And Iran's industrial base was by all accounts far ahead of that across the Gulf. The loss of foreign support among the GCC militaries would probably lead to a rapid depletion in their capabilities. If foreign help were to stand fast, then force capabilities would depend on the operating skills of trained native personnel.

The Threat from the Military

Few GCC rulers will discuss their fear of the internal threat posed by their own militaries. Yet such a fear can be inferred from actions they take or refuse to take. In the Saudi case in particular a fairly clear pattern of decisionmaking can be distinguished in which Saudi rulers have sought to balance modernization with internal control. The smaller states in the GCC, however, lack Saudi Arabia's defense burden and hence its problem with a large military. Here it is less what rulers do than what they are unwilling to do that suggests concern for the internal threat that their forces might pose. Three techniques of control can be identified.

ORGANIZATIONAL POLICIES. Today's Saudi rulers employ the method King Abd al-Aziz invented to control his ground forces, that of divide and rule. When the Ikhwan forces that King Abd al-Aziz used to consolidate his hold on most of the Peninsula revolted in 1929, the king organized an army from other areas of his growing kingdom and with it subdued the rebellious tribes. Thereafter he allowed the two forces to exist in balance as a means of controlling either one, and this practice continues today. The Ikhwan was allowed to regroup and became first the White Army and later the Saudi Arabian National Guard (SANG). Other forces were grouped under a regular army, since renamed the Royal Saudi Army (RSA).[27]

26. That the homofars ultimately rose against the shah probably has reinforced the aversion to training such local technical experts among GCC rulers. See William F. Hickman, *Ravaged and Reborn: The Iranian Army, 1982* (Brookings Institution, 1982), p. 6.

27. Dyer, "Saudi Arabia," 607–12. For a discussion of continuing tension between the National Guard and army, see Michael Collins, "Riyadh: The Saud Balance," *Washington Quarterly*, vol. 4 (Winter 1981), p. 204.

Today the split between the SANG and the RSA only partly reflects a desire to divide and control the military. The SANG draws on the noble tribes of the Najd and Hasa, has been a means of subsidizing these tribes, and is commanded by Crown Prince Abdullah of the Shammar branch of the Saudi family. The army draws on other parts of the state (including the Hijaz) and comes under Prince Sultan, the minister of defense and aviation and a member of the Sudayri branch of the Saudi family. To some extent the cleavage between these two forces reflects tribal and family politics as much as fear of the military.

The two forces have also been modernized differently. Beginning in 1964 King Faisal initiated programs that make the RSA today a mixed armored and mechanized infantry force. The SANG languished until early in the 1970s when the Saudis, with U.S. assistance, began to convert it into a light mechanized force, a process that continues today. From a purely military perspective the two forces are no longer balanced. But the National Guard's disadvantage in weaponry may be balanced by the deployment of major guard units close to Riyadh and in all other major Saudi cities, while army units have been deployed quite far from the capital. Moreover, the Saudis have employed other techniques to limit the RSA's capabilities, making the RSA-SANG balance a more even match.

Other organizational approaches to controlling military forces are fairly common across the GCC. Except for Oman, the oil kingdoms have only recently introduced technological or organizational means of communication between air and ground forces, despite the usefulness of close air support in actual combat. They have also resisted placing aircraft and air defense missiles under a unified air defense command, despite its advantages for air defense. Such policies amount to divide and rule, although on a smaller scale than that evident in Saudi Arabia.

PERSONNEL POLICIES. GCC military forces, especially ground forces, tend to be fairly small as a percentage of population. The two major exceptions to this rule, Oman and the UAE, both involve heavy concentrations of foreign mercenaries (Omanis in the case of the UAE, Baluch in the case of Oman).[28] While small size is valuable in its own

28. On the UAE, see Cottrell, Hanks, and Bray "Military Affairs in the Persian Gulf," p. 164. In 1982 Pakistanis and Baluch constituted 23 percent of the Sultan of Oman's Land Forces (SOLF); the percentage has been declining for some time as Sultan Qabus has sought to increase the number of native Omanis in his forces. Interview with SOLF officials, May 1982.

right from the standpoint of internal control, it also reflects a preference among these rulers for taking recruits from the dwindling Bedouin portions of their societies. This preference, and the tendency of indigenous personnel to prefer jobs in the lucrative private sector, have left some Saudi units (especially their armored forces) chronically understrength, while many of Saudi Arabia's manpower-intensive Improved-Hawk air defense systems remain in storage. Other GCC forces simply remain small.

Conscription might solve these problems but is unpopular with constituents. Moreover, in the Saudi case conscription might bring more potentially disloyal Hijazi, urban, and modern elements into the armed forces.[29] Kuwait enacted a conscription law in 1978, but it is not well enforced, and Kuwait's rulers seem content recruiting primarily from among the poorer Bedouin tribes along their borders with Iraq and Saudi Arabia.[30]

Promotion in the officer ranks continues to be based on loyalty as well as on merit, especially in the smaller sheikhdoms where family members dominate all forces.[31] Expatriates and seconded foreign personnel also fill key officer as well as advisory positions, especially in Oman, where the British are only now transferring command to Omani officers. Elsewhere Pakistanis and Jordanians are spread throughout indigenous forces. Although these individuals compensate for the lack of local technical expertise, they also tend to be sources of intelligence and control for rulers.

MODERNIZATION POLICIES. The purchase of high-technology weaponry also helps GCC rulers deal with the internal military threat. Modern weapons tend to raise the status and satisfaction of military officers. Because modern weapons depend far more heavily than traditional Bedouin forces on logistics and support, GCC rulers can control their

---

29. Dyer, "Saudi Arabia," p. 619. Also, U.S. LOC, CRS, *Saudi Arabia and the United States,* p. 53.

30. Cottrell, Hanks, and Bray hold that one-third to one-half of Kuwait's army consists of poorly educated Iraqi or Saudi tribesmen. "Military Affairs in the Persian Gulf," p. 167. On conscription in Kuwait, see Mansur, "The Military Balance in the Persian Gulf," p. 59.

31. Pascal and others, *Men and Arms in the Middle East,* pp. 44–45. The Rand study also notes the deleterious effects on military performance of a tendency to strip the best officers and soldiers out of line units and assign them to elite units. Usually the most elite units are the Royal Guard units, which have an internal rather than external security role.

forces by keeping tight rein over ammunition and spares.[32] They also control the salaries—and hence presumably the loyalties—of the large foreign support communities that accompany modern weapons.

Although the tendency of these rulers to buy weapons from a variety of national suppliers is driven primarily by their desire to retain independence from any single supplier state, this policy, too, may be related to their internal situation. In particular, this policy may curb the potential threat to them of their own forces by making coordination more difficult. The Royal Saudi Army, for example, has an armored component based on French tanks, advised by French experts, and trained in French tactics. Its mechanized component is based on U.S. equipment (including M-60A1 and A-3 tanks), U.S. advisors, and U.S. tactics. The two components constitute two armies (the SANG is a third) that rarely train together. They would probably have problems coordinating any action—internal or external.

There will always be some degree of uncertainty about how much GCC rulers still fear their own militaries. Direct evidence is scant; GCC rulers are loath to discuss military issues, let alone perceptions of their own militaries. And indirect evidence is ambiguous; buying weapons from various countries, for example, serves a variety of purposes besides meeting the internal military threat. Finally, things do seem to be changing, however slowly. Under the duress of the Iran-Iraq war, for example, Kuwait announced in the summer of 1984 that it would place its air defense aircraft and missiles under the same command.[33]

Still, circumstantial evidence suggests that fear of large, centralized, and otherwise efficient military forces remains strong in these countries. If change comes, it will come at a pace set by the rulers themselves, a pace impervious to the advice of foreign advisors. Finally, because past practice has led to the development of diverse and decentralized military organizations in these countries, change is not likely to come easily or quickly due simply to organizational momentum. Note, for example, the difficulties that plague U.S. defense planners who wish to encourage greater coordination among the U.S. services. The inefficiencies and anomalies that characterize GCC forces will not disappear for some time, even under the most auspicious political circumstances.

32. U.S. LOC, CRS, *Saudi Arabia and the United States,* p. 21.
33. Melissa Healy, "U.S. to Buttress Kuwaitis' Air Defenses," *Defense Week,* vol. 5 (July 30, 1984), pp. 7, 13.

The Dangers of Using Military Force

Ultimately, fear of the domestic threat these forces might pose affects not only their organization or equipment but also the willingness of GCC rulers to use them. As William Quandt points out, doing so might give rise to an internal threat. "Serious problems could arise if the political leadership were to order the military into some action that exceeded Saudi capabilities. A humiliated armed forces could turn on the politicians, as occurred in Egypt in 1952."[34]

Such considerations may account in part for the tendency of both Kuwait and Saudi Arabia to deploy forces symbolically—to the Arab-Israeli fronts, for example—yet assiduously to keep them out of combat. But by acting this way rulers deprive their armed forces of any chance to develop the competence that only combat can breed and thus reinforce their own reluctance to engage those forces in combat.

Even under favorable conditions, however, dangers are connected with the use of indigenous military forces. In June 1984, after all, a Royal Saudi Air Force F-15 did shoot down an Iranian F-4 that was apparently seeking to attack an oil tanker off the Saudi coast. The Saudis could hardly have expected to lose; they enjoyed the support of U.S. AWACS aircraft, and their F-15s carried advanced Sparrow and Sidewinder air-to-air missiles, while Iran's aircraft suffered from a lack of spare parts and general deterioration. Yet the defensive manner in which the Saudis announced the incident,[35] and their failure thereafter to engage other Iranian aircraft despite continuing Iranian attacks on oil tankers near the Saudi coast, suggest that they had no wish to antagonize their large neighbor unnecessarily. The Saudis realize that they must live with revolutionary Iran for some time to come. They recognize their vulnerability not only to the revolutionary forces unleashed by Iran in 1978 but also to the kind of terrorism occasionally threatened by Iran's leadership. Under these conditions they are always likely to prefer diplomacy to force, especially the use of their own forces.

---

34. *Saudi Arabia in the 1980s,* p. 103, n. 18.

35. As Prince Bandar ibn Sultan, the Saudi ambassador to the United States, put it, "Our sovereignty was violated and we reacted, as we said we would all along, in a defensive manner. We think it is a pity we had to be dragged into this conflict." See the discussion in "Pushing the Saudis Too Far," *Time,* June 18, 1984, p. 44.

Local Forces and the Prospects for Cooperative Defense

In general, the constraints outlined yield forces marked by (1) organizational cleavages that leave components of the same military ill equipped or trained to deal with one another, let alone with the military of another member of the GCC; (2) serious logistical problems because these rulers buy from several suppliers and keep tight rein over fuel and ammunition; and (3) fairly small indigenous support, reinforced by large numbers of foreign technical experts. These features, and the uncertainty of assessing forces that have rarely been seen in combat, make it difficult to draw conclusions about GCC military capabilities. In the worst case, these rulers may well have purchased little more than "a deterrent shell."[36]

Nevertheless, GCC forces are real and growing; presumably they can function at some level of effectiveness even within current political strictures. Moreover, political strictures may change slowly, raising the potential of these forces still further. Thus a best case can be made as well, one that considers political and logistical constraints but nonetheless posits some capability in portions of these forces. If the best case does not represent what the GCC forces can do now, it nevertheless can serve as a realistic guide for U.S. military assistance. Based on the descriptions of the GCC military organizations detailed in the Appendix, this assessment looks at the prospects for cooperative defense of GCC territory.

The Prospects for Ground Force Cooperation

Saudi units will be well deployed to face likely threats once King Khalid Military City (KKMC), near the Kuwaiti border, is occupied, but ground force units will probably be fixed along specific borders. The Royal Saudi Air Force, by contrast, represents a swing force, dispersed for its own protection as well as to cover various fronts, but capable of being quickly concentrated against a specific threat.

Saudi Arabia and Kuwait could each contribute about two brigades to meet the northern overland attack threat, while Saudi Arabia and Oman would be the GCC principals involved in containing the Yemens. Air

---

36. Spoken in reference to Kuwait's military by Mansur, "The Military Balance in the Persian Gulf," p. 59.

assets of the GCC might be more flexible, although currently so many different types of aircraft are in use that reinforcement to specific fronts would be severely limited. Thus it might be assumed that Saudi F-5s and Kuwaiti A-4s could fly strike (but not close air support) missions in the north, while Saudi and Omani aircraft (and possibly the UAE's A-10s, should they purchase any) could deal with Yemeni threats.

No amount of ground force cooperation will defend the GCC from the kind of overland threat that could materialize to the north of Kuwait. A reinforced Yemeni threat with Cuban and Soviet support would also be too large for GCC forces alone. By contrast, the marginal military threats posed by the Yemens (unreinforced) might conceivably be handled by Saudi Arabia and Oman, with a GCC rapid deployment force possibly providing limited help. Thus it seems reasonable to think that any GCC ground force cooperation will remain geared principally for the internal security of the Arabian Peninsula as a whole.

The Prospects for Cooperative Air Defense

Air defense has been second only to internal security as a focus for cooperative effort within the GCC. Defense ministers have spoken of purchasing a common GCC fighter aircraft, for example, and even of developing a GCC defense industry around it. Far more often, however, GCC officials talk of coordinating their air defenses, and so far that coordination has consisted primarily of efforts to link the air defense of other members of the GCC with Saudi Arabia's air defense network, in particular to the U.S. (and later, Saudi) AWACS stationed at Al Kharj. Questions remain, however, about how likely and productive various cooperative schemes would be.

The major benefits of purchasing a common aircraft would be logistical. A common aircraft would produce a dispersed, uniform structure of support across the GCC. Other GCC air forces could then take advantage of Saudi Arabia's strategic depth, reducing their vulnerability to preemption. (Aircraft of different makes could be dispersed to Saudi bases for defensive reasons but could not sustain operations from them.) Cooperative maintenance, with each state responsible for a set of key components, would make maximum use of scarce manpower resources. It might also lead to the development of a GCC industrial structure based on a similar division of labor. Purchase of one of the U.S. FX aircraft—designed to be easy to maintain—would enhance prospects for independence from foreign suppliers, at least for this portion of the GCC's military forces.

The tactical advantages of commonality are less clear. Pilots flying the same aircraft would probably find it easier to coordinate their actions in aerial combat. In this sense purchase of a common aircraft would ultimately produce the best air defense possible for the members of the council. Yet the best GCC air defense is not likely to be—or at least need not be—substantially better than the air defenses these states could produce even without a common aircraft. For example, aircraft of various makes can be linked to one another and to AWACS if compatible communications equipment is purchased. Joint exercises can produce teamwork among pilots flying different aircraft, while the absence of joint exercises would hamper coordination even among pilots flying the same aircraft. Thus the tactical benefits of commonality are marginal at best and in any case dependent on how the plan is implemented. A common support structure would benefit sustained operations rather than help the members of the GCC cope with the sporadic air threat that they are more likely to see. Passive measures, such as revetments for aircraft, might be just as effective as a common support structure in protecting aircraft.

Moreover, purchase of a common aircraft must be placed within the context of the diverse array of aircraft already in or on order to the GCC states. None of these states is likely to cease development of other elements of its inventory. Saudi Arabia in particular would be loath to sideline its F-15s in favor of the Mirage F-1, the F-16, or the Tornado. Consequently, development of a common inventory would occur as part of broader efforts by each state to develop its arsenal independently. The real issue would be the importance that each state might attach to the common program. At best, a common program might emerge as a dominant part of what would remain a mixed fleet.

Even this best case is not likely to occur soon. Saudi Arabia's F-5 program, based on a fairly simple aircraft, emerged from decisions made in 1971. Aircraft were delivered between 1974 and 1978. The Saudis assumed all front-line maintenance responsibilities in 1983, although higher-level maintenance remains in the hands of foreigners. Similar decisions concerning a GCC aircraft made in the mid-1980s thus would probably not produce a fully equipped common inventory until the early 1990s. Independence—if that were a goal—would not come until much later in the decade. GCC rulers could improve their ability to coordinate aircraft in combat more quickly simply by purchasing proper communications devices for the aircraft they now own.

It is far more likely that the GCC will continue to field a diverse array of aircraft, and that GCC cooperation will include efforts to integrate these aircraft, and ground-to-air missiles like the U.S.-made Improved-Hawk, into a more elaborate and resilient network. That will not be easy insofar as command and control is the weakest link in the GCC's defense chain. Whether this problem stems from the technical complexity of communications links, or from political fear in GCC capitals of a unified command structure, the difficulty is not likely to disappear soon.[37] But even minimal efforts to provide AWACS information to other GCC states, or to coordinate sectoral defense over the Gulf, would greatly improve the current state of affairs.

The Prospects for Coastal Protection

The naval forces of the GCC are too new to be assessed on a state-by-state basis, let alone collectively. Still, if individual states are able to deploy their new missile craft effectively, it seems reasonable to assume that, with minimal cooperation, the GCC could develop a limited coastal denial capability, using these ships in a standoff mode around key targets. The capability might extend to protecting tankers docked or afloat in the Gulf. But it would not extend much beyond the Strait of Hormuz and Oman's coast.

The Limits of the Best Case

Even a realistic best case is not very comforting, either to the council members or to those who support them. In it, the GCC states can be expected at best to police the Peninsula, to deal with various threats from the Yemens, and to settle disputes among themselves amicably. However, a ground force attack on GCC territory from Iran or Iraq might involve a third of the divisional strength that either Iran or Iraq possesses, and even a third of fifteen to twenty divisions would easily overwhelm the understrength brigades that Saudi Arabia and Kuwait

37. As one Western diplomat put it, "It is astonishingly complex to have a joint control and command system. . . . I don't think the [GCC's] military capability will frighten anybody for a long time." Quoted in David B. Ottaway, "Saudi Arabia, Iran Struggling for Control of Gulf Sheikdoms," *Washington Post*, November 25, 1982.

could deploy along their northern borders. The same could be said of the air balance between GCC states and potential adversaries like Iran, Iraq, Egypt, or Israel, although Saudi Arabia's AWACS and the capabilities of GCC air forces make the air balance more even than the ground balance. The GCC states can hope at best to deter external attackers by promising some damage to the attackers to limit initial damage to themselves, thus buying time until reinforcements arrive. These goals are worthy, but even meeting them fully is unlikely to protect the members of the GCC from coercion or serious attack by their larger neighbors.

The Approach To External Defense

Unable to defend themselves fully, council members have tried to protect themselves by getting help. And regional dynamics have in fact enhanced their security by providing both the military and the diplomatic forces needed to deflect or deter any military attacks into the GCC area. That approach to external defense, far more than developing their own forces, has ensured their security in the past and is likely to ensure it in the future.

Allies Past and Present

Several cases over the past two decades exemplify how help from others has enabled peninsular rulers to overcome threats by outside powers. Some examples are Egypt's entry into the Yemeni civil war in 1962; Iraq's involvement in the Dhofar rebellion in Oman in the early 1970s; and major Iraqi threats to Kuwait in 1961–63 and 1973–76.

COUNTERING THE EGYPTIANS IN YEMEN. Egypt's President Gamal Abdel Nasser officially supported North Yemen's Republicans almost immediately after they toppled the Yemeni Imamate in September 1962. During the next five years Egypt deployed as many as 70,000 of its own soldiers to North Yemen and offered air support and supplies as well. Nasser's goal was to achieve a position in North Yemen which in turn would allow him to pressure Saudi Arabia, with its vast oil reserves.

Both Nasser and the Republicans seriously underestimated the strength of the Yemeni Royalists, and both also faced enormous military difficulties overcoming North Yemen's rugged terrain. In this sense Nasser's chances of success may have been slim from the start. Yet Saudi

Arabian, Iranian, and Jordanian financial and military aid to the Yemeni Royalists reduced those chances still further. When Egyptian aircraft strafed villages in Saudi Arabia in 1963, King Faisal was able to call for deployment of a squadron of U.S. aircraft as a show of support. U.S. F-100s were deployed to Jiddah for some time, with apparent effect, since Egyptian attacks on Saudi territory ceased.[38] Ultimately, however, it was less the Saudis or the United States than the Israelis who ended Nasser's Yemeni adventure; their smashing defeat of Egypt in 1967 forced Nasser to withdraw his forces entirely from North Yemen.

COUNTERING IRAQ AND THE PDRY IN THE DHOFAR. Iraqi financial and ideological support to Oman's Dhofari rebels grew as the movement became more radical, especially after 1968, and it essentially supplemented the considerable support from the People's Democratic Republic of Yemen (PDRY). Oman's British-trained security forces quickly stopped PDRY attempts to mount a campaign of urban terror in the north, while in the Dhofar area itself British advisors and Special Air Service troops, Jordanian special forces and engineers, and Iranian paratroopers supported Oman's counterguerrilla forces in suppressing the rebellion by 1975.[39] Beginning in 1974 Iraq began to withdraw its support for the Omani rebels as part of its rapprochement with Iran. In June 1976 Iraq closed all the offices of the Popular Front for the Liberation of Oman in Iraq.[40]

COUNTERING IRAQI THREATS TO KUWAIT. Major Iraqi threats to absorb all or part of Kuwait occurred in 1961–63 and 1973–76.[41] In 1961, 5,000

38. Nyrop and others, *Area Handbook for Saudi Arabia,* p. 316. In this case the United States sent a squadron of F-100 fighters on a demonstration visit to Saudi Arabia. In March 1979 the Saudis asked for and received the deployment of two U.S. AWACS aircraft to cover a small crisis on the Yemeni border. In October 1980 four AWACS were deployed to Saudi Arabia to cover the Iran-Iraq war. These represent the major crisis deployments of U.S. forces to the Peninsula.

39. See J. E. Peterson, *Oman in the Twentieth Century: Political Foundations of an Emerging State* (London: Croom Helm, 1978), pp. 187–94; and Nyrop and others, *Area Handbook for the Persian Gulf States,* pp. 385–99.

40. Robert Litwak, *Security in the Persian Gulf: Sources of Inter-State Conflict* (Montclair, N.J.: Allanheld, Osmun for the International Institute for Strategic Studies, 1981), p. 76.

41. On the 1961 crisis, see Elizabeth Monroe, "Kuwayt and Aden: A Contrast in British Policies," *Middle East Journal,* vol. 18 (Winter 1964), pp. 65–67; and Majid Khadduri, *Republican Iraq: A Study in Iraqi Politics since the Revolution of 1958* (Oxford University Press, 1969), pp. 166–73. See Majid Khadduri, *Socialist Iraq: A Study in Iraqi Politics since 1968* (Washington, D.C.: Middle East Institute, 1978), pp. 156–59, for a general study of the 1973 crisis.

British soldiers, staged through bases in Bahrain, manned the Kuwait-Iraq border soon after Iraq first made its threat.[42] These troops were quickly replaced by Egyptian, Sudanese, Jordanian, and Saudi forces under Arab League mandate.[43] Egyptian forces departed soon thereafter, but other Arab League forces remained deployed until 1963, when a new regime in Baghdad promised improved relations with Kuwait.

Border violence in 1973 was met by a similar Arab League response, with Syrian and Saudi representatives visiting capitals of both countries to mediate the dispute. The Saudis moved forces to their border, and Iran offered troops in Kuwait's support. Jordan and Iran both offered troops to Kuwait in the event of future crises.[44] Kuwait reportedly threatened to reconsider its aid to the Arab states directly confronting Israel, bringing Egyptian diplomatic pressure to bear on Iraq.[45] Under military pressure in the Kurdish area, and in need of Arab backing in its broader confrontation with Iran, Iraq withdrew its troops.[46] Tensions ran high until 1976, when the issue subsided in the context of a major relaxation in tensions between Iran and Iraq.

In these incidents and in lesser cases over the past two decades three sources of security can be identified. At one level, security has been ensured almost inadvertently by shifting balances elsewhere in the

42. See Frank Fukuyama, "Iraq and Kuwait: Past Policies and Future Options" (Marina del Ray, Calif.: Pan Heuristics, February 1980), p. 18. Significantly, the United States offered to support the British move and began moving a small flotilla, then visiting Mombasa, toward the Strait of Hormuz. The British declined the offer "with thanks." Hermann F. Eilts, "Security Considerations in the Persian Gulf," *International Security,* vol. 5 (Fall 1980), p. 108.

43. The presence of Egyptian forces is noteworthy given the sour state of Saudi-Egyptian relations at the time. Robert R. Sullivan notes that this was the only time in this period that Saudi Arabia and Egypt cooperated. "Saudi Arabia in International Politics," *Review of Politics,* vol. 32 (October 1970), p. 448.

44. IISS, *Strategic Survey, 1973* (London: IISS, 1974), p. 97.

45. Nyrop and others, *Area Handbook for the Persian Gulf States,* p. 185. Freedman suggests that the Kuwaitis may also have found their relations with Moscow useful in controlling Iraq during this period. Robert O. Freedman, *Soviet Policy toward the Middle East Since 1970,* rev. ed. (Praeger, 1978), p. 216.

46. Iraq had broken diplomatic relations with Iran in 1971, after the shah forcibly occupied three small formerly Arab islands in the southern Gulf. No other Arab Gulf states followed suit, leaving Iraq isolated even before the 1973 crisis began, and possibly more susceptible to pressure from other Arab states, especially Egypt. As John Duke Anthony notes, in Kuwait's case, deterrence of Iraq "is mainly political and diplomatic. In short, not a single Arab dynastic state could be expected to extend a meaningful level of support to any serious Iraqi attempt to violate Kuwaiti territory." John Duke Anthony, "The Persian Gulf in Regional and International Politics: The Arab Side of the Gulf," in Hossein Amirsadeghi, ed., *The Security of the Persian Gulf* (St. Martin's, 1981), p.176.

region. Israel hardly acted to defend the Saudis when it attacked Egypt in 1967, for example, but that is partly what Israel did by defeating Egypt. At a second level, the members of the GCC have benefited from the help of long-standing regional friends. Jordan, in particular, has become involved in virtually every peninsular security crisis since 1962, and Great Britain has been a constant source of help to Oman. Finally, outside help has been obtained in an ad hoc fashion, as when U.S. fighter aircraft were stationed for a time at Jiddah to deter Egyptian attacks on Saudi territory. The shah of Iran was another essentially ad hoc ally who supported Saudi Arabia and Oman for his own reasons, yet on other occasions he was viewed with great suspicion from the Peninsula.

Allies Future

If past patterns suggest that members of the GCC will protect themselves from external threats by getting help, where are they likely to get help in the future? What forces can others bring to bear in the council's favor? Under what circumstances? These questions must be addressed by examining the force postures of likely helpers, the threats that council members must deal with, and the probable political constraints affecting the availability of the helping forces for Gulf contingencies.

THE HASHEMITE KINGDOM OF JORDAN. Although the Al Saud drove the Hashemite family from the Hijaz in 1926, common conservative values, similar political systems, Saudi aid, and Jordanian military prowess have helped these families overcome their past antagonism. In 1957 the Saudis sent troops to Jordan to bolster King Hussein's defense against a Nasserist coup, and since then King Hussein has offered forces almost every time that the members of the GCC have been threatened, externally or internally.

Jordan's forces are considered by most observers, including the Israelis, to be the most effective of any Arab force on a unit-for-unit basis. They consist of four divisions (two armored, two mechanized), three separate infantry brigades, and a small but well-trained air force of about one hundred combat aircraft.[47] In general, Jordan's divisions are tied down by the Israeli threat to the west and the Syrian threat to the north. That leaves the infantry brigades and parts of Jordan's mobile police

47. Except where otherwise noted, basic order of battle information throughout this section is taken from IISS, *Military Balance, 1983–1984.*

force as ground forces potentially available for GCC reinforcement. This outline could change if Jordan's political situation changes (peace with Israel, better relations with Syria). A much larger proportion of Jordan's air force would probably be available to the GCC, except when Jordan itself faced imminent hostilities.

PAKISTAN. Although Pakistanis in both official and unofficial capacities are conspicuous throughout the GCC militaries, since 1979 the Saudis appear to have formalized and enlarged their security arrangements with Pakistan. In return for the promise of financial aid, the Pakistanis are said to have contributed combat units, composed of Sunni Muslim troops, to Saudi Arabia. These troops have apparently been stationed around Tabuq, although reports indicate that they may be destined for the Yemeni border. Both Saudi Arabia and Pakistan deny the arrangement, although it is clear that the Saudis requested deployment of Pakistani forces, and satisfactory evidence suggests that Pakistani units of limited size are in fact in Saudi Arabia.[48]

With its comparatively large population and high level of technical competence, Pakistan has the greatest military potential of any of the regional sources of reinforcement to the GCC. Moreover, Pakistan's president, General Mohammed Zia ul-Haq, has stated that in the event of a crisis on the Peninsula he will "leave Pakistan and lead the military contingent in case it is required by the Saudi government."[49] Yet Pakistan faces threats from India and from Soviet forces in Afghanistan. It has also experienced serious internal problems. Like Jordan, it needs most of its forces for its own security concerns. A shared border with Iran and long-standing efforts to improve Pakistan's relations with Iran make it quite unlikely that Pakistani ground forces could be used to counter an Iranian threat. Finally, the presence of growing numbers of Pakistani units in Saudi Arabia is likely to stir resentment in the military forces of both countries. Consequently, for political as well as military reasons Pakistan's ground force contribution to the GCC may be limited to small forces confined to fighting on the Yemeni or the domestic fronts. But Pakistan could probably make a larger contribution to GCC air defense, especially through its involvement in the UAE's air force.

48. See Devlet Khalid, "Pakistan's Relations with Iran and the Arab States," *Journal of South Asian and Middle Eastern Studies,* vol. 5 (Spring 1982), pp. 20–21; and Quandt, *Saudi Arabia in the 1980s,* pp. 40–41.

49. "American Arms to Pakistan: 'A Test of U.S. Credibility,' "*U.S. News and World Report,* September 21, 1981, pp. 45–46.

EGYPT. Nasser's rhetorical and subversive attacks on the peninsular monarchies ended with his defeat at the hands of Israel in 1967. Beginning in that year the Saudis in particular began to funnel substantial quantities of aid to Egypt, quantities that grew in the 1970s, as the moderation of Sadat's foreign policy toward the sheikhdoms became clear. Much of this aid went to bolster Egypt's military capabilities. There was hope, too, of setting up an Arab defense industry based on oil kingdom money and Egyptian technical talent. These efforts stopped after Egypt signed its peace treaty with Israel in 1979, although GCC rulers have been rather moderate in condemning Egypt in the years since.

Possessed of the largest population in the Arab world, Egypt has fairly large military forces: eleven ground force divisions (three armored, three mechanized, and five infantry), five regiments of fighter/ground attack aircraft, and a regiment of bombers.[50] Given the treaty with Israel, Egypt's main enemy is Libya, whose tiny forces pose little threat. Outwardly, Egypt appears to have great flexibility in coming to the aid of the GCC.

That is not true, however, for two reasons. First, the ongoing conversion of Egypt's forces from aging Soviet to sophisticated Western equipment will seriously decrease its overall military potential for at least five years. Second, Egypt's Western arms purchases have been guided primarily by a desire to maintain independence from a single foreign supplier rather than to develop military effectiveness. In the ground force area, Egypt is in the process of buying 650 M-60A3 tanks and associated M-113 personnel carriers. But Egypt is also maintaining its old Soviet inventory and buying Romanian tanks to augment this force. Over the long term Egypt's air force will probably have more F-16s (80 to 120) than any other single aircraft, but in fact Egypt's inventory of aircraft is now more diverse than that of the GCC as a whole.[51] Thus Egyptian forces can operate coherently only in packages considerably smaller than the overall size of the force posture suggests.

50. See IISS, *Military Balance, 1983–1984,* p. 53.
51. Interview with Egyptian military officials, June 1982. According to the IISS, *Military Balance, 1983–1984,* Egypt currently owns or has ordered the following types of tactical aircraft: F-16, MIG-17, MIG-21, SU-7, Chinese F-6, F-7, Mirage 5, Mirage 2000, and Alpha Jet. Of these, the F-16s and Mirage 5s will be the most numerous. See the series on Egypt's air force in *Aviation Week & Space Technology,* vol. 115 (December 14, 1981), pp. 40–54; vol. 115 (December 21, 1981), pp. 34–37; vol. 116 (January 4, 1982), pp. 41–47; and vol. 116 (January 18, 1982), pp. 61–66.

A more serious question concerns the political acceptability (to either Egyptians or the GCC) of deploying Egyptian forces to the Arabian Peninsula. Both Egyptians and Saudis remember Yemen's civil war; in different ways it has caused both parties to be wary of an Egyptian presence on the Peninsula. Egypt signed the peace treaty with Israel to allow for concentration on internal economic problems and to avoid war. After bearing isolation from the Arab world as a consequence, Egyptians may not be willing to see their forces deployed to defend Kuwait or Saudi Arabia. Nor is it certain that Egypt sees any important connection between Egyptian interests and GCC defense.

Size and location alone inevitably make Egypt important to the GCC, but the same factors also make Egypt the source of worrisome threats. Like U.S. rapid deployment forces, Egyptian troops will probably always be seen by peninsular rulers as part of a two-edged sword. Like U.S. rapid deployment forces, Egypt's forces are best kept over the horizon. That is where they are currently, the result primarily of Egypt's own choices. While events may prompt the GCC to call for Egyptian help, GCC rulers will probably always be more interested in Egypt's diplomatic support than in its military assistance.

FRANCE. French involvement on the Peninsula is of recent origin and is mainly the result of arms transfers. Arms deals with the Saudis, the UAE, Qatar, and Kuwait have brought French advisors to these countries. In Saudi Arabia, the French-run armor school and support staff for the Royal Saudi Army's AMX-30s have brought with them about 2,000 French military personnel. Saudi naval officers train in France, and the sale of French naval vessels to Saudi Arabia has brought French naval personnel to that country.

Although French forces have not been used on the Peninsula, the military resources that France could bring to bear there are considerable. The forward portion of the French Maritime Forces of the Indian Ocean (FMOI) operates out of La Reunion and consists of three Exocet-armed frigates and supporting vessels. Reinforcing elements connected with the FMOI but not necessarily on station in the Indian Ocean include an antiship-missile ship, supporting elements, and a marine commando group of about 600 men. From ports in France could come a naval intervention force of a carrier (with about forty fighter/ground attack aircraft), a helicopter assault carrier, support vessels, and perhaps 2,300 marine commandos with limited armor (AMX-30) capabilities. Other forces available would include about 3,600 Foreign Legionnaires, supporting tanks, and a small squadron of Mirage 3As at Djibouti, and a parachute and marine division stationed in France.[52]

GREAT BRITAIN. Oman will probably remain the focal point of British activity on behalf of GCC defense. Still, during the Falklands war the British moved about 9,000 soldiers (mostly infantry), more than 100 combat aircraft (42 of them Harriers, which, armed with AIM-9L Sidewinder missiles, scored most kills against Argentine aircraft), and 2 carrier groups to the South Atlantic in just over two months.[53] The size and composition of this force suggest that the British could handle threats larger than those prevalent during the Dhofar rebellion.

THE UNITED STATES. The United States has been involved in GCC security chiefly through Saudi Arabia, with which it has had close ties since World War II. The U.S. contribution to crisis security has been specialized —a squadron of F-100s during the Yemeni civil war, and AWACS to oversee Yemeni border conflict in 1979 and the Iran-Iraq war beginning in 1980. Such a contribution has beneficially minimized U.S. visibility on the Peninsula but has also employed the United States in areas of its comparative advantage—sophisticated general purpose forces. In this sense the United States has been wisely used as a force of last resort.

Of all the potential sources of reinforcement, the United States can bring the most impressive set of military resources to bear. U.S. projection forces are those belonging to the U.S. Central Command. These could be applied to all GCC defense requirements. The constraints on deploying these forces are political and derive from the fears that GCC rulers may have of the "American threat," from their concern for the domestic political ramifications of obtaining U.S. help, and from concern in the United States about the commitment of U.S. forces abroad.

---

52. See Stephen S. Roberts, "French Naval Policy Outside of Europe," Professional Paper 294 (Alexandria, Va.: Center for Naval Analyses, September 1980), pp. 21–23; *Jane's Fighting Ships, 1983–84* (London: Janes's Publishing Co., 1983), ship reference section, pp. 150–79; and Drew Middleton, "French Force in a Vital Area," *New York Times,* May 7, 1981.

53. See Neville Trotter, "The Falklands and the Long Haul," and Samuel L. Morison, "Falklands (Malvinas) Campaign: A Chronology," *U.S. Naval Institute Proceedings,* vol. 109 (June 1983), pp. 111, 124, respectively; and Lawrence Freedman, "The War of the Falkland Islands, 1982," *Foreign Affairs,* vol. 61 (Fall 1982), pp. 201–02.

Peninsular Defense and Reinforcement

If in peacetime GCC military forces have an international character, in a crisis their character becomes even more international. Military forces liberally sprinkled with expatriates, foreign advisors, and support crews are usually reinforced or replaced with foreign military forces. Because the forces of external powers will always be larger than the forces GCC members can muster in their own defense, that pattern of reinforcement will probably remain critical to GCC external defense. Consequently, the problem confronting the GCC changes from that of building local capabilities to that of facilitating the delivery of help. Viewed from this perspective, some of the problems and anomalies of GCC military capabilities seem more understandable.

The presence of foreign advisors, for example, begins to look reasonable. Foreign advisors serve as a useful resident team able to coordinate the delivery and deployment of external forces who may not speak Arabic and who probably are not familiar with either the terrain or local politics. Some foreigners may assume control of local weapons, less to improve technical performance than to facilitate coordination with incoming forces.

Arms transfers also take on larger significance. In most cases GCC members implicitly buy a logistical base capable of supporting reinforcement, as well as the weapons themselves. For instance, Saudi Arabia's F-15 purchases, replete with large stocks of spares, munitions, and maintenance equipment, ease substantially the logistical problems connected with bringing in U.S. Air Force F-15s. This holds true, though to a lesser extent, for the smaller sheikhdoms, where French and British equipment dominates. Since the most likely regional sources of help are also states that rely on Western equipment, GCC purchases provide logistical bases for the council members as well as for Western suppliers themselves.

Indeed, if the centerpiece of the GCC defense problem is reinforcement rather than the development of local capabilities, then the diversity that marks local weapons inventories works to the GCC's advantage. Saudi Arabia and Kuwait have purchased the tanks of all three major Western suppliers, for example, allowing themselves flexibility to call for help in accord with the threat and local political constraints. Likewise the presence of French aircraft in Kuwait, Qatar, and the UAE, or of British aircraft in Oman, allows flexibility in reinforcing air defense. The military advantages of a common GCC aircraft—or any other common weapon—must be weighed against its cost in flexibility.

Under these circumstances, absorption of weaponry and the development of independent local forces are undesirable as well as unlikely. Purchase of simpler systems like the F-5 or the new FX undoubtedly promises the greatest indigenous capability in the shortest possible time. But precisely for that reason such a purchase threatens to eliminate foreign advisors. And because weapons like this are fairly simple they are not likely to be in use in Western inventories, limiting reinforcement potential. Finally, even if the weapons are used by potential helpers, they are not the best available systems and thus do not promote the best possible defense under conditions of reinforcement. Saudi F-15s are the entree for an effective air defense overlay based on one of the best fighter aircraft available. They are flashy deterrents less in their own right than in what they promise.

This logic can be pushed too far. Legitimate interest may exist among some circles in the GCC to develop indigenous capabilities, and there are probably domestic political incentives to do so. Moreover, large foreign communities in these states, underscoring Gulf rulers' reliance on foreign help, carry potential costs. As always, GCC rulers must balance competing pressures. If important components of their security system would need reinforcement, however, the balance they have chosen is not a bad one.

Conclusions

Notwithstanding the logistical and organizational disarray of their military forces, Saudi Arabia and its GCC associates have developed a reasonably effective security system. It has worked fairly well in protecting them from internal as well as external threats. The system employs what amounts to a division of labor in which outside help is integrated into GCC security efforts at every level.

Members of the GCC focus principally on internal security and on the Peninsula as a whole. Here they use diplomacy, familial and political intrigue, and traditional methods of political control far more than force to control internal violence, and in so doing keep external adversaries at a distance. Against external threats they employ the services of others as available and appropriate. The system relies primarily on ad hoc arrangements; it has worked so far largely because in crises enemies' enemies have become friends, tacitly or explicitly, and because geographic and political circumstances make it difficult to attack the Peninsula.

Western military planners might prefer to see these states develop more organized military institutions, central command structures, and carefully laid plans for reinforcement in a crisis. Yet if the West understands the inherent weakness of these regimes and the tension between their need to meet threats and the threat posed by meeting their security needs, then it is easy to understand that the GCC security system evinces a wisdom all its own. Given the newness of the enterprise, the development of GCC military forces could not be expected to produce extraordinary results in any case. But GCC military forces are disorganized for a purpose and will continue to be disorganized as long as these forces seem to pose a threat to GCC rulers. The very diversity that these rulers introduce into their forces as a means of controlling them makes it easier for other states to reinforce them in a crisis.

These rulers choose partners carefully. The United States might be only too happy to provide Saudi Arabia with all the security help it needs—in return for bases, a U.S. presence, and a common front against the Soviet Union. But the six members of the GCC clearly see drawbacks to such an arrangement. Instead, GCC rulers have turned to Jordan— militarily able, yet small and politically compatible—and Pakistan— technically capable, yet distant, non-Arab, and Islamic. Among Western powers, GCC rulers have turned to France and Great Britain as well as the United States. GCC rulers buffer themselves from external helpers for the same reason that they emasculate their own military forces; doing otherwise could be dangerous.

Such an approach has worked well for the GCC states so far. But to the extent that it is a strategy of weakness that relies on overarching balances in the surrounding region, important questions arise about limits on the ability of these rulers to act in their own interests. What if the balances collapse? If these rulers faced a serious external threat, could they tolerate the extended presence of U.S. forces without grave internal disorder? Could they possibly build more effective forces that wouldn't constitute a serious threat to themselves? The answers to these questions depend in part on the nature of the threat; the internal repercussions of a direct Soviet threat would probably differ greatly from the repercussions of a local threat clothed in the trappings of Pan-Arabism or Islam. The answers would also depend on the relative strength of national as opposed to local or regional loyalties among citizens in the GCC.

In fact, GCC rulers probably do not know the answers to all of these questions, and their actions suggest that they are not eager to find out. They have constructed their security system to deal with most likely threats because serious planning to meet worst cases may be threatening in its own right. Should they ever be forced to face the worst case, accommodation may seem less risky than confrontation, but no course of action will be free of danger. How much external threat to their security can GCC regimes tolerate before any cure—even accommodation—becomes as dangerous as the disease? Thus far GCC rulers have not had to answer this question.

CHAPTER SIX

Toward a Flexible
U.S. Security Policy

U.S. POLICYMAKERS should be no more anxious than GCC rulers to discover the limits of the Gulf Cooperation Council's approach to security. The delicate political and military balances affecting the Arabian Peninsula suggest, first, that a respect for the constraints within which Gulf rulers operate must inform U.S. policy. Traditional U.S. military advice, urging greater centralization and standardization among GCC forces, must change to take account of the dangers that lurk in implementing that advice. Second, a broader U.S. security policy must include an appreciation of the wisdom of the GCC's multinational division of labor. A more visible U.S. role in the security of these states might lead to a weakening of their internal security, where most of their security problems rest. Finally, insofar as the political and military balances around the Arabian Peninsula facilitate the GCC rulers' approach to security, U.S. policy must seek to maintain those balances. Concern for GCC security inevitably draws attention outward from the Peninsula to the surrounding region.

A policy of enhancing the GCC's approach to security would directly benefit the United States. It would free the United States from major involvement in the area's internal problems, which neither U.S. forces nor the U.S. public is better disposed to handle than countries that have long histories of involvement in the Gulf's internal affairs. The tendency of members of the GCC to involve outside powers in their security affairs has engaged U.S. allies in Gulf security without the need for grand, and usually unsuccessful, cooperative schemes within NATO. Finally, for the United States as well as for GCC forces, protecting the Peninsula as a whole is easier militarily than protecting individual states on it. Enhancing the GCC's approach to security thus promises to focus U.S. military planning on interdiction missions that U.S. forces are comparatively well designed to handle.

Even if approached skillfully, GCC security will remain uncertain, as will the security of U.S. interests around the Gulf. These regimes will not last forever, nor will they always pursue policies that satisfy U.S. interests as well as their own. Regional changes may place them in a squeeze that ultimately works to their detriment as well as to the detriment of the United States and its allies. Energy conservation and stockpiling provide useful hedges against the uncertainties of this situation. But U.S. military planners cannot avoid planning for the worst. They must face the possibility of having to use force in defense of U.S. interests in the area.

This chapter treats both aspects of U.S. security policy: a cooperative, understated support of the GCC's traditional security mechanisms, and the possibility of the offensive use of force. The first part of the chapter takes the threats outlined in chapter 4 and the security framework outlined in chapter 5 and derives from them a set of guidelines for security policy toward the region. The second part of the chapter examines the conditions under which force might be used to protect oil and outlines the costs and benefits of doing so under differing circumstances. Significantly, neither section offers a cure for the uncertainties that hamper the United States' ability to secure its interests on the Arabian Peninsula. U.S. leaders, like GCC rulers themselves, must make the best of a bad situation. But there are better and worse ways of doing this. Overall, this chapter suggests that a selective, low-key, and somewhat detached approach to these GCC security issues is most useful.

U.S. Policy and Peninsular Security

Enhancing the GCC's approach to security does not imply that the United States should take a laissez-faire approach to securing its interests on the Arabian Peninsula. Clarifying roles and missions with interested parties in Europe and the Gulf region, offering technical solutions to specific security problems, and planning for the rapid insertion of U.S. forces are demanding tasks. Often, avoiding involvement may pose choices as difficult as those linked with increasing commitments. Indeed, handling GCC security is demanding because it cannot be done unilaterally and because Gulf rulers are ambivalent about U.S. support. The maxim "less is more" may be a proper guide to U.S. involvement in GCC security affairs. But doing less—skillfully and consistently—is no less challenging than doing more.

U.S. Policy and Internal Security in the Peninsular States

Prudence alone suggests that the United States has a stake in the internal security of the GCC states. Internal violence could produce regimes more willing than present ones to sell oil and stabilize the oil market. But this scenario is unlikely. It is more likely that internal pressures would impede smooth relations between Western powers and existing regimes. Coups or revolutionary violence could produce a fundamentalist regime opposed to selling oil at rates common in the past. And oil facilities could be damaged by internal violence, be it of strictly internal origin or the result of infiltration by an outside adversary. Finally, internal turbulence in the five smaller oil states could produce an external threat to Saudi Arabia. Violence within any of the six GCC states thus could certainly endanger the interests of the United States and its allies.

Yet direct U.S. involvement in the internal security of these states raises questions. Arming and training internal security forces is not something the United States can do better than others. Indeed, U.S. advisors are likely to be considerably less sensitive to internal political dynamics than Jordanians, Egyptians, or the British. This is especially true in the more traditional internal security areas, about which the United States knows little compared with other countries whose involvement is already well established. Closer cooperation in internal security affairs could involve the United States directly in domestic issues—retaking the Mecca Mosque, repressing Shi'as in Al Hasa, or keeping track of Palestinian residents of the Gulf states.Those are not missions the United States should seek to acquire.

Nor have the GCC rulers encouraged the United States to take on such internal missions, with one exception: U.S. assistance to the Saudi Arabian National Guard (SANG). Although a private firm (the Vinnell Corporation) implements the SANG program, it remains an official U.S. assistance program under U.S. Army direction. It deals with a small portion (eight battalions) of the guard and has sought, apparently with limited success, to convert these units into a light, conventionally armed force designed to defend the oil fields. Yet SANG units are not structured to meet the main external threats to the fields, which would come by air or sea, or would involve ground attack by armored forces out of the north. Their more likely role remains internal security, as their involvement in repressing the Shi'a demonstrations in 1979 and 1980, as well as in retaking the Mecca Mosque, suggests. Accordingly, the United States should minimize or curtail its assistance to the SANG.[1]

Technical assistance is a different matter, especially with regard to the two new internal security problems that GCC rulers have acquired in recent years: oil field security and protection against infiltration, especially by Iranian terrorists. In both cases the United States and its allies have both technical expertise and technologies—ground-surveillance radars, intrusion detection devices, computers, and other equipment—that could be useful to GCC regimes. Passive security measures such as perimeter security, facility architecture, and hardening of key oil technologies would also be useful. Elaborate arrangements to deliver such assistance are unnecessary. Much of the assistance could be provided by private U.S. firms and individuals. The United States should try to focus the attention of GCC rulers on these problems and offer U.S. expertise when appropriate.

The principal role for U.S. forces in the event of internal turbulence on the Peninsula is to prevent outside intervention. The usual scenario depicts a U.S.-Soviet race to support opposed factions in a Saudi civil war. But more likely possibilities would involve regional powers—Iran, Iraq, and Egypt have all meddled on the Peninsula in the past—seeking to intervene in the smaller sheikhdoms rather than in Saudi Arabia. External adversaries could mount two-stage attacks, finding a foothold anywhere on the Peninsula and then exploiting it unhampered by geographic barriers. These antagonists could pose to the Saudis and their remaining GCC associates a serious long-term threat that might be difficult indeed to meet. It may not always be possible to deter such intervention, or to interdict the actual military operations involved

---

1. A decade's involvement with the Saudi Arabian National Guard (SANG) makes it difficult politically, and perhaps dangerous to U.S. credibility, for the United States to curtail its SANG program abruptly. At least, however, the United States should refrain from expanding its involvement with the SANG. Perhaps the best course would be to focus attention on that part of the SANG involved in oil field security, since it is this part of the force that is most likely to be used for external security, including defense against infiltration and terrorists.

quickly enough. But U.S. naval forces on station in the Gulf and the Indian Ocean could play an important role by helping to counter threats before they materialized on the Peninsula, where they would become much more serious.

Clearly, neither the United States nor GCC rulers can expect to prevent outside adversaries from providing diplomatic and possibly material support to dissident factions within the GCC. Clandestine infiltration of combatants may also be possible. But GCC forces can handle those problems with their usual sources of help. If by threatening interdiction the United States can force the GCC's adversaries to adopt a low profile in their support to dissidents on the Peninsula, the United States will be performing a useful service to the GCC.

The actual deployment of U.S. forces to deal with internal threats cannot be ruled out. If internal conflict were to endanger oil technologies, port facilities, and storage depots, it would present the United States and its allies with the choice of protecting those facilities from attack or choosing sides in the internal conflict. Insofar as the United States remains detached from internal turmoil, its direct entry into conflict is likely to be delayed, allowing U.S. policymakers time to assess the conflict's significance and determine how U.S. forces can play a useful role. Closer discussions with allies and friendly regional powers more deeply involved in the GCC's internal security affairs, rather than greater U.S. involvement in those affairs, is the recommended policy.

U.S. Security Assistance, Peninsular Forces, and External Defense

The GCC states are cash buyers in the world arms market, and political considerations encourage them to purchase arms from various states besides the United States. Indeed, the presence of British and French weapons in GCC arsenals bears witness less to the excellence of their marketing techniques than to the power of political considerations in GCC capitals. Rulers are not likely to be receptive to a strong U.S. push to increase the presence of its weapons and advisors in their countries.

Moreover, a broad-based push by the United States to increase its presence on the Peninsula would probably be counterproductive. To the extent that it could be implemented successfully, such a policy might risk increasing internal problems in these states by creating more obvious and tangible links to the United States. Successfully applied to ground forces in particular, such a policy might increase the internal threat that these forces posed to existing regimes. Similarly, a forceful U.S. effort to compete with France and Great Britain across the entire range of arms might only limit the positions that these European countries maintain within the GCC, thus ultimately decreasing the GCC's flexibility to handle military problems. At what point, for example, would a growing U.S. position among Saudi conventional forces leave the Saudis with no choice but to turn to the United States for help with internal as well as external security?

Encouraged by these considerations to focus its security assistance policies on a narrow set of issues that best serve its interests, the United States should seek to conduct an assistance program aimed at three goals. First, the United States should facilitate reinforcement by outside help. Second, it should develop GCC air and coastal defenses sufficiently to buy time for reinforcement to occur. Third, the United States should develop components of the GCC's ground forces to a point at which these states can handle the military threat from the Yemens. In short, U.S. policy should strive to help the GCC states police the Peninsula while facilitating the entry of other forces to handle more demanding defensive tasks. These goals suggest a number of specific policies.

ARMS TRANSFERS AND OVERBUYING. Reinforcement is facilitated by the presence of spare parts, support facilities, and munitions in these countries in quantities larger than those required for local forces alone. The Saudis have already adopted a policy of overbuying in regard to their F-15s and air-delivered munitions, and they have built airfields large enough to handle major reinforcement. Policies of the smaller GCC states are harder to discern, yet clearly it is in the U.S. interest to encourage them to overbuy and overbuild as well.

U.S. ASSISTANCE AND SAUDI GROUND FORCES. Saudi ground forces are now organized to neatly balance Saudi Arabia's internal and external security requirements. U.S. security assistance should not aim to change that situation. There is little to be gained in external defense, and potentially much to be lost in internal security, by trying to turn Saudi Arabia's ground forces into a large, rationalized, and perhaps centrally deployed army.

Rather, to the extent that the United States wields leverage over Saudi ground forces, U.S. policy should seek to improve the functioning of the two small armies into which the Saudis have divided their forces. The two brigades in the south might well be capable of handling what will probably remain sporadic and unsophisticated threats from the Yemens. At any rate, meeting the Yemeni threat should be the focus for the training of these forces. In the north, Saudi Arabia and Kuwait together cannot be expected to defend against likely overland attacks, but they could protect Kuwait's border until reinforcements arrived. Both sets of rulers would feel compelled for domestic political reasons to use their forces this way. The use of Saudi and Kuwaiti forces would also probably be a prerequisite for U.S. public support of involvement in the defense of that area.

This approach to security assistance to local ground forces gives the Saudis the lead in shaping these forces as they see fit. Constraints on U.S. action, besides those imposed by the Saudis themselves, stem from the possible requirement for the projection of U.S. ground forces to meet major external threats to the Peninsula. The need for a logistical base to support incoming U.S. forces makes it wise, where possible, to transfer major pieces of equipment that will also be found in U.S. projection forces.[2]

THE PROBLEM OF PENINSULAR AIR DEFENSES. Improving GCC air defenses should be a principal goal of U.S. security assistance policy. This is the defense sector in which surprise attack is most likely; hence GCC air defense forces are more likely than others to face threats alone, at least temporarily. And GCC rulers have already focused attention and resources on their air defense, an area where recruiting problems are fairly minor. The GCC states may be able to put up a defense against sporadic air threats (assuming that foreign support personnel stand fast), as the Saudis demonstrated in June 1984 when their F-15s shot down an Iranian F-4 over the Gulf. Air defense aircraft capable of strike missions would provide a flexible addition to GCC ground defenses especially in Saudi Arabia, whose enormous size makes the idea of a swing force of

2. From this perspective rumored sales of M-1 Abrams tanks to Saudi Arabia are of questionable value since these tanks are new and are being sent primarily to U.S. forces in Europe. Still, the goal of matching exported equipment with equipment deployed with projection forces is only one factor in what are usually complex calculations. If, for example, the Saudis are set to choose between the M-1 and the Leopard II of West Germany, a country unlikely ever to project force to the Gulf, it makes no sense to forgo the sale simply because the M-1 is not found among U.S. rapid deployment units. To the extent that sales of the M-1 to Saudi Arabia lower its unit cost to the U.S. Army, the sale might at least be said to benefit the overall U.S. defense posture. However, when there is a choice, the effects of a specific U.S. sale on the logistical base available in the region for U.S. projection forces should be considered.

strike aircraft especially appealing. Finally, while Saudi air force officers have been politically active on several occasions, the forces themselves do not pose the internal threat posed by ground forces. Thus developing effective air defense capabilities is subject to fewer political constraints.

The focus of so much GCC attention on sophisticated aircraft should not distract U.S. policymakers from pressing—and from encouraging their allies to press—for the implementation of passive air defense measures. Dispersing aircraft; hardening key oil, air terminal, and port facilities; and building shelters or revetments on runways are the only defensive measures likely to be in place for a "bolt from the blue" air attack. Some of these may be expensive, but once constructed they have no manning requirements and are politically inert. Consequently, they accord well with GCC resource and political constraints.

A more expensive and manpower-intensive elaboration on this theme would involve constructing more air bases in Saudi Arabia to complicate preemptive attack, giving resilience to Saudi air operations and easing the process of bringing in reinforcements should they be required. The Saudis may not be interested in provoking Israel by pursuing such construction in their northwest quadrant. But bases north and south of Riyadh would help them meet or deter attacks from Iran or Iraq.

The presence of valuable fixed targets in these states raises questions about the usefulness of fixed air defense missile installations. Like passive measures, these systems pose little threat to GCC rulers. They strain local manpower, however, and many of the systems currently deployed in the GCC remain partially unmanned, even undeployed. It would still be useful for these rulers to buy and deploy more, on the assumption that, at the very least, these units could be manned in a crisis by experts from various reinforcing states, including the United States. As of this writing the Iran-Iraq war—in particular the air war against oil tankers that peaked in May and June of 1984—seems to have increased the interest of GCC rulers in their air defense missiles. Any move to improve the readiness of these weapons would add measurably to GCC security.

The interest of both Kuwait and the UAE in linking their Improved-Hawk air defense systems to Saudi Arabia's AWACS aircraft suggests another direction for U.S. assistance. The effectiveness of I-Hawk and all other GCC ground-based radars would improve with long-range warning provided by AWACS. Although little seems to have been done yet to link Saudi Arabia's AWACS to its own forces, over the long haul linking radars and missile sites across the GCC would dramatically improve the potential effectiveness of GCC air defenses. Observers may be properly skeptical of the GCC's ability to exploit such capabilities, but this does not mean that reinforcing states could not use the capability, or that GCC forces could not learn to exploit the capability over time.

However useful steps like these may be, aircraft will remain the dominant concern within the GCC, as well as among Western suppliers. Militarily, aircraft are especially flexible and can deal with threats from several directions. The presence of sophisticated Western aircraft on GCC runways also bears witness to the political commitment of Western suppliers to Gulf security. For the supplying countries, the presence of these aircraft near the Gulf creates at least a modest base for reinforcement. And aircraft sales lower unit costs to Western militaries. Thus various pressures combine to emphasize aircraft in discussions of GCC air defense, as well as of peninsular security in general.

Aircraft sales are among the most controversial that the United States can undertake, however. Sales of F-15s and AWACS to Saudi Arabia were approved by Congress only after considerable debate about the threat that such systems would pose to Israel, and sales of other U.S. aircraft to Kuwait or the UAE are likely to be viewed with similar concern. These controversies deter not only the executive branch of the U.S. government but also the Gulf's rulers, whose desire for discretion and quiet diplomacy is offended by vitriolic public debate in the United States. This may be one reason why some Gulf rulers have chosen European aircraft in the past. Even the Saudis themselves may opt for a European addition to their air force (most likely one of the French Mirage series) rather than face repeated controversies over additional requests for U.S. weaponry.

The political volatility of these issues in the United States makes it pointless to offer strong recommendations as to what weapons should or should not be offered to Saudi Arabia or the GCC. Ultimately, these issues are decided in a political process that takes account of far more than the increment to GCC security, or the threat to Israel, that a given sale portends. Military strategists can only outline the basic strategic issues at stake, giving decisionmakers military guidelines on which to proceed should all else be equal.

First, it makes little sense to push hard to see the GCC states buy a common aircraft. As long as Gulf rulers are ambivalent about such purchases, such a push would incur diplomatic costs for marginal military benefits. To the extent that the United States succeeded it might well reduce the British and French positions on the Peninsula, undermining an important basis for allied cooperation in GCC security affairs. Finally, insofar as the GCC standardized its aircraft (around any model), its ability to accept reinforcements from the various states that have helped it in the past would be reduced.

Members of the GCC may nonetheless approach the United States on the issue of a standard aircraft; then it will be difficult to avoid discussing specific aircraft. From a military perspective it makes sense to discuss dual-capable, fighter/ground attack (FGA) aircraft like the F-16 or Northrop's F-20, one of the FX aircraft. Unlike the F-15, both the F-16 and the F-20 are capable of striking ground and naval targets as well as defending airspace. Thus they accord better than the F-15 with the full range of threats the GCC states may have to face and would permit more efficient use of the limited number of GCC pilots. On balance, sale of either of these aircraft would make more military sense than the sale of F-15s.

Of the two, the F-16 is preferable from a U.S. perspective. Easier to maintain than the F-16, the F-20 could be expected to produce a relatively independent GCC air capability. But the F-20 is not likely ever to enter the U.S. inventory, or the inventories of other likely reinforcing powers. Thus its sale would do little to facilitate reinforcement of the GCC states in a crisis. Sale of the F-16 would satisfy the need for a logistical base in the region for an aircraft currently in U.S., Egyptian, and Pakistani hands while also satisfying the GCC's need for a common, dual-purpose aircraft.

This logic applies to aircraft sales to Saudi Arabia as well as to the GCC as a whole. On the one hand, the Saudi air force will always be larger than other GCC air forces, making the logistical base associated with aircraft sales better developed in Saudi Arabia than elsewhere on the Peninsula. On the other hand, the military value of FGA aircraft is especially high for Saudi Arabia; indeed, they provide a uniquely flexible defense capability that can be swung around the entire Saudi domain. Putting aside the question of a standard GCC aircraft, then, the Saudis may consider the F-16 for themselves alone.

A request for F-16s, whether from the Saudis or the GCC as a whole, would be intensely controversial in the United States, since it would breach an important threshold in the level of U.S. arms sales to the peninsular states. The F-15's single-mission status and the seemingly defensive character of a pure air defense aircraft played importantly in winning congressional approval for the Saudi F-15 sale in 1978. To be sure, fighter aircraft can be used offensively, as the Israelis know very well; introduced into an Arab-Israeli conflict, Saudi fighter aircraft could draw off Israeli air defenses, leaving the skies open to other Arab strike aircraft. Thus the military difference to Israel of selling sophisticated fighter or FGA aircraft to Saudi Arabia or the GCC is probably not as great as the 1978 debate suggested. But the symbolic importance of introducing a new, mainstream, dual-capable U.S. aircraft into one or more GCC inventories would make the issue controversial nonetheless. Faced with this prospect, neither the Saudis nor CENTCOM's military planners may be interested in pursuing this option, despite the military logic behind it.

Whatever decisions are reached about the purchase of new aircraft, GCC inventories are likely to include a diverse array of makes and models for years to come. Consequently, U.S. policy should encourage these states to purchase technologies that enable their aircraft to communicate with one another, whatever their make. Transponders for facilitating "identification, friend or foe" by ground radars as well as other aircraft are available commercially as well as through military sales. Even if they avoided purchase of a common aircraft, GCC rulers could buy the same transponder, giving them commonality in an area where NATO has yet to achieve it.

U.S. ASSISTANCE AND PENINSULAR NAVAL FORCES. There seems to be no political danger in the development of larger GCC naval forces. Moreover, both the naval vessels and antishipping helicopters these states have ordered recently have a high technology to manpower ratio that accords well with shortages of skilled manpower in these states. The forces are new, and it would be surprising if they were not beset with many of the operational problems that plague other components of GCC forces. But the GCC has the potential to develop a standoff coastal protection capability. Encouraging that development should be the goal of U.S. assistance. The GCC rulers will probably not become interested in an oceangoing fleet in the foreseeable future; their concern is likely to remain the Gulf, their coasts, and in Saudi Arabia's case, the Red Sea. Any attempt to go beyond the kind of forces now being purchased would be a waste of resources.

As is true with air defense, attention tends to have been diverted to sophisticated ships, helicopters, and missiles when other, often less expensive and elaborate, means exist to perform the same task. Hardening of coastal installations, such as piers and harbor facilities, would limit the damage of both air and coastal strikes. Shore-based gun and missile batteries could back up ship- and air-based defenses.

U.S. Forces and Peninsular Security

No amount of arms aid will alleviate the GCC's need for help in meeting the major military threats its members might face. In the past, reinforcement was often an ad hoc affair, as when small units from Egypt, the Sudan, Jordan, Kuwait, and Saudi Arabia lined up on Kuwait's border with Iraq late in 1961. In that case no real military threat materialized; troop deployments were designed merely to bring diplomatic pressure to bear on Iraq. In the future the GCC may not be so lucky. The religious zealotry of Iran's Revolutionary Guards, the practical military experience gained by the forces of Iraq as well as Iran in their war, the growing importance of the peninsular states, and their increasing exposure to regional political currents suggest that they may well have to face threats demanding the deployment of effective military forces in response.

Whether or not U.S. forces are required, reinforcement in the face of serious threats cannot be as haphazard as it was in 1961. Besides encouraging the peninsular states to overbuy military equipment to establish the infrastructure to support reinforcing powers, three military issues are paramount. First, air defense, already an important requirement of GCC defense, is made still more important by the vulnerability of land or sea convoys, or arriving aircraft, and of ports, roads, and airfields to air attack. Second, delivery of reinforcing units may be complicated by the need for speed and by the size and weight of weapons required for modern combat. Delivery of infantry or mechanized forces from Jordan might pose no problems, given Jordan's proximity to the Peninsula and Saudi Arabia's large and growing fleet of transport aircraft. But delivery of heavy units over long distances—from France or Great Britain, for example—would fall well outside the transport capabilities of local actors. U.S. air transport assets could play an important role in expediting reinforcement, even when other U.S. forces are not needed.[3]

3. The United States has played this role on rare occasions in the past. U.S. aircraft

Finally, serious military operations require a degree of centralized control missing in previous GCC security crises.[4] The requirement for unity of command will vary with the intensity of the threat. Against reinforced Dhofari rebels in Oman, for example, Jordanian, Iranian, Omani, and British forces divided the defense and operated in different sectors under only loose British and Omani control. Against a serious armored thrust into GCC territory from the north, or sustained air attack, however, coordination of all elements of the defense would be essential. Piecemeal or loosely organized defenses might work reasonably well against low-key or sporadic threats, but major threats would require virtually the complete replacement of GCC forces by reinforcing units.

U.S. forces must expect to assume the major threats. Two in particular are important: defense against overland attack and air defense. Because any overland attack threat would probably involve an air threat, and because reinforcement would require air defense at the outset, U.S. reinforcement of GCC air defenses will be discussed first.

REINFORCING OR REPLACING AIR DEFENSES. Conceivably, U.S. help to the GCC might be much like U.S. air support to Saudi Arabia in 1963. The Egyptian threat then was sporadic and small, reinforcement amounted to a deterrent show of force, and the problem was solved. The U.S. reinforcement hardly disrupted Saudi air defenses, as meager as those were in 1963. In the future, however, the GCC may face much larger sporadic or even sustained air attacks, and then it is probably best to plan to replace or take over local air defenses. An effective defense requires that radars and aircraft be linked, otherwise elements of the system might threaten each other more than they threaten the enemy. Ideally, pilots should operate on the basis of common tactics and know

---

helped move British troops and supplies from Lebanon to Jordan during the 1958 Lebanon crisis. And in May 1978 U.S. aircraft lifted both Belgian and French forces to Shaba province in Zaire during insurgency there. See, respectively, William B. Quandt, "Lebanon, 1958, and Jordan, 1970," in Barry M. Blechman and Stephen S. Kaplan, *Force without War: U.S. Armed Forces as a Political Instrument* (Brookings Institution, 1978), p. 239; and Philip D. Zelikow, "Force without War, 1975–82," *Journal of Strategic Studies,* vol. 7 (March 1984), p. 39.

4. Even in Lebanon in 1983, operating on the margins of fighting around Beirut, the U.S., French, British, and Italian forces found that conducting sporadic offensive operations without prior coordination is dangerous, as the artillery fire of one contingent threatened the low-flying strike or reconnaissance aircraft of another. See Thomas L. Friedman, "Beirut Flaw: 4-Nation Force Isn't United," *New York Times,* September 28, 1983.

the capabilities of each other's aircraft. Few of these links are available in the GCC itself, and none exists between GCC and reinforcing air defenses. An attempt to construct an air defense net based on both local and foreign components could be dangerous to the participants.

U.S. assets are far and away the largest and best prepared to take over the GCC's air defenses. The basic ingredients for U.S. reinforcement are already in place. Saudi Arabia's F-15 purchases have given that country a resilient base for accepting U.S. interceptors, whether these would come from bases in Europe or the United States. AWACS aircraft are already in place for directing the air battle. Meanwhile, U.S. aircraft carriers in the Indian Ocean provide an entirely different venue for bringing U.S. air power to bear quickly. Assuming that these carriers cannot be sailed into the Gulf itself, the range and sortie rate of the naval air defense will be limited, although in-flight refueling of naval aircraft, using tankers based on carriers or in Oman, would substantially enhance naval capabilities. Meanwhile, U.S. I-Hawks are available in the GCC, as are various U.S.-built radars and communications facilities.

The course of reinforcement would vary depending upon whether or not air attack had already begun. Were the members of the GCC to come under attack before reinforcement began, there would be an immediate need to put an air defense cap over key targets, as well as over the reinforcement process itself. The cap might be supplied by the GCC. Against the air force available to Iran in 1984, for example, the Royal Saudi Air Force could probably have been very effective. Against a refurbished Iranian air force or Iraq's air force, the GCC might still be able to put up a limited defense. Otherwise, reinforcing aircraft would have to fight their way in. U.S. F-15s could land at Khamis Mushayt and work north and east against an Iranian or Iraqi threat, for example. Or U.S. carriers off Oman could cap at least the southern part of the GCC area to allow land-based aircraft to enter the region. With an effective cap in place, technicians could be brought in to man local I-Hawks, ground-based radars, and AWACS aircraft.

In a crisis where the air threat had not yet materialized, reinforcement could be more relaxed, even piecemeal. U.S.-Saudi cooperation just after the start of the Iran-Iraq war provides a partial model. U.S. AWACS aircraft were deployed to Saudi Arabia within weeks after Iraq's attack began. With them went additional ground radars and several hundred technicians and advisors to train the Saudis on this equipment. Presumably these technicians would also have run the equipment in the event of

attack. The process was designed to deter either combatant from expanding the conflict, but it also produced additional military capability had
deterrence failed.[5]

The Israeli case is a special one from the standpoint of local powers as
well as the United States. The Israeli threat is so large and sophisticated
that local powers have shown no great interest in defense. The United
States would not be willing to help them defend themselves in this case.
The local assumption seems to be that their only effective defense would
be U.S. diplomatic pressure on Israel. Whether or not this assumption is
valid remains to be seen. But clearly the introduction of U.S. forces in
this case is quite unlikely.

MEETING THE NORTHERN ATTACK. At this point only the United States
fields forces capable of handling a major attack from the north, which
could involve several Iranian or Iraqi divisions along with air support.
Egypt appears to be the only other state with the potential (far from
realized at the present) to do so in the future. For political as well as
military reasons, GCC units might throw up a preliminary defense
against the invading force. But the requirement for unity of command
over the air-ground battle and the need to coordinate with air and coastal
defenses would, in the worst case, require a virtual replacement of GCC
forces with reinforcements.

Reinforcement would have to begin with the movement of air defenses onto the Peninsula. A direct defense of the Peninsula's northern
corner against armored attack would require a force capable of engaging
in maneuver warfare in relatively open terrain. Kuwait City could be
protected initially by a fairly small (possibly local) ground force contingent and capped with air defenses. The defending force could then push
attacking units westward into open country where there would be ample
room for battling them, primarily with strike aircraft. The difficulties
posed by such operations would vary with the size of the threat, and with
how effectively attacking forces were able to use their sophisticated
weapons. U.S. rapid deployment forces geared to meet the Soviet threat,
however, appear to be capable of meeting an Iranian or Iraqi overland
threat.

The politics of meeting this threat are likely to be more demanding

5. See, for example, Philip Shabecoff, "Brown Discloses U.S. Sends Saudis Ground
Radar and 100 Personnel," *New York Times*, October 6, 1980; and Bernard Gwertzman,
"Carter Considers Sending Aircraft to Saudi Arabia," *New York Times*, September 30,
1980.

than military operations. A large Egyptian force—were one available—might be no more acceptable politically to GCC rulers than U.S. forces. Although the past behavior of these rulers suggests that political constraints decline rapidly as the situation deteriorates, incentives remain to find less obtrusive ways of meeting the threat. Air bases in Turkey, Jordan, and even Israel—as well as the air forces of those states—might be used to take the attack on its flanks. Any military action that drew threatening forces away from Kuwait's border would be useful. A major U.S. naval buildup off Bandar-Abbas might pull Iranian troops back toward Iran, while Jordanian reinforcement of the Iraqi front might also draw Iranian troops away from the GCC border. The military and political feasibility of these attacks would depend on the circumstances. But there is no reason to confine the GCC's defense to the GCC's border.

COASTAL AND TANKER DEFENSE IN THE GULF. Uncertainty about the performance of the GCC's new and untested naval forces leaves open the possibility that here, too, reinforcement might be required. Naval forces would probably come from the three Western powers, who maintain fleets in the Indian Ocean. Support comes with each fleet, making reinforcement much easier than it is with ground or air forces. Allied naval forces could easily accomplish missions such as convoying tankers under threat and protecting coastal facilities against a range of local threats. Allied cooperation might involve working on effecting such protection jointly.

U.S. Security Assistance and the Peninsular States' Regional Helpers

Because GCC security depends critically on help from nearby powers—Jordan, Pakistan, and perhaps Egypt—U.S. policy toward those states must be seen as indirectly related to U.S. interests in the GCC. In no case is that idea likely to be the primary influence on U.S. policy. U.S. military assistance to Jordan is shaped principally by Jordan's proximity to Israel. Assistance to Pakistan is based on assessments of the Indo-Pakistani balance, the Soviet position in Afghanistan, and Pakistan's nuclear ambitions. Aid to Egypt is based on the need to give political support to the one Arab state that has signed a peace treaty with Israel. Egyptian military choices seem designed primarily to ensure Egypt's independence by diversifying suppliers. The idea of equipping the Egyptian military to help it intervene on the Peninsula would cause apprehension among GCC rulers.

In specific instances, however, concern for the role that those three states could play in peninsular security might affect U.S. security assistance at the margin. Sale of advanced aircraft is perhaps the most important example. Recent sales of F-16s to Pakistan and Egypt suggest that little thought has been given to reinforcement of the GCC by these states, the F-16 being one of the few aircraft not represented in GCC inventories. In the latter half of this decade Jordan and many of the GCC states will probably make important aircraft purchases. Given Jordan's importance to GCC defenses, the notion of matching sales to Jordan and the GCC should influence the determination of which U.S. aircraft is sold.

U.S. plans to arm a brigade of the Jordanian Arab Army as a mobile strike force for Gulf contingencies suggests growing awareness of Jordan's Gulf role.[6] But the threats that Jordan faces on the Peninsula are not likely to require the high-technology forces envisioned by U.S. planners. Conversely, Jordan's contribution to GCC security is likely to be a function primarily of its overall security situation, given the threats it faces from Israel and Syria, rather than the composition of a single brigade. Although equipping a brigade might make a marginal contribution to Jordanian security, the untimely exposure of plans for so doing only added to King Hussein's security problems. Hussein's situation will be affected far more by diplomatic actions aimed at easing tensions among Jordan, Israel, and Syria than by security assistance policy narrowly defined.

Indeed, the critical point is not that regional forces need to be specifically equipped for helping the peninsular states; these forces are most likely to face internal threats on the Peninsula. Such threats are likely to be less militarily demanding than they are politically delicate. More important, the security of Jordan, Pakistan, and Egypt is related to GCC security and hence to U.S. interests in the Gulf. Jordan is especially important given its vulnerability to attack by Israel as well as Syria, its growing (and increasingly risky) role in Arab-Israeli peace initiatives, and its participation in peninsular security. Jordan tends to be seen primarily in the Arab-Israeli context. U.S. policy must also take account of Jordan's role in securing U.S. interests in the Arab world.

---

6. See Bernard Gwertzman, "U.S. Seeks to Equip Jordan's Soldiers as a Strike Force," *New York Times,* October 14, 1983.

The United States, Iran, and Iraq

Jordan and Pakistan are related both directly and positively to the GCC's security; each provides assistance, while neither is likely to pose a serious military threat to the GCC. The relationship of Iran and Iraq to GCC security is more complicated. Either country could act in the GCC's interests. The shah's Iran did this when, for example, Iraq threatened Kuwait in 1973, or during Oman's Dhofar rebellion. In defending Iraq's border with Iran from massed Iranian forces in 1984, Iraq's forces implicitly defended GCC territory from Iranian attack. Yet either state, unchecked by the other, could pose perhaps the most serious military threat that the GCC states could face. A balance between these two states is crucial to GCC security and hence to the protection of Western interests.

Although the confusion of the Iranian revolution opened that country to Iraq's attack in 1980, the subsequent course of the Iran-Iraq war has highlighted Iraq's inherently weaker position in this balance. Iraq's population is less than one-third that of Iran. Historically, Iraq has compensated for this disadvantage by enlisting a larger share of its population in the military than Iran, but Iraq remains comparatively less able than Iran to sustain the casualties of a war of attrition. Iraq's coastline is pitifully small in comparison with Iran's, making it less able to conduct its oil trade by sea in wartime. Although both countries' oil facilities lie close enough to their common border to be within reach of the other's forces, Iran's political center lies far from Iraq, while Baghdad lies a scant hundred miles from Iran along a well-defined invasion route.

If Iran is the stronger of these two countries, it is also the more important strategically. Iran has by far the largest population of any Gulf state, and it dominates the northern Gulf coast. Moreover, Iran remains the strategic buffer between the Soviet Union and the Gulf. U.S. military action to deter Soviet involvement in Iran is likely to require Iranian acquiescence, if not active support. Conversely, internal upheaval in Iran and the possibility of fragmentation among Iran's minorities make Iran the most likely scene of serious U.S.-Soviet military confrontation around the Gulf.

From a military perspective Iran's strength makes Iraq important. By the summer of 1984 Iraq appeared to be militarily stronger than Iran, or at least capable of defending its border from massed Iranian forces. Yet Iraq's superiority depended largely on Iran's isolation, in particular its dwindling sources of arms supplies and the continuing deterioration of its war materiel. Over the course of the Iran-Iraq war, however, the Iranians have demonstrated considerable military prowess despite a deteriorating arsenal. Over the long haul this and Iran's comparatively large population are likely to give Iran a decided military edge over Iraq. A regime in Tehran with reequipped military forces and the will to use them might pose the most serious threat to regional stability imaginable.

Beginning in mid-1983 both superpowers, as well as other states, sought to preserve the Iran-Iraq balance both by bolstering Iraq and by tightening the embargo on the sale of arms to Iran. U.S. policy began a cautious tilt toward Iraq focused mainly on U.S. efforts to help finance an oil pipeline from Iraq to Jordan's port at Aqaba. U.S.-Iraqi relations grew increasingly cordial in 1984, and in November the two countries resumed diplomatic relations, which had been severed during the 1967 Arab-Israeli war. It is doubtful, however, whether the exchange of ambassadors will lead to rapid growth of commercial and military ties between the two countries.

A fundamental change in Iraq's position on Israel might loosen existing constraints on U.S. dealings with Iraq over the long run. But Israeli arms transfers to Iran during the Iran-Iraq war suggest that Israel still sees Iran as the strategic counterweight to Iraq, despite Khomeini's references to the "Zionist enemy." Under these circumstances a meaningful shift toward Iraq would be politically difficult in the United States.

Still, the Iran-Iraq war has encouraged a warming of U.S.-Iraqi relations and a cooling of Iraq's hostile rhetoric toward Israel. U.S. policymakers now have an opportunity to enhance the U.S. position in Iraq. At the same time, the war provides an opportunity for the American public to see vividly the importance of the Iran-Iraq balance, and to come to terms with the fact that Iraq's forces are defending U.S. friends in the GCC as well as Iraq itself. An enhanced U.S. position in Iraq need not yield greater leverage; the Soviets were not warned of, and indeed were unhappy with, Iraq's September 1980 attack into Iran, despite their long-standing relationship with Baghdad. By the same token, there is no reason for the United States to pass up an opportunity for enhanced relations with Iraq, if only to see where they might lead. Iraq's importance to GCC security surely makes the effort worthwhile.

Enhanced U.S.-Iraqi relations need not undermine the prospects for the future development of U.S. ties to Iran, however unlikely that appears to be at this writing. The Soviet Union's simultaneous courting of Syria and Iraq, and to a lesser extent its warming relationship with Egypt, suggest that explicitly choosing sides in the Middle East is unnecessary. Indeed, the visit by an official of Iran's Foreign Affairs Ministry to Moscow in June 1984, apparently in an unsuccessful bid to curb Soviet arms shipments to Iraq, suggests that leverage may flow from playing, or at least seeking to play, many sides.[7] The United States may not wish to draw too close to either side, but under current circumstances this is hardly likely.

Indeed, at this writing, and into the foreseeable future, U.S. allies are likely to have stronger positions than the United States in either or both of these countries. In the military sphere, France in particular has continued its policy, initiated in 1968, of supplying Iraq with arms.[8] The visit to Tehran in the summer of 1984 by West Germany's foreign minister signaled that in Iran, too, one of the United States' European allies was taking the lead in opening a relationship. Meanwhile, both Turkey and Japan stand out conspicuously as U.S. friends that have managed to retain ties to both Iran and Iraq over the course of the war. Whatever the status of its own relations with Iran and Iraq, the United States should encourage its allies to continue to develop their relationships with these two countries.

The United States and Its European Allies

Historical reasons prevent West Germany and Japan from major engagement in GCC military security, although each has developed reasonably strong ties to Iran and Iraq that might serve in tempering the regional setting of GCC security. By contrast, Britain and France are engaged actively with GCC security efforts. Britain maintains relations through its position in Oman and its lingering ties to the other sheikhdoms. France has influence through strong, apparently growing ties to the Saudi ministries of defense and aviation as well as interior, and through its arms sales to the smaller sheikhdoms.

Doubtless, at some levels the positions of Britain and France are

7. "Iran," *Middle East Economic Digest,* vol.28 (June 15, 1984), p. 19.

8. Although the wisdom of certain French transfers can certainly be questioned, on the whole French policy has served Western interests both by balancing Moscow's position in Iraq and by sustaining Iraq in its war with Iran. Although it seems wise to discuss specific objections and problems with the French, French involvement with Iraq in the military realm should be encouraged.

competitive with that of the United States, politically as well as commercially. Neither Britain nor France is anxious to rely on U.S. security measures for protecting the flow and price of oil. Both are critical of U.S. ties to Israel, the U.S. tendency to overemphasize the Soviet threat, and the seeming inability of U.S. policymakers to deal with Gulf security issues in the consistent, low-key way that Gulf rulers prefer. Thus politically both countries seek to distance their own policies and personnel from those of the United States. Meanwhile, commercial British and French arms manufacturers, backed strongly by their respective governments, compete with U.S. firms in the arms market.

Under these circumstances, cooperation by European powers with the United States on Gulf security issues is not only neglected but purposely avoided. In any case, efforts to develop so-called out of area policies for NATO with regard to the Persian Gulf distract NATO from demanding requirements within Europe itself, where NATO's members have hardly exhausted the possibilities for greater cooperation. A sound U.S. policy, however, would sidestep the problems inherent in pushing formal understandings among allies. Instead, U.S. policy should encourage allies to independently sell assets or offer aid to the GCC with an eye to complementarity that would ultimately enhance GCC security. Then, the British and French might be more willing to discuss cooperation at margins where it might be both useful and feasible. Specifically, in what areas would such cooperation help the GCC?

MAKING THE BEST OF ARMS TRANSFERS. Arms transfers from Western powers to the peninsular states may be viewed cynically as a way to recycle petrodollars, lower unit costs of weapons to home services, or, in Europe, sustain domestic arms industries that could not subsist on the domestic arms market alone. Or Western powers could see arms transfers as helpful to establishing a position on the Peninsula that enhances security, intelligence capability, political relations, and the prospects for easy reinforcement of GCC forces. The possibility of large external threats to the GCC and domestic political constraints on the development of indigenous forces encourage the second view, and to some degree all three Western powers adhere to it. The French advisory presence among Saudi Arabia's ground forces or U.S. support behind its AWACS or F-15 sales exemplifies the positive view.

French aircraft sales to the coastal sheikhdoms, by contrast, do not seem to be motivated by the ideal. The Mirage F-1 is known as a relatively unreliable aircraft, yet minimal French assistance accompanies the aircraft to the sheikhdoms that have purchased it. The same can be said for support connected with recent Mirage 2000 sales.[9] Pakistanis have often substituted for French support teams, especially in the UAE. But Pakistanis can only act as substitutes when older French aircraft also found in Pakistan's inventory are used. For Mirage F-1 and 2000 inventories, there seems to be no substitute for the French support teams.

This doesn't mean the United States should try to drive France out of the arms market, although future arms sales to the peninsular states will be fiercely competitive, and France could just as well lose as win. Rather, the United States should discuss with France the importance of arms transfers in the West's approach to GCC security, particularly the potential entree arms sales provide for reinforcing powers. A U.S. overture to France that emphasizes the usefulness of French arms transfers rather than their drawbacks, and one that requires no overt signs of cooperation with the United States, might encourage a more cooperative French approach on key issues such as stocking spares and munitions and providing adequate support personnel.

REFINING THE DIVISION OF LABOR. The United States must also discuss scenarios in which European forces could support the GCC. The British have already demonstrated their willingness to support the sultan of Oman in extended conflict. The French, who have forces in nearby Djibouti, need to be queried about their willingness to become actively involved (if invited) in Saudi internal affairs. Beyond that, both Britain and France have positions in the coastal sheikhdoms, and the British have a keen understanding of the politics of these states. What are the limits of their willingness to aid the GCC with the introduction of their own forces? Overt cooperation among Britain, France, and the United States is not at issue. But an enhanced understanding of who is likely to do what in a complementary division of labor would be valuable.

PREPARING FOR COOPERATION. Little threats can become big threats. Internal violence in particular can start small but build to major proportions. Given the populations of five of the six members of the GCC, "major" need not signal anything like the kind of insurgency the United States dealt with in Vietnam. But in Saudi Arabia fairly large-scale civil violence could occur, and in all six states internal factions

9. The UAE's purchase of eighteen Mirage 2000s with eighteen more on order is to be accompanied, apparently, by only nine French technicians. "Emirs Go for French Plane," *Defense Week,* vol. 4 (November 7, 1983), p. 2.

might seek outside support in a way that would escalate the scale of violence. The GCC's neat division of labor would be in danger of breaking down as external antagonists entered the conflict.

The principal role for U.S. forces in these scenarios would be that of deterring outside involvement. But deterrence might require the commitment of U.S. forces, or these might be called for in any case. Moving slowly is mandatory. A quick, substantial U.S. military move, surrounded with the fanfare usually required to sustain such operations among the U.S. public, might further endanger the beleaguered regime and is even more likely to deter British and French involvement. Instead, with uncertainty running high initially, the United States ought to let others—if not its European allies, then Jordan and Pakistan—become involved before committing itself, if it is asked and if it chooses to do so.

Countries likely to become involved in the internal violence of these states should engage in discreet discussions about their prospective responses. Intelligence sharing on internal affairs, or at least preparation for intelligence sharing in a crisis, will be vital in these situations.

On the Benefits and Costs of Selectivity

The United States has a right to be selective in its approach to GCC security. Members of the GCC offer no unqualified promises about future performance and are selective in their dealings with the United States. The United States also has the opportunity to be selective. Other countries are as interested in GCC security as the United States, and most field military forces that could be used effectively against the kind of threats most likely to plague the GCC. Finally, the United States ought to be selective in its approach to GCC security. Seeking a closer embrace of these states might actually decrease their security, while it would threaten to enmesh the United States in the kind of shadowy internal or internecine conflict that it is neither politically nor militarily well disposed to handle.

The policy recommendations offered here make the U.S. role in GCC security less burdensome. By seeking to enhance the division of labor that has protected the GCC states in the past, these recommendations implicitly relieve the United States of principal responsibility for dealing with internal and peninsular conflict. This does not mean that the United States can expect to remain safely out of internal conflict on the

Peninsula. But it does mean that the United States will enter such conflict only in conjunction with others and preferably only after events have clarified the nature of the threat. Meanwhile, U.S. military planners can fix their attention primarily on a limited number of conventional military threats to the GCC that U.S. forces, and the U.S. political temperament, are better able to handle.

To achieve these benefits, however, the United States must tend to a wider range of issues than would be true were it willing or able to handle GCC security unilaterally. Because other countries are involved in GCC security, U.S. arms transfers, assistance and, in the broadest sense, its diplomacy toward other regional actors all relate to GCC security. Because the GCC's approach to security functions best if these states have ample room to maneuver, U.S. policy must consider the setting of GCC security. Other countries may often have more leverage there than the United States. The military and political requirements of the policy recommended here may be less burdensome, but a conceptual challenge remains. U.S. policymakers must fit small pieces into a coherent whole; see the wide-ranging connections between security on the Arabian Peninsula and events and actors beyond its borders; and accept the uncertainties inherent in this approach to GCC security.

Oil and the Offensive Use of Force

The analysis so far has focused on how U.S. military planning can be integrated into broader policies designed to influence events around the Persian Gulf by supporting key Gulf oil producers. A decade ago, in 1974–75, some analysts discussed the quite different goal of wresting control of oil from oil producers whose interests were assumed to be at odds with U.S. interests. Those oil producers were viewed as capable of raising prices enough to strangle the economies of industrialized nations. This discussion took place in the aftermath of the 1973–74 oil embargo, which the 1973 Arab-Israeli war precipitated. Although only a few analysts and commentators participated in the discussion, their arguments achieved notoriety.[10]

---

10. The most notable were Robert W. Tucker, "Oil: The Issue of American Intervention," *Commentary*, vol. 59 (January 1975), pp. 21–31; and Miles Ignotus (pseud.), "Seizing Arab Oil," *Harper's* (March 1975), pp. 45–62. A more objective look at the

Today much less is heard about the so-called oil grab scenario, and for good reason. OPEC is hardly the coherent organization it was perceived to be in 1974; even the Gulf states, as a subgroup of OPEC, have hardly agreed easily on production decisions in recent years. Moreover, oil-producing countries have learned that their interests are in many ways tied up with the economic vitality of industrialized states in which they have invested heavily. A move to strangle the West would only work against the interests of oil producers in the long run, since a sharp increase in oil's price ultimately would decrease demand for oil. Significantly, this decrease in demand would be registered most directly in the Gulf, which is the swing producer within OPEC. Thus it is difficult to argue that OPEC or the Gulf's oil producers would capriciously seek to cut production sharply, even under conditions of high demand for oil.

Still, unless it is simply impossible for rulers of the Gulf states to deliberately[11] lower production so as to bring great harm to the world's economy, military planners cannot avoid thinking about this worst case. What kinds of military responses would be appropriate? What are their costs? And what is the preferred U.S. role? Strangulation of the world economy has not occurred, and there are no hard data on how and at what cost oil fields might be captured and held. Still, tentative answers to these questions can be offered.

Scenarios

It is not impossible to conceive of scenarios that could approximate the strangulation that some observers feared in 1974–75. One scenario resembles the oil embargo of 1973–74. It would involve a political act by

---

military issues involved can be found in U.S. Library of Congress, Congressional Research Service, *Oil Fields as Military Objectives: A Feasibility Study,* prepared for the Special Subcommittee on Investigations of the House Committee on International Relations, 94 Cong. 1 sess. (Government Printing Office, 1975). (Hereafter U.S. LOC, CRS, *Oil Fields as Military Objectives.*)

11. Deliberate choice is important in these scenarios. Strangulation implies intention. Internal turbulence in Saudi Arabia might shut down oil production for some time, as happened in Iran in 1979. Iran might coerce the peninsular states into cutting oil production levels substantially. Assuming a fairly tight oil market, both circumstances would cause a sharp increase in oil's price. In neither case, however, would it be fair to say that Saudi Arabia was trying to strangle oil consumers. Force might play a role in dealing with either of these two scenarios. But invading oil wells against the will of the host government requires, at the least, a situation in which that government has voluntarily chosen to cut production sharply.

all or some Gulf states aimed at extracting political concessions from the United States, probably in the wake of another phase of the Arab-Israeli conflict. Recalling that the earlier embargo was circumvented by shifting tanker destinations on the high seas, oil producers in this embargo would actually cut production. Consequently, they would bring harm to all oil consumers, who would then be expected to pressure the United States on the oil producers' behalf. Economically rational rulers could engage in the embargo since it would amount to a bargaining ploy; the hope would be to return to previous levels of production as soon as the embargo had produced its intended effect on U.S. policy.

In a more threatening scenario, conservative religious leaders might come to power, or they might successfully pressure regimes for large cuts in oil production as a matter of principle, despite the long-term economic consequences of such action. Indeed, those leaders would genuinely eschew economic development. They might face a great deal of domestic unrest from classes and elements less repelled by oil wealth than they. Nevertheless, so long as the power of those religious groups remained intact little or no prospect would exist for a return to previous production levels. In contrast to the first scenario, no amount of bargaining on the part of oil consumers could influence this policy.

Either scenario would increase the price of oil. Under tight market conditions, or when a large enough number of oil producers agreed to cut production, that price increase could be large indeed. With it would come suffering, social dislocation, lost economic growth, and other harmful consequences. At a high enough level, such suffering might be expected to produce a consensus among members of some group (the U.S. citizenry; the United States and its allies; the oil-consuming states as a bloc) that further pain would be intolerable. Strangulation would thus be defined as it was experienced, through an essentially ad hoc political process precipitated by production cuts themselves.

The use of force would not be the only possible response to the scenarios just outlined. Political bargaining could take place, for example, with rulers who had enacted an embargo to pressure the United States or its allies. Simply waiting might appear to be a reasonable option in cases where leaders committed ideologically to cutting oil production were embroiled in domestic turbulence that could eventually topple their regimes. Covert operations (not necessarily mounted by the United States) might be used to hasten the downfall of such rulers. Even if only partially successful, such operations might precipitate a civil war in which outside powers would at least be able to intervene militarily on behalf of some local faction rather than in a naked grab of territory. Presumably, the attractiveness of these options would depend in part on the perceived costs of pursuing a strictly military option, and it is that option that military planners must consider.

The Military Option

The military option would be aimed at taking and holding a piece of territory rich enough in oil to allow the aggressors to bring oil back onto the market in quantities large enough to force prices down to an acceptable level. Military planners must assume that oil-producing states not involved in cutting production themselves might respond to an oil grab by cutting their own production in order to pressure the invaders. The captured territory must be rich indeed in oil to compensate for this possibility,[12] and Saudi Arabia inevitably tops the list of desirable objectives. Its Ghawar field alone contains more known oil reserves than any other oil-producing country. Saudi Arabia's huge reserves make it an essential party to any successful effort to cut production; thus Saudi Arabia, or at least that territory extending from Ras Tanura southwest across the Ghawar field (figure 6-1), can be made the explicit objective of military planning for the offensive use of force.

Planners must assume that the operation would be a long-term venture. Critics properly point out that delicate oil field technologies would be vulnerable to destruction before invading forces arrived,[13] yet this is no argument against the operation. Invading powers would have

12. Assume, for analytical purposes, that conservative religious rulers throughout the Gulf were to take most of the Gulf's oil exports (close to 20 mbd during periods of high world demand) off the market. Invading powers might wish to assume that, in reaction to their military action, even OPEC's more economically rational leaders might nonetheless take their production off the market as well, at least until the invaders had made it clear that they could accomplish their objectives. Invading powers would have to take an area capable of sustaining at least 20 mbd of production over the long run, but ideally able to sustain 30 mbd as a means of keeping the rest of OPEC in line. Producing 30 mbd for ten years would require reserves of more than 100 billion barrels, larger than the known reserves of any oil-producing country except Saudi Arabia. By contrast, Saudi Arabia's Ghawar field contains at least 70 billion barrels and could alone produce nearly 20 mbd for a decade, or 30 mbd for nearly six and one-half years.

13. See, for example, Jeffrey Record, *The Rapid Deployment Force and U.S. Military Intervention in the Persian Gulf* (Cambridge, Mass.: Institute for Foreign Policy Analysis, 1981), pp. 29–32.

Figure 6-1. *Persian Gulf Oil Fields*

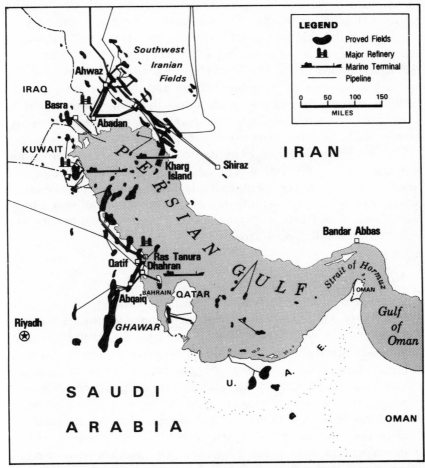

Source: U.S. Library of Congress, Congressional Research Service, *Oil Fields as Military Objectives*, prepared for the Special Subcommittee on Investigations of the House Committee on International Relations, 94 Cong. 1 sess. (Government Printing Office, 1975).

every incentive to move quickly to minimize damage to the fields, but they should be willing to accept short-term reductions in oil output in anticipation of long-term gains. Barring a lucky seizure of the wells intact, much of the real work of the invasion would be carried forward by construction crews and technical experts capable of bringing oil production back on line. Military forces would simply protect those operations.

Determining how invading powers would end their involvement is difficult. Withdrawal would be complicated; a truly committed Islamic government in Riyadh, for example, might move back into vacated territory and destroy much of the oil technology. Or a peninsular regime might never be able to control terrorism, in which case withdrawal would lead to a slow deterioration in the oil equipment. It is possible to define conditions under which withdrawal would be feasible. But the military weaknesses of peninsular regimes and the sheer fragility of oil facilities make it difficult to envision how invading powers could be reasonably certain that withdrawal would not produce disaster. Invading powers might have no choice but to occupy the territory indefinitely.

Thus the phrase "oil fields as military objectives" does not convey the full scope of the undertaking. The oil grab itself might induce needed flexibility in Arab governments and might change the political composition of the Arabian Peninsula. But more likely an invasion would be the start of a long-term occupation; invading powers would be carving a non-Arab state out of Arab territory.

Military Feasibility and Costs

Is the operation described militarily feasible? Within reasonable limits the feasibility of military action is largely a matter of the costs those using forces would be willing to bear. The United States, for example, presumably could carve out a new state on the Arabian Peninsula if it were willing to commit enough forces, accept a certain number of casualties (immediately and over the long haul), invest enough money to rebuild sabotaged wells and port facilities, sustain a long occupation and possible counterinsurgency campaign, and accept whatever international repercussions the operation might provoke. Military feasibility is ultimately a political issue, and in this sense results influence its assessment. International approbation and Soviet counteractions would definitely figure in popular calculations of results. Consequently, a discussion of military feasibility must include those issues as well as military costs narrowly defined.

Because no one has invaded an oil field lately—at least not one on the Arabian Peninsula—nothing certain can be said about the specific costs and problems connected with the military option. Nonetheless, those favoring an invasion of peninsular oil fields argued that since the area "has no substantial centers of population and is without trees, its effective control does not bear even remote comparison with the experience of Vietnam."[14] Even some who opposed the idea of an invasion seemed willing to admit its technical feasibility, resting their opposition instead on the attendant international political repercussions.[15] Only I. F. Stone challenged sanguine assumptions about the difficulty of running guerrilla operations in opposition to the U.S. move, citing T. E. Lawrence's success with precisely these kinds of operations during the Arab revolt against the Turks, 1916–18.[16]

On one issue most accounts are simply wrong: the area does have at least one substantial and important center of population, the Dhahran–Qatif–Ras Tanura urban-industrial complex, through which run virtually all Saudi pipelines. Census data are scarce, but the population of this area appears to be between 500,000 and 1 million. This is about the size of Beirut, a city that has proven difficult to control in recent years. The comparison to Beirut may be unfair; that city's hilly terrain and long-standing confessional antagonisms make control more difficult. But the Ras Tanura area's delicate network of oil technologies makes control that much more urgent, the consequences of failure that much more grave. Clearly, urban areas of this size cannot be dismissed casually.[17]

Invading powers might seek to move port facilities to an unpopulated area, but doing so would take considerable time and effort. Alternatively, invaders might in time be able to bring the Ras Tanura area under control. In either case, the major problem appears to lie in protecting the area's critical oil technologies at the outset, as foreign forces prepare for their attack and sort themselves out in the first hectic days and weeks of the invasion. There would be no way to stop a certain amount of terrorism and sabotage in this period, perhaps aimed at compressors and turbines that are difficult to replace. Invading powers would have to be prepared to move very quickly and in considerable force. They would also be wise to stock replacement parts in advance and to bring construction crews in early.

On other issues the costs of military operations in the peninsular oil region are more difficult to assess. Modern technology might make

14. Tucker, "Oil: The Issue of American Intervention," p. 25.

15. See, for example, Earl C. Ravenal, "The Oil-Grab Scenario," *New Republic*, January 18, 1975, pp. 14–16.

16. "War For Oil?" *New York Review of Books,* February 6, 1975, p. 7.

17. If the French experience in calming Algiers provides any useful analogy, it suggests that cities need not tax forces (the "paras" brought in for the battle of Algiers numbered less than 5,000), but may well require draconian interrogation, search, and seizure. See Alistair Horne, *A Savage War of Peace: Algeria, 1954–1962* (Viking Press, 1977), pp. 183–208.

guerrilla activity against invading forces and oil fields much more difficult today than it was sixty years ago. Detection technologies—airborne radars, intrusion sensors, and the proliferation of observation aircraft—would make surprise raids difficult. Modern air power would make massed ground attacks on the defensive perimeter nearly impossible. Yet the recent experience of both superpowers confronted by low-technology guerrilla fighters cautions against optimism or arrogance. The ability of such fighters to adapt to and ultimately to exploit the weaknesses of high-technology occupying forces, not to mention their ability to maintain commitment despite sustained casualties, has been painfully surprising.

Significantly, in placing local Arab forces on the defensive, invading forces would be pushing these soldiers back to a form of warfare more comfortable to them than what they have learned from Western advisors. Lightning raids by small bands of lightly armed Bedouins constituted the bulk of peninsular conflict through the mid-twentieth century. Such action might be largely tribal in nature, as has been true in Afghanistan. Driving the invaders from the Peninsula itself would probably be out of the question. But producing a sustained casualty rate, and harassing oil production so that the overall objective of the operation would become more difficult to achieve, might be well within the capabilities of local warriors.

Terrorism would be as much a problem for the occupying powers as it is now for GCC rulers. Presumably, Arab workers in the oil region would have to be expelled, and other laborers—mostly foreigners—would have to be screened, if not replaced wholesale. Acts of sabotage against oil facilities nonetheless would remain a distinct possibility. Infiltration of individual terrorists from inside the Peninsula would border on guerrilla activity but would be harder to spot. Infiltration over the coast, notably from Iran and Iraq, would require a fairly impressive coastal constabulary. Both forms of terrorism would demand constant protection of oil and military facilities.

Putting aside the immediate problem of securing the Dhahran–Qatif–Ras Tanura area, taking oil wells is likely to pose less of a problem than holding them. Assuming no Soviet counterintervention, GCC military forces would pose only a meager defense against invading forces. Controlling captured territory effectively enough to increase oil production seems likely at the very least to require the acceptance of a sustained, low-level casualty rate. Accepting some level of sabotage to oil facilities would also be required. Sabotage would endanger the overall benefits of the operation—the flow of oil at reasonable prices—and casualty rates would raise its human costs.

How much force would be required for the outright invasion of oil fields? A Congressional Research Service estimate of two to four divisions to take and hold the Saudi core area seems reasonable.[18] Deployment of units in northern Kuwait, which Robert W. Tucker wisely suggested as a means of deterring outside intervention, would add perhaps another division.[19] At least a division, and naval forces, would be needed to take and hold territory on either side of the Strait of Hormuz, to protect the operation's logistical lifeline. Four divisions would be the minimum. Even so, unilateral U.S. commitment of this size force would commit most of the nation's strategic reserve, giving the United States little flexibility in dealing with OPEC retaliation, Soviet countermoves, or crises elsewhere in the world.

If this is true, the magnitude of the operation alone favors multilateral action. U.S. involvement in the operation would be almost essential, because of the size of U.S. forces and the country's logistical capabilities. But unilateral U.S. action would pose grave risks on military grounds. The problem is not that U.S. forces are not large enough to take on the oil grab, although uncertainties surrounding the question of force requirements should make planners skeptical even on this point. Rather, the problem is that, having taken the oil fields, the United States would have no forces left to do anything else.

Broader Diplomatic and Strategic Costs

The oil grab would clearly violate international law by violating the sovereignty of an oil-producing state, even though the grab would be a response to extortionate pricing policies. Smaller states, who rely on the principle of sovereignty for a certain amount of protection from predatory neighbors and superpowers, might find the economic consequences of extortionate pricing policies unbearable. Yet they still might recoil from the precedent of U.S. intervention, especially if they had no say in

18. U.S. LOC, CRS, *Oil Fields as Military Objectives*, p. 60. The CRS study considers a four-division force to be "austere, given the size of the area, counterintervention threats, and the sense of urgency." (n. 24.)

19. "Oil: The Issue of American Intervention," pp. 25–26.

it. NATO's European members would no doubt be offended if they were not consulted, or if the United States ignored their counsel. No matter how much the world's oil consumers might ultimately benefit from successful U.S. action, there would be an element of fear in their reaction induced by the demonstration of U.S. willingness to operate beyond the control or moderating influence of even its closest allies.

Measuring the tangible consequences of such concern is difficult. Still, prudence dictates taking steps to limit diplomatic costs, even if they cannot be measured in advance. Other things being equal, these considerations, like the military considerations outlined, would encourage the United States to make the military option a multinational enterprise.

There are more tangible potential costs to the oil grab beyond those specific military issues just raised. Some of these costs might be minimized through multilateral action. Some might have to be paid in any case. These costs fall under three headings: potential Soviet responses; the OPEC reaction; and the Arab and Islamic reaction.

POTENTIAL SOVIET RESPONSE. Those sanguine about the prospects for using force to secure oil discount the possibility of direct Soviet counterintervention. At the moment there appear to be good reasons for doing so. Militarily, the physical objectives of an oil grab might lie closer to Soviet than to U.S. borders, but they would still lie well away from Soviet territory. The balance of interest and resolve would favor the United States. Even if the United States acted unilaterally, other oil consumers might be sympathetic to the U.S. move, giving Soviet action to stop the United States potentially broad diplomatic costs to the Soviet Union.

Moscow might apply pressure elsewhere—at Berlin, through the PLO or some other regional client, or possibly on the high seas—if it saw advantages in doing so. If NATO's European members were squeamish about the operation, for example, pressure on Berlin or a partial mobilization of Soviet forces in Eastern Europe might add to U.S. problems with its NATO allies. Of course, a successful attempt to secure oil at reasonable prices might alleviate these problems. Presumably, Arab states in particular would oppose U.S. action even if many other oil consumers supported it (quietly or actively), creating the possibility for major Soviet diplomatic initiatives in the Arab world. Iran, finding itself wedged tightly between the two superpowers, might move closer to Moscow. Such events are difficult to predict. But it is fair to say that Moscow's diplomatic opportunities would largely depend on how much international support the United States marshaled for its action.

Missing from many discussions of Soviet responses to a U.S. invasion of the Arabian Peninsula is an understanding of how an invasion would change Moscow's sense of its defensive security problem. While a U.S. attack would severely limit U.S. military flexibility by committing its strategic reserve to the Gulf, it would also cause Moscow to perceive a military threat to its southern flank where none had existed before. At the least, this would induce the Soviets to upgrade forces in the southern military districts. Depending on the internal state of Iran at the time, the Soviets might move into the northwestern quadrant of that country, both to extend their military power southward and to buffer their border from possible U.S. action. Similarly, they might upgrade their forces in Afghanistan, and they would probably improve air bases on the western and southern sides of that country. Although these moves might involve the Soviets in offensive military action, they would be defensive moves strategically.

Nonetheless, these actions would fundamentally alter the nature of the superpowers' interaction around the Gulf. The quality of Soviet forces in the southern military districts critically affects U.S. military strategy. As the quality of Soviet forces and the depth of Moscow's interest in the region increase, so do the demands on U.S. forces required to balance Soviet power. Thus even if the United States were able to create circumstances on the Peninsula that favored complete withdrawal of its forces, it might find it difficult to do so; the status quo ante would be irretrievable. As in Western Europe, the line between U.S. and Soviet interests and forces would become more precise, more costly to sustain, and possibly more prone to crisis.

THE OPEC REACTION. If the goal of military action were to increase production at Saudi wells beyond current capacity, and if that goal were achieved, then the OPEC reaction to the invasion would ultimately cease to matter. As production increased, the United States, or whatever consortium of states gained control of the Saudi core area, would gradually take control of the oil market. Under the best circumstances, OPEC would have a limited—but hardly insignificant—amount of time in which to retaliate, if retaliation were its goal. Stockpiled oil could protect Western economies during part of this period, but the amount stockpiled would have to be considerably larger than is currently planned.

The most obvious form of OPEC retaliation would be cutting oil production. Perhaps OPEC would promise to reconsider the OPEC-wide price structure just as soon as foreign soldiers left the Peninsula. Such a strategy might have considerable appeal, especially if the invasion and occupation were going badly. It might drive a wedge between the United States and its allies if the allies had shown weaker enthusiasm for the operation. And it might bring considerable world pressure to bear on the United States if it had acted unilaterally. If the operation were going smoothly, however, many countries might accept the short-term costs in expectation of much lower oil prices in the future.[20]

If the invasion and occupation did not go well, however, the risks would be substantial. Consider, for example, even a moderately success-ful operation in which oil production fell initially and then rose, but only slowly, sporadically, and at considerable human cost. To achieve com-plete success, more forces would have to be deployed to the Gulf coast. Under these conditions OPEC might retain considerable leverage that could last for some time. Moreover, U.S. military flexibility would decrease as its own forces were tied up in the Gulf. The spectacle of its problems there might make other oil consumers less willing than ever to use force against other OPEC members.

THE ARAB AND ISLAMIC REACTION. Among non-oil-producing states, the Islamic or Arab ones would be most likely to oppose the invasion of peninsular oil fields. Such states might find their loyalties to the Arab nation or Islam strained by their fear of economic disaster. The promise of side payments, however, by the Gulf's oil states might encourage loyalty. Conversely, the promise of lower energy prices by invading powers might undermine that loyalty. It is impossible to predict how such events would unfold.

Past patterns suggest that volunteers could decide to join peninsular military or guerrilla forces opposing the invasion and occupation. For example, Jordan contributed to Iraq's defense in the Iran-Iraq war, and Jordan and Iran contributed to Oman's counterinsurgency in the Dhofar. Volunteers from these countries would join those opposing the invasion, whatever their government's official policy.

20. Although many countries in the world might care no more for the United States than they do for OPEC, in this instance even the most skeptical would certainly expect better prices than the ones that had provoked military action in the first place. Still, many oil-consuming states might worry that, over the long haul, U.S. control of oil prices might be no more advantageous for them than OPEC control. Some might fear, for example, that the United States would use its oil power selectively to coerce or punish. Much would depend on the production and distribution apparatus that the United States or other invading powers put into place.

Terrorism has been a tool of weaker powers against strong and should be expected whatever the official policies of Arab and Islamic governments. A truly unified Arab or Islamic rejection of the oil grab might breed terrorist attacks on U.S. embassies in these countries, leading, for example, to multiples of the Iranian hostage crisis of 1979–80. Or U.S. commercial interests and personnel might come under siege. Long-term occupation of the Gulf's major oil area might precipitate waves of terrorism in the Islamic world. If the United States were involved in making a hostage of Arab oil fields, there would be plenty of U.S. hostages that Arabs or other groups could take in reprisal.

On Moving Last Rather Than First

Although some of the costs of the oil grab are fairly certain, clearly the worst case would be costly indeed. The oil grab would involve the most flagrant kind of imperialist aggression, even though in response to reprehensible behavior by one or several oil producers. An oil grab would violate international norms and values that the United States professes to cherish. It could also be very messy in the narrow military sense; large-scale terrorism, in particular, might breed reactions of the most ugly sort. If the operation failed—that is, if the flow and price of oil from the Peninsula could not be stabilized at levels that substantially lowered oil prices—then the perpetrators of the grab would find themselves in an incredibly embarrassing and costly military and diplomatic position the world over.

These considerations place the oil grab in the realm of desperate acts, to be taken under desperate circumstances. Still, there are better and worse ways to conduct the military operation, and the oil grab scenarios most discussed in 1974–75 are among those likely to be most costly. Articles written at that time implicitly discussed unilateral U.S. military action ("because we have a vital interest in the fate of those unwilling—and unable—to act")[21] or U.S. action supported by Israeli forces.[22] Yet clearly the more states brought on board the operation, the fewer would be the diplomatic opportunities likely to open up to the Soviet Union. Getting poor Arab states to support the move might sound improbable, but the payoffs of doing so would be high. Bringing others into line

21. Tucker, "Oil: The Issue of American Intervention," p. 28.
22. Ignotus, "Seizing Arab Oil."

behind the action would also limit terrorism outside the Peninsula itself and enlist other governments in fighting it where it occurred. Involving the military forces of other countries would allow the United States military flexibility that would otherwise be almost completely absorbed by the grab. Finally, given that the U.S. public has shown little tolerance for sustaining casualties and international disapprobation over the long haul, sharing that burden, as it was shared in Beirut in 1983, might contribute to U.S. staying power.

A joint U.S.-Israeli invasion would be potentially worse than unilateral U.S. action. Nothing could more effectively weld local populations together in their resistance to the operation than seeing Zionism and imperialism descend together onto their patrimony. Nothing would be more likely to generate popular opposition elsewhere in the world. Although Israel could no doubt contribute useful military facilities and support to the operation, its small population and beleaguered position in the Levant would minimize its force contribution to sustaining the operation, leaving the United States alone. The military benefits would be small, the diplomatic—and possibly military—costs, large.

Impatience appears to be the greatest U.S. liability. There are military grounds for developing the capability to project force into the Gulf oil fields very quickly. But even when all other alternatives appear to be failing, the United States faces compelling reasons to refrain from projecting its forces until it has the diplomatic, and in important cases military, support of others—the more the better. Rather than strong U.S. leadership, the situation encourages the United States to outwait others. U.S. natural resource wealth makes such a strategy feasible. The experience of past price shocks emphasizes that waiting is advisable where possible. And the costs of moving unilaterally make it wise for the United States to let other states ask for help rather than take action alone.

Insofar as others would indeed be unable to act without U.S. military support, the United States would retain veto power over the operation. But in the case of a multilateral decision to go ahead with military action, the United States would be deferring to others who had decided what constituted truly intolerable events. At best, the United States would be one voice among many. There is much to recommend this approach on ethical grounds. But more important, it makes good sense in terms of hard political and military realities.

Significantly, this approach leaves open the widest opportunities for other responses. In particular, it enhances the prospects for successful covert action aimed at those states who had removed their oil from the market in the first place, thus precipitating the crisis. Indeed, patient waiting by the United States leaves disgruntled constituents in the oil states maximum leeway in which to work their own covert designs. Whether or not any of these alternate efforts would be successful, exhausting them all before moving ahead to grab the fields would be the wisest possible U.S. response.

Conclusions

U.S. military planners must prepare to secure U.S. interests around the Persian Gulf in opposite ways. They must develop a security policy that emphasizes a low-key, cooperative approach to the region, which would enhance the Gulf Cooperation Council's own approach to peninsular security. And they must plan for the much less likely prospect of using force offensively to seize oil wells. Both ways have in common the premise that the United States ought to share the peninsular security burden with others, and in important cases should move last rather than first. Unilateral U.S. military action is not the most prudent course nor particularly necessary, except when it is clear that only U.S. forces could handle the threat.

Barring major improvements in the capabilities of regional powers like Iran and Iraq, U.S. forces structured to deter the Soviets in Iran are probably capable of handling regional scenarios. Nothing in the conduct of the Iran-Iraq war, for example, suggests that meeting the forces of either of these countries need tax U.S. forces as much as meeting Soviet forces in Iran. By contrast, should seizing oil fields become necessary the operations would absorb virtually all of CENTCOM's present force structure, making cooperation with other countries useful from a military as well as a diplomatic standpoint.

A low-key, diplomatic approach by the United States to peninsular security allows military planners to focus on a few key scenarios for which the forces amassed under CENTCOM seem to be well suited. More important, concentrating U.S. military efforts principally on the most extreme security threats brightens the prospects for gaining public support for military operations. The United States would also be kept clear of the inherently more complicated, lesser conflicts on the Peninsula where the rhetoric required to generate public support for U.S.

involvement, not to mention U.S. involvement itself, might damage U.S. relations with those it wished to support. In the extreme the United States could inadvertently exacerbate the very conflict it wished to settle.

A massive reorganization of U.S. forces or a reorientation of the U.S. position on the Arabian Peninsula is less crucial than a refinement of relationships among the United States, the GCC states, and those regional and Western powers intimately involved in peninsular security. Cooperation must be improved on margins where the payoffs are likely to be highest. And the United States must clarify how it prefers to handle future conflicts in the area. Given the vicissitudes of American politics, accomplishing such goals may pose as formidable a challenge as facing the military threats that could confront the United States around the Gulf.

OPEC's Investments and the International Financial System

Richard P. Mattione

Few events of the past decade have affected the global economic and political landscape as much as the sharp increase in the price of oil in 1973-74 and again in 1979-80. The massive transfer of real resources from mostly Western oil-consuming nations to oil-producing countries, especially to members of the Organization of Petroleum Exporting Countries, raised widespread fears that actions of OPEC nations could disrupt world financial markets, that oil markets and energy supplies would become unstable, and that a significant shift of political power would increase international tensions.

In this study of how OPEC nations have used and learned to invest their wealth, Richard P. Mattione shows that the fears, if not groundless, have not in any significant way been realized. Mattione is the first to analyze in detail the size and distribution of the investments, their effects on the international financial system, and the motivations behind each OPEC member's investment strategy. Analyzing hard-to-find data from a variety of sources, he argues that investments in the United States and elsewhere have been motivated at least as much by conventional financial considerations — the need for liquidity, diversification, safety, and adequate rate of return — as by oil policy, development policy, or political considerations. He also traces the growth of these countries' abilities to absorb funds through internal development, their growing sophistication in financial planning and in moving Arab banks into international financial markets, and their mixed success in using aid to third world countries to further their foreign policy goals. The book concludes with an analysis of the interplay of oil prices and policy, development needs, and financial strategies and their implication for the investments of each OPEC member in the 1980s.

Richard P. Mattione, a former research associate in the Brookings Foreign Policy Studies program, joined Morgan Guaranty Trust in 1984. He is coauthor (with Richard Dale) of *Managing Global Debt* and (with Thomas O. Enders) of *Latin America: The Crisis of Debt and Growth,* both published by Brookings.

201 pp./1985/cloth and paper

CHAPTER SEVEN

U.S. Military Policy
in Its Strategic Context

IN 1980 the challenge of securing U.S. interests around the Persian Gulf set in motion a series of actions to improve the U.S. capability to project forces to the Gulf region. Some of these moves were ridiculed by U.S. critics, who pointed out that no new forces were being created and that ships and aircraft to move forces to the area were in short supply. Other moves were resisted by regional leaders unwilling to host a U.S. base or an enlarged U.S. miiltary presence. The sense of crisis precipitated by Iran's revolution and the Soviet invasion of Afghanistan was matched by a sense of frustration among U.S. military planners, who seemed unable to do much about the situation.

Yet the frustrations borne at that time by U.S. military planners may not have been in vain. Fiscal and regional political constraints on U.S. military activities helped prevent the United States from rushing too quickly into a complicated and politically delicate situation where its presence could make things worse. Local rulers have kept the U.S. military at a distance for good reason. To do otherwise risks exacerbating the kind of internal problems that are the most likely and potentially dangerous threats they face. To handle these threats themselves these rulers need a freedom of maneuver within the region that would be denied them by obvious close ties to the United States. Ironically, such ties might only embroil the United States in murky internal conflicts that it is not well disposed to handle. And a strong U.S. military position around the Gulf would risk further militarizing Moscow's approach to the region, setting off a competitive dynamic with dangerous consequences for both superpowers.

Clearly, unrealistic assumptions about regional stability and the efficacy of local security arrangements must be avoided. There are threats to U.S. interests in this area and limits to the development of local capabilities. The demand on U.S. diplomats and military planners, however, is to balance their sense of the region's importance and vulnerability with a sense of the dangers in seeking a U.S. solution to the region's security problems. This calls for reasonable assessments that balance the risks of failure, which military analysts seek to minimize, with the risk of making things worse, which regional analysts also seek to minimize. These assessments need not be static; threats may change; local rulers may become more flexible about military access; and Moscow may take a more aggressive and militant approach to the region than it has in the past. In this part of the world it is wiser to adjust plans to changes rather than to plan to cover all possibilities at the risk of producing the more alarming among them.

Taking such an approach does not require grandiose budget proposals. Indeed, $10 billion (in 1984 dollars) in life-cycle costs—hardly a large sum in comparison with the total defense budget—would significantly enhance the U.S. ability to handle Gulf contingencies. Much of this money should be used to purchase strategic lift assets, which are usually slighted in the defense budget process. That fact emphasizes that the challenge of securing U.S. interests around the Gulf is distinguished less by its enormity than by its subtlety. The United States must do well things it has not traditionally done well. The challenge starts with spending defense monies wisely—on lift rather than on more forces. It ends with integrating military plans into a regional diplomacy that makes effective use of the security framework that is already there.

Buying Agility Rather Than Forces

This is not the first study to call attention to the United States' lack of air- and sealift. A deficiency has existed for years.[1] It stems partly from lift's lack of a powerful constituency in the congressional budget process. The army, which is the principal user of lift, must rely on the air force and navy to purchase lift, but these services tend to place higher priority on combat systems. Meanwhile, commercial shipping firms, which

---

1. See William W. Kaufmann, *Planning Conventional Forces, 1950–80* (Brookings Institution, 1982), pp. 16–17.

make a profit carrying military cargoes, often see military lift as a competitor and lobby against it in Congress. In the 1970s legislators opposed to the Vietnam War resisted purchasing more strategic lift on grounds that lift assets would allow the services to intervene elsewhere as well. And in the 1980s a focus among many in the executive branch on improving strategic nuclear forces and on threatening the Soviet Union around its periphery decreased the sensed need for new lift assets.

To some extent the services have compensated by prepositioning equipment overseas. For example, prepositioned overseas materiel customized in units sets (POMCUS)—whole sets of army divisional equipment stored in the Federal Republic of Germany—makes it possible for U.S. forces to reinforce NATO quickly. Since 1980 a portion of a Marine Corps unit has also been prepositioned near the Persian Gulf. For the most part, however, in areas outside Europe U.S. military planners must live with a need for more lift.

Aiming to improve the agility of U.S. forces inevitably focuses attention on airlift. Yet while airlift is the most rapid delivery means available, it is also the least efficient. For the price of airlift to move a single mechanized division to the Gulf the Defense Department could preposition seven division sets of equipment. Or the department could buy enough fast sealift to move four divisions. Arguments in favor of buying more airlift often tend to overlook these rather large cost disparities.

In any case, more airlift alone would not solve the problem facing U.S. military planners in the Persian Gulf region. The Defense Department can already deliver small units to the Gulf rapidly, and more airlift would do little to improve delivery times for small units. Furthermore, the strategic problem of confronting the Soviets is not that of preemptively positioning a small unit in their path. Rather, the United States must confront the Soviets with forces large enough to confuse and confound Soviet conventional operations. That requires an increase in the speed with which a substantial force—four to six divisions—can be moved to the Gulf. Airlift required for this mission would be prohibitively expensive, and the delivery of this many units by air to one region would constitute a complicated operation. The United States thus needs a balanced fleet of lift assets, combining air- and sealift discussed earlier with prepositioning of another unit set of equipment on ships near the region.

These investments are essential to securing U.S. interests in the Gulf region. The investment required is fairly small, both as a portion of the annual defense budget and in relation to the interests at stake in the Gulf. If the services cannot establish among themselves a constituency for more lift of the proper type, then the Pentagon's civilian leadership would do well to try to correct lift inadequacies. Adding firepower to military units, or increasing the size of U.S. forces without also increasing the speed with which they can be brought to bear in the Gulf, makes no sense.

Planning to Surge the Force

A review of CENTCOM's planning documents would not reveal the full range of capabilities that the United States could bring to bear in Southwest Asia. The deployment of specific systems is usually governed by due regard for their survival; aircraft carriers, for example, are expected to remain outside the Persian Gulf. The capabilities of specific systems are calculated with due regard for service life; airlift load and range factors, for example, take account of normal maintenance and life-cycle availability. Finally, the range of forces available to CENTCOM is constrained by prudent concern that conflict may occur in more than one place at one time. Such guidelines, supplied to all U.S. military commanders by the Joint Chiefs of Staff, provide the basis for CENTCOM's plans.

But these guidelines need not always be applied. CENTCOM's access to forces is based on planning for the defense of U.S. interests worldwide. If a threat were clearly confined to the Gulf, there would be no absolute bar to using additional forces if they could be helpful and if it were physically possible to do so. Officials could order carriers into the Gulf if the air threat were small or if their value in the Gulf would outweigh the survival risk of deploying them there. And individual weapons capabilities can be stretched: airlift can be pushed to lift more, carry it further, and fly more sorties than air force planning regulations suggest is advisable, for example, if the value of doing so is high and the prospects that competing needs will emerge is low.

Conservative planning is sensible. But in the context of U.S. security policy toward the Gulf region, especially with regard to possible Soviet threats, its limits as well as its strong points are evident. When the agility and speed of U.S. forces are more important than the weight of force brought to bear, the difference between the conservatively planned force and the force that could be available is critical. For example, the United States has many more long-range strike aircraft than those assigned to CENTCOM. In some scenarios it would be prudent to fix those assets in place. But in others they could be shifted to the Gulf with little risk, almost doubling the interdiction capability that CENTCOM could bring to bear off the Soviet Union's southern flank. Likewise C-130s could be borrowed from other commands to accomplish intratheater lift more rapidly. Speeding the tactical deployment of forward units by days or a week and increasing their support could make a big difference in the prospects for deterring and confusing Soviet forces in Iran.

Force reallocations of this size would be difficult if not impossible, however, unless steps were taken in advance to provide ready support for more aircraft than CENTCOM has formally been given. It makes little sense to move F-111s from Europe to Saudi Arabia, for example, unless fuel and munitions are available to support the enlarged interdiction force this would create. It makes little sense to borrow C-130s from other commands unless enough people, equipment, and ramp space are available to support an enlarged intratheater lift operation. It makes sense not only to buy and position but also to train for larger operations than conservative planning guidelines permit.

This means that CENTCOM's planners must be willing to think beyond the constraints of conservative planning. It also means that they must seek to influence the budget process and plan for coordination among commands. Doing so would challenge ingrained thinking about force structure as well as the prerogatives of separate commands. Neither challenge is easily met, but there are high payoffs to doing so.

Sharing the Security Burden Informally

The United States can handle unilaterally the task of buying the appropriate mix of forces and planning for their use. The United States cannot, however, handle Gulf security unilaterally. The technical limitations of U.S. weaponry mean that the exercise of U.S. military power around the Gulf would almost always require local cooperation. Consequently, the deployment of U.S. forces in this region depends on diplomacy in a way that makes the vicissitudes of U.S. relations with its NATO allies look trivial.

The United States is, of course, importantly involved in the informal division of labor that GCC rulers have employed for some time to preserve their security. Yet formal agreements with Gulf rulers, not to mention an expanded U.S. role, are unlikely. Formal coordination of policies among the United States, Gulf rulers, and European allies is also unlikely.

Fortunately, formal coordination among these groups of states is not essential for Gulf security. Indeed, informal arrangements and ad hoc reinforcement have helped preserve peninsular security for years. The absence of formal arrangements has not prevented local rulers like the Saudis from consulting the United States on a wide range of security issues. The structure of agreements is not vital. Rather, the United States is challenged to hear what the Gulf rulers are saying and to act in ways that are sensitive to their security problems, as well as to U.S. security needs.

U.S. military planners would like more secure basing agreements with local powers. But basing access will always depend on the immediate consent of the state whose bases are sought. CENTCOM can hedge against these uncertainties by planning to use a diverse set of bases in a variety of countries. And it can ameliorate short-term logistical problems through wise use of arms transfers. But there is no substitute for good diplomacy, before and during a crisis, if basing access among the Gulf states is to be achieved.

As for European allies, an underlying compatibility of interests ensures a certain compatibility of policies, however uncoordinated. In some respects, the United States benefits from the policies of its allies precisely to the extent that it does not seek to control them. Independence allows countries like France and Great Britain (or the Federal Republic of Germany and Japan, if the comparison is extended beyond military security to broader diplomatic contacts) to deal more freely with Gulf security problems that might be inaccessible to the United States.

These arguments might be less powerful if the GCC states were able to develop coherent and effective military forces. A rationalized defense posture would require a more concerted arms transfer policy, since competition among allies would stand in the way of regional security efforts. But even a rationalized defense posture among the GCC states would not be particularly strong, and political realities discourage rulers from developing such a posture anyway. Defense against external threats will probably always require reinforcement, in which case the polyglot arsenals of these states are at worst unimportant, but on balance an asset rather than a liability.

Seeking loose coordination among allies only on the margins where it yields a payoff poses the major challenge to U.S. policy. To enhance the Gulf region's security, modest technical cooperation that produces compatibility among weapons of differing national origins is more useful than competition aimed at covering the market with one kind of weapon system. Plans to coordinate defense of sea lanes and tankers in the Gulf would also be helpful. In approaching the Gulf states, agreeing on a division of labor is preferable to competing to supplant it.

Doing these things means that the United States must forgo attempts to impose grand organizational schemes on the Gulf. It also means that the United States must be willing occasionally to move last rather than first in responding to events in the Gulf region. Finally, it means a diplomacy toward the Gulf states that is sensitive to their regional and domestic political concerns. Although U.S. policy has achieved all of these goals at times in the past, meeting them consistently would be a major improvement over past practice.

Placing Strategy over Military Planning

From the military planner's perspective, these arguments amount to a call for military planning to give way to strategy. Military planning separates parts—military theaters, or areas in which U.S. interests are at stake—from the whole, and seeks to minimize military risk in those theaters. Military planning implicitly rejects priorities and political realities. It is fairly easy, since it eliminates bothersome detail in favor of the worst military case. But for these reasons it is also unrealistic, both in regard to what is fiscally possible and in regard to the military weight that various theaters of the world can bear.

Strategy, by contrast, begins by fitting pieces into the whole. It fits the military instrument into the broader fabric of U.S. foreign policy and into the political context in which U.S. forces must operate abroad. Strategy is very much a matter of priorities. Devising strategy is more difficult than constructing military plans, because strategy demands that complex political dynamics and an array of military and political uncertainties be faced squarely.

Each year U.S. military planners on the Joint Chiefs of Staff develop a low-risk force posture for protecting U.S. interests around the world. The realities of U.S. military policy are then shaped by a budget process that has not, in the postwar era, allowed for financial support of the full low-risk posture, and by friends and allies abroad who have some say about the way U.S. forces are deployed. Strategy is in effect imposed on U.S. military planning.

The U.S. relationship to the Persian Gulf is illustrative: since 1979 neither the U.S. budget nor regional powers have been friendly to U.S. military plans. But the costs of seeking to impose these plans on the Gulf are higher than they are in Europe, for example, where political systems are more stable and where the threat is more clearly defined. Gulf security is a matter of balances. Local powers seek a balance between diplomacy aimed at heading off military threats and judicious use of military force. They also seek to balance themselves among a range of potential helpers, the United States only one among them. And for the United States, the balance between diplomacy and threats of force in the U.S.-Soviet relationship is worth preserving as long as it can be preserved. Even unsuccessful U.S. efforts to impose itself more visibly in the region could upset that balance.

The rewards of learning to do well that which the United States has traditionally not done well are also significant. Perhaps the United States will not need to change or learn; there is a slim chance that the Gulf will not figure as importantly in the future as most analysts think. But the more likely prospect is that the Gulf will grow in importance and continue to demand of the United States skills not traditionally found in the U.S. military or diplomatic arsenal. Whether or not the United States comes to terms with this region remains to be seen. If the United States does not, and if the Gulf's importance indeed grows, the security of important U.S. interests there will depend on sheer good luck.

The Gulf Cooperation Council's Forces, 1984

THIS ASSESSMENT is grouped around the security demands imposed on the GCC states by the external threats that they face. These states must be able to meet an overland invasion from the north; handle harassing border attacks from the Yemens; and handle air and coastal strikes, especially from the north (Israel and Iraq) and east (Iraq and Iran). Ground forces and strike air forces are treated first, air defense is considered separately, and then coastal defense forces are discussed. Detail is supplied only for those forces that seem able to contribute to GCC external security. Finally, the prospects for cooperation and further development are assessed.

GCC Ground Forces

The GCC ground forces outlined in table A-1 vary greatly in size and structure. The small, lightly armored forces of Qatar and Bahrain serve principally to guard the ruling family and are unlikely to be deployed beyond token strength against external threats to the GCC area. Oman's is a combat-tested counterinsurgency force currently lacking the armor for significant deployment against the potential threat from Iran or Iraq. But both Kuwait and Saudi Arabia field armored units capable of deployment against the larger and heavier threats around the Peninsula.

SAUDI ARABIA. The structure of the Royal Saudi Army (RSA) has changed over the past decade from a predominantly infantry force in 1970 to one having two brigades each of infantry, mechanized infantry, and armor. One of the armor brigades is a cadre unit because of recruitment difficulties. The armor brigades employ AMX-30s, while

Table A-1. *Peninsular Overland Defense Forces*[a]

Item	Saudi Arabia	Kuwait	Bahrain	Qatar	UAE	Oman
Army strength	35,000	10,000	2,300	5,000	46,000	19,550
Organization (combat brigades)	1+ armor 2 mechanized 2 infantry 1+ artillery	1 armor 2 mechanized	⅓ armored carrier ⅓ infantry	⅓ armor 1⅓ infantry	1⅓ armor/ armored carrier 3 infantry	1 armor/armored carrier/infantry 1 infantry
Tanks	300 AMX-30 150 M-60A1/3	70 Vickers MK-1 10 Centurian 160 Chieftain	...	24 AMX-30	100 AMX-30 18 OF-40 60 Scorpion (18 OF-40 MK-2) (20 Scorpion)	6 M-60A1 12 Chieftain (15 Chieftain)
Armored personnel carriers/armored cars	200 AML-60/90 350 AMX-10P 20 VCC-1 800 M-113	100 Saladin 80 Ferret 175 M-113 130 Saracen	8 Saladin 20 AML-90 8 Ferret	10 Ferret 30 AMX-10P (8 Commando)	6 Shorland 90 AML-90 VBC-40 AMX10P	36 Saladin
Strike aircraft	65 F-5E	30 A4KU	(6 F-5E/F-20?)	2 Hunter 1 T-79 8 Alpha Jet	3 Alpha Jet 10 MB-326KD (3 Alpha Jet) (A-10?)	19 Jaguar 12 Hunter
Air-surface munitions	Maverick	Super 530 SS-11/12	...	...	AS-11/12	...

Source: International Institute for Strategic Studies (IISS), *The Military Balance, 1983–1984* (London: IISS, 1983), pp. 52, 57–58, 60–62, 64.
a. Verifiable orders in parentheses.

the mechanized units rely on M-60A1s (currently in transition to M-60A3s). The Saudis expect to buy more tanks, and it seems likely that one of the mechanized brigades will be converted to armor, while they mechanize one of the infantry brigades. Reports also suggest that the Saudis may deploy an airmobile unit over the course of this decade.[1]

The Saudi Arabian National Guard (SANG) has also been modernized, principally by the SANG program, a U.S. effort involving the Vinnell Corporation and U.S. military advisors.[2] In March 1973 the Saudis began to try to modernize four SANG battalions by using V-150 armored cars, TOW antitank weapons, towed howitzers, 81mm mortars, trucks, and small arms. In 1978 the Saudis asked to have another four battalions and a logistics battalion modernized along the same lines. This effort has created within the SANG the structure, if not the reality, of "a lightly armored reconnaissance screening force . . . ideally suited for the security of the cities and surrounding areas, or the oilfields."[3] Some discussion of purchasing heavy tanks for SANG has occurred, but as yet no action has been taken.[4] Interviews suggest that the SANG program has been marginally useful and that the SANG remains the tribally based internal security force it always was.

The Saudis do not publicize precise deployments, but in general the RSA is deployed to the west and south of the country (figure A-1). Most of its armor and its armor school, the parachute units, and commandos are deployed at Tabuq. Completion of a three-brigade complex, King Khalid Military City (KKMC), at Wadi al-Batin near the western edge of Kuwait, will allow the Saudis to move heavy units to this area to meet possible threats by ground forces without compromising the security of the royal family. Mechanized units are stationed along the Yemeni

1. U.S. Library of Congress, Congressional Research Service, *Saudi Arabia and the United States: The New Context in an Evolving "Special Relationship,"* prepared for the Subcommittee on Europe and the Middle East of the House Committee on Foreign Affairs, 97 Cong. 1 sess. (Government Printing Office, 1981), p. 51. (Hereafter U.S. LOC, CRS, *Saudi Arabia and the United States.*)

2. On the SANG program, see *Proposed Arms Sales for Countries in the Middle East,* Hearing before the Subcommittee on Europe and the Middle East of the House Committee on Foreign Affairs, 96 Cong. 1 sess. (GPO, 1979), pp. 2, 35.

3. Ibid.

4. A Saudi request to the Federal Republic of Germany for 300 Leopard IIs apparently originated in the National Guard. See John Vinocur, "Saudi Weapons Deal Starts Bonn Debate," *New York Times,* March 26, 1981. Late in 1983 the Germans formally declined to sell the tanks for historical and political reasons. "Germans Won't Sell Saudis Leopard," *Defense Week,* vol. 4 (October 17, 1983), p. 18.

Figure A-1. *Saudi Arabian Force Deployments*

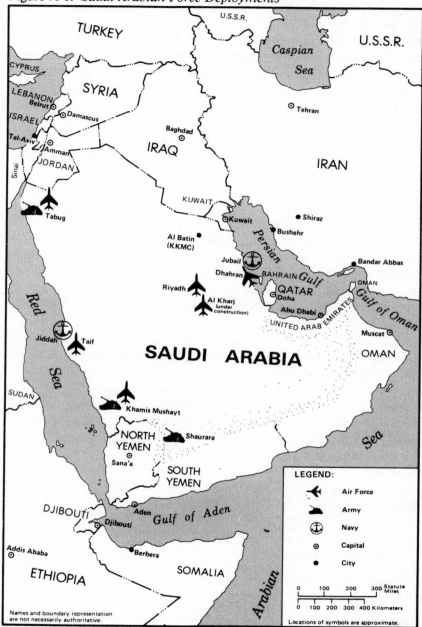

Source: *The Proposed AWACS/F-15 Enhancement Sale to Saudi Arabia*, prepared for the Senate Committee on Foreign Relations, 97 Cong. 1 sess. (Government Printing Office, 1981).

border at both Khamis Mushayt and the smaller outpost at Shaurara, built after the 1969 border problem with the PDRY. The infantry is scattered about the country, including at outposts along the Iraqi border. The RSA's headquarters and logistical center, though few combat troops, are based at Al Kharj, near Riyadh. SANG units are stationed in all major towns and along the borders, with units at Hofuf in the oil region and a headquarters near Riyadh.

Given logistics, equipment, and deployment patterns, Saudi ground forces can be considered separate one-to-two-brigade armies of questionable capability, likely to operate alone in defending the country's far-flung borders. As armored units are moved to KKMC, the deployment of these small armies will come reasonably into line with the location, if not the size, of likely threats. The SANG's modernized units will fall in behind whatever larger units the Saudis and Kuwaitis might move north to meet an attack from that direction. In the south deployment of Saudi mechanized units might be seen as a screen against likely Yemeni threats.

KUWAIT. Kuwait's 10,000-strong army began life as protector of the ruling family, growing after Kuwait became independent in 1961 to the small size of 2,500 soldiers. The soldiers were lightly armed (but for a few British Centurion tanks), and officers were almost exclusively members of the Al Sabah, Kuwait's ruling family.[5] Iraqi threats to Kuwait in the early 1970s produced a series of budget supplements, however, that refurbished and expanded all services. As shown in table A-1, Kuwait's army today owns 160 of Britain's heavy Chieftain tanks—certainly inappropriate for internal security—and deploys two armored brigades as well as three infantry battalions. Little is known about these forces save their basic outlines. But Kuwait's tendency to recruit relatively unskilled Bedouins raises questions about the effectiveness as well as the endurance of Kuwaiti tank units against a serious external threat.[6]

OMAN. The Sultan of Oman's Land Forces retain much of the struc-

5. J. C. Hurewitz, *Middle East Politics: The Military Dimension* (Praeger, 1969), p. 352.

6. According to Cottrell, Hanks, and Bray, in 1978 one-third to one-half of Kuwait's army consisted of poorly educated Iraqi or Saudi tribesmen. See Alvin J. Cottrell, Robert J. Hanks, and Frank T. Bray, "Military Affairs in the Persian Gulf," in Alvin J. Cottrell and others, eds., *The Persian Gulf States: A General Survey* (Johns Hopkins University Press, 1980), p. 167. Nyrop and others note that in the mid-1970s Bedouin tribesmen composed up to 80 percent of the Kuwaiti army and the National Guard. Richard F. Nyrop and others, *Area Handbook for the Persian Gulf States* (GPO, 1977), p. 193.

ture they acquired during the Dhofar rebellion; they consist primarily of light infantry forces geared for counterinsurgency warfare.[7] This is especially true of the Southern Brigade, whose four battalions (mostly Baluch in composition) are stationed in the Dhofar region. These units still train principally for counterinsurgency missions, although they have begun to acquire antitank weapons to deal with a Yemeni armored threat. Beneath these four units is a 3,700-strong force of Firqats, local Dhofaris (many of them former rebels) first trained by the British beginning in 1974, who are used as tribal police, scouts, and border guards.[8] The Northern Brigade, headquartered near Seeb, now has eighteen tanks in its inventory and fifteen more Chieftains are on order. Barring an uncharacteristically rapid expansion in the size of Oman's tank units, however, they are likely to be of little help to Saudi Arabia and Kuwait in facing Iraqi or Iranian threats.

Strike Aircraft

Table A-1 also highlights data on GCC ground attack (strike) aircraft.

SAUDI ARABIA. The sixty-five F-5Es that constitute the Royal Saudi Air Force's strike capability are distributed to bases at Khamis Mushayt, Taif, Dhahran, and Tabuq. These aircraft will probably also be stationed at KKMC when it is operational. Purchases made since 1975 have given Saudi Arabia a large inventory of ground attack munitions. These include more than 2,000 Maverick TV-guided missiles useful for attacking armor and several thousand laser-guided bombs and cluster bomb units for use against point and small area targets like supply depots, antiaircraft installations and radars, and forward staging areas.[9] Although at the moment none of these munitions can be delivered in close support to Saudi ground forces, they could prove useful against massed forces even if used independently of ground forces.

The Saudis claim to have just enough native pilots to fly their full

---

7. Interview with Sultan of Oman's Land Forces officials, May 1982.

8. On the Firqats, see Nyrop and others, *Area Handbook for the Persian Gulf States,* p. 394.

9. For a discussion of the Saudi munitions inventory, see *Proposed U.S. Arms Sales to Saudi Arabia,* Hearing before the Subcommittees on International Security and Scientific Affairs and on Europe and the Middle East of the House Committee on Foreign Affairs, 96 Cong. 1 sess. (GPO, 1980), pp. 9, 10, 35.

combat inventory of F-5s and F-15s, giving them as yet no depth and hence limited tolerance for combat losses. Assuming that the best F-5 pilots move on to F-15s, overall strike force effectiveness will probably drop until a new crop of pilots learns to fly F-5s skillfully. In 1983 the Saudis assumed full ground support responsibilities for their F-5s, but here too the transfer of the best mechanics to the F-15 and AWACS programs is likely to sap the effectiveness of F-5 support for some time. Although indigenous support is quite shallow, Saudi modernization predates that in other GCC states and is further advanced than elsewhere on the Peninsula.

OMAN. The core combat power of Oman's air force lies in its twelve Hunters (provided by Jordan) and its seven Jaguars (twelve more are on order). Both can be used for ground attack (including close air support), and the Omani inventory of munitions includes cluster bomb units for use against attacking armor. Oman's aging BAC-167 Strikemasters may also be used in the ground attack mode, though these aircraft are more appropriate against insurgents than against external attack from the PDRY. These aircraft are based principally at Thumarit, Masirah, Salalah, and Seeb, near Muscat. Thumarit is the main base for offensive aircraft and includes hardened facilities for one squadron of aircraft.

Having emerged from near-complete isolation in 1970, Oman's indigenous manpower problems top even those of Saudi Arabia. In the past the Sultan of Oman's Air Force relied on British seconded and expatriate pilots, and although about fourteen Omani pilots are being trained annually, the British would still probably have to participate in defending against any PDRY attack. British officers outnumber Omani officers in the air force. Most maintenance is done by civilians on contract; about 10 percent of the maintenance personnel are native Omanis. Although the sultan is anxious to have his forces composed of Omanis, he is also currently searching for a new interceptor which, as in Saudi Arabia, will require help from foreign personnel.

OTHERS. Kuwait's force of about thirty McDonald-Douglas A-4s is the only other ground attack air capability currently available to the GCC. Little is known about this force, however, save that the Kuwaitis seem to have enough pilots to fly the aircraft. Support probably lies with contract hire laborers. These aircraft are aging, and the Kuwaitis may well enter the market for replacements in the near future.

Also entering the market is the United Arab Emirates, or more properly Abu Dhabi, which has test-flown the Fairchild (and USAF)

Table A-2. *Peninsular Air Defense Forces*[a]

Item	Saudi Arabia	Kuwait	Bahrain	Qatar	UAE	Oman
Interceptors	42 F-15C/D 34 Lightning 30 F-5E[b] (20 F-15)	19 Mirage F-1B/C (12 Mirage F-1C)	...	(14 Mirage F-1)	30 Mirage 5 (36 Mirage 2000)	(Tornado?)
Surface-air missiles (batteries, where known)	16 I-Hawk 2 Shahine Redeye (Shahine)	4 I-Hawk SA-7	RBS-70[c]	Tigercat (I-Hawk)	Rapier Crotale RBS-70[c] (7 I-Hawk)[d]	Rapier Blowpipe
Antiaircraft guns	AMX-30SA (30mm) M-42 (40mm) Vulcan (20mm)	ZU-23/4SP[e]	...	...	(Skyguard 35mm)	4 ZU23-2
Passive measures	Dispersion, revetments on some runways[f]	...	...	...	Shelters being built for Mirage 2000s[g]	...

Source: IISS, *The Military Balance, 1983–1984*, pp. 52, 57, 60–61, 64, except as noted below.

a. Verifiable orders in parentheses.
b. When F-15 deliveries are completed, about 30 percent of Saudi Arabia's F-5E force will be allocated to air defense. *Proposed U.S. Arms Sales to Saudi Arabia,* Hearing before the Subcommittees on International Security and Scientific Affairs and on Europe and the Middle East of the House Committee on Foreign Affairs, 96 Cong. 1 sess. (Government Printing Office, 1980). p. 36.
c. The RBS-70 is a Swedish laser-beam-riding, short-range missile.
d. See "Hawk Missile Deal Signed," *Middle East Economic Digest*, vol. 27 (March 25, 1983), p. 56. Verified with Raytheon.
e. Mark Heller, ed., *The Middle East Military Balance, 1983* (Tel Aviv University, Jaffee Center for Strategic Studies, 1983), p. 146.
f. Ibid., p. 202.
g. "Mirage Shelter Plans for Abu Dhabi Air Base," *Jane's Defence Weekly*, vol. 2 (November 24, 1984), p. 916.

A-10.[10] If completed, such a purchase would probably be made in conjunction with Pakistan. An A-10 fleet would be the only one among the GCC air forces designed strictly for low-altitude ground attack missions.

Air Defense

Table A-2 lists the air defense portions of GCC air forces with air defense missile inventories, radars, and known passive measures, most of which come under ground force control. Table A-2 clearly illustrates Saudi Arabia's commanding lead in air defense. It also raises questions about the prospects for standardizing an aircraft within the GCC, given the predominance of French aircraft in three states, U.S. aircraft in two, and British in one. There is considerably more standardization in the category of air defense missiles, where it is not as useful.

SAUDI ARABIA. Although some of the British Lightnings from Saudi Arabia's earlier air defense modernization still fly out of Tabuq, these aircraft are nearing the end of their structural life. The core aircraft for air defense will be, when conversion to F-15s is complete, about thirty F-5s configured for this role, and fifty-two F-15s (the other ten F-15s in the inventory being needed for training and "float"). Variations of the U.S. AIM-9 series Sidewinder air-to-air missiles will serve as the principal weapon for these aircraft. Behind these missiles stand sixteen Improved-Hawk (I-Hawk) surface-to-air missile batteries and their associated radars, and two batteries of the shorter-range Shahine, with more on order.[11] Most of the I-Hawk batteries remain in storage, however, ostensibly because of manpower limitations.[12] The 400 U.S. Stinger shoulder-fired air defense missiles (with 200 launchers), delivered to Saudi Arabia in late May 1984, add little to this basic air defense array.

Above these will fly the five AWACS aircraft that the United States

---

10. "UAE Checks Out A-10," *Defense Week*, vol. 4 (January 17, 1983), p. 4.

11. In January 1984 the Saudis announced the signing of a $4 billion air defense agreement with France, with a package based on the Shahine. Significantly, the Saudis claim to have invested in the development of the system they are buying. See "Saudi Arabia Says It Funded French Missile Program," *Wall Street Journal*, January 27, 1984.

12. During congressional debates concerning the F-15 sale to Saudi Arabia it was claimed that an air defense screen of I-Hawks would require five times the skilled personnel required by the F-15 fleet. "Middle East Aircraft Package: Reference Papers" (Washington, D.C.: U.S. Department of State, March 1978), p. 4.

will transfer to the Saudis in a three-phase program beginning in 1985 and extending into the 1990s—although four AWACS aircraft under U.S. control have been stationed in Saudi Arabia since 1980. At cruise altitude (29,000 feet) these aircraft are deemed capable of detecting low-flying aircraft at ranges of more than 200 miles. By comparison, the ground radars associated with Saudi I-Hawks can pick up low-flying aircraft at perhaps thirty miles, assuming no terrain interference. As part of the 1981 air defense enhancement package in which the Saudis purchased the AWACS they also sought to purchase an elaborate command and control net to link those aircraft to their air defense missiles as well as to the F-15s and F-5s.[13] But little has been done to develop such a system. Links between AWACS and Saudi I-Hawk batteries remain vocal radio links, if even that exists.

Saudi Arabia's enormous size works both for and against it in the realm of air defense. The Saudis have a great deal more to defend than the other GCC states, and this necessity prevents them from concentrating all of their fairly large air defense apparatus on the eastern coast, where it would be of direct value to the GCC. But size allows the Saudis to disperse their aircraft and take advantage of this, the cheapest form of air defense. Purchase of extended range (conformal) fuel tanks for Saudi F-15s, also part of the 1981 enhancement package, was justified on grounds that it would allow aircraft based at Khamis Mushayt to respond quickly to attack on the Dhahran area.

OTHERS. The UAE's fleet of thirty-five Mirage 5s is configured for air-to-air combat. These were originally heavily supported by Pakistanis,[14] but in recent years Jordanians and Moroccans have assumed some support duties, and the UAE has developed a small coterie of skilled native pilots. Late in 1983 the UAE ordered eighteen Mirage 2000s with an option for eighteen more, and although these aircraft will provide additional capabilities, they will also demand additional support crews and pilots.[15] The UAE has also recently ordered seven batteries of

13. For details on the AWACS sale and capabilities see *The Proposed AWACS/F-15 Enhancement Sale to Saudi Arabia*, prepared for the Senate Committee on Foreign Relations, 97 Cong. 1 sess. (GPO, 1981).

14. See Paul Beaver, "Gulf Air Power in Profile," *Islamic World Defence*, vol. 2 (April–June 1983), p. 21.

15. "Emirs Go for French Plane," *Defense Week*, vol. 4 (November 7, 1983), p. 2. Reports suggest that delivery of the first eighteen Mirage 2000s will occur in 1985 or early 1986. *Jane's Defence Weekly*, vol. 2 (November 24, 1984), p. 916.

I-Hawks, to include communications links not only to other elements of the UAE's air defenses but also to Saudi Arabia's AWACS. Raytheon, the I-Hawk manufacturer, will supply technical advice to the UAE, while the U.S. Army will train UAE citizens in the United States.[16]

Little is known about the effectiveness of Kuwait's fleet of about twenty Mirage F-1s. Support arrangements are probably similar to those in the UAE, with Kuwait supplying native pilots to complement largely Pakistani support crews. Four batteries of I-Hawks complete Kuwait's inventory of air defense assets; deployment of these is uncertain.

The other three GCC states have no interceptor assets, but they will soon obtain some. Qatar has fourteen Mirage F-1s on order, though it is doubtful that Qatar has the indigenous skills needed to support these aircraft in even the limited numbers available in the UAE or Kuwait. Bahrain has expressed an interest in Northrop F-5s, but in small numbers (four to six aircraft to start). These aircraft might be usefully seen as a small addition to the Saudi F-5 fleet. Finally, Oman is in the market for an interceptor, and the United States has made clear that Oman can buy even sophisticated U.S. models like the F-15. The strong British presence in Oman, however, makes it likely that Oman will turn to the Tornado (in which they have reportedly expressed an interest).[17] As for missiles, Bahrain has some I-Hawks on order which will probably fit into the Saudi I-Hawk net, while Qatar and Oman currently have shorter-range systems. In all cases, however, the newness of these assets makes it unlikely that they will contribute to air defense, except perhaps in the hands of experienced foreign personnel.

Coastal Defense

Beginning with Saudi Arabia in 1972, all GCC states have begun to purchase fast attack craft armed with precision-guided antiship missiles (mainly the French Exocet and the U.S. Harpoon), resulting in the inventories and orders shown in table A-3. Like GCC air defense forces, fast attack craft inventories are mostly on order; even in the Saudi case they are brand new within the past three years. Still, these orders suggest a long-term conversion from shore patrol and coast guard activities

16. "Hawk Missile Deal Signed," *Middle East Economic Digest,* vol. 27 (March 25, 1983), p. 56. (Hereafter *MEED.*)

17. "Tornado Leads the Field," *MEED,* vol. 28 (March 2, 1984), p. 41.

Table A-3. *Peninsular Coastal Defense Forces*[a]

Item		Saudi Arabia	Kuwait	Bahrain	Qatar	UAE	Oman
Missile frigates (with main armament)		4—Otomat[b]	...	...	...	...	...
Fast attack craft/corvettes	Missile	13—Harpoon	5—Exocet (3—Exocet)	(2—Exocet)	2—Exocet (1—Exocet)	6—Exocet	3—Exocet (2—Exocet)
	Gun	1	...	2	...	6	4
	Torpedo	3	...	...	...	...	...
Antiship helicopters		(24 Dauphine)	...	...	...	...	...
Coastal patrol craft[c]		20	15	...	35	22	4 1+ royal yacht
Minesweepers		4	...	...	...	...	...
Coastal defense		Otomat	...	...	3 Exocet CD systems	...	...

Sources: IISS, *The Military Balance, 1983–1984*, pp. 52, 57, 60–61, 64; and *Jane's Fighting Ships 1983–84* (London: Jane's Publishing Co., 1983).

a. Verifiable orders in parentheses.
b. Status of the Saudi-France "Sawari 2" contract remains uncertain. If financed, however, the contract would add two 4,000-ton frigates armed with Crotale missiles to the Saudi inventory. See Paul Betts, "France Set to Sign Saudi Arms Deal," *Financial Times*, May 12, 1983.
c. GCC coastal patrol craft often belong to coast guards and are split between ministries of defense and interior. Numbers shown here are for armed craft of either ministry.

(which are more properly internal security functions) to some degree of "sea denial" capability. But the very newness of the effort makes evaluation even more difficult in this than in other defense sectors.

Interest in missile-firing fast attack craft is in keeping with the overall GCC approach to defense procurement. Navies are technology intensive in comparison with other military services, and the development of precision-guided antiship missiles increases their firepower dramatically without changing their basic character. In most cases guidance systems in the missiles themselves relieve operators of all but initial lock-on responsibilities. Thus it may be more possible here than in other sectors of the GCC defense apparatus to absorb new weaponry. Significantly, as part of the U.S. Navy's Saudi Naval Expansion Program (SNEP), Saudi crews trained and qualified in the United States took charge of their ship in the United States and sailed it home on their own.

Coastal defense and sea denial need not be performed by ships alone. As was demonstrated during the Falklands war, aircraft properly armed can also take on the antiship mission. GCC inventories and orders reflect this fact, though purchases have been of rotary- rather than fixed-wing aircraft, most notably the French Super Puma armed with Exocets. Coastal facilities can be important in coastal defense, and shore-mounted guns and missiles have begun to appear in the arsenals of both Saudi Arabia and Oman.

Again, Saudi Arabia's inventory is the largest and most interesting from a U.S. perspective, although Oman's deserves attention both because of the country's naval tradition and its key position on the Strait of Hormuz.

SAUDI ARABIA. The main impetus to Saudi naval expansion was Iran's seizure of Abu Musa and the Tunbs, small islands off the coast of the UAE to which the shah asserted a claim. In 1972 the Saudis initiated the SNEP with the United States, calling for the purchase of thirteen small (400- to 800-ton) antiship-missile craft armed with Harpoon missiles, four minesweepers, and the construction of shore installations. The first of the thirteen ships was delivered in 1980, with the rest following by 1982. Meanwhile, U.S. engineers began construction of a base and training center at Jubail, on the Gulf coast; port facilities near Jiddah, on the Red Sea; and a headquarters complex in Riyadh.[18]

In October 1980 the Saudis signed a $3.35 billion contract with France

18. See U.S. LOC, CRS, *Saudi Arabia and the United States*, p. 49.

(the so-called Sawari naval contract) for four fairly large (2,000-ton) frigates armed with Otomat antiship missiles, twenty-four Dauphin helicopters armed with AS-15 air-to-surface missiles, supporting radars and tankers, and some shore batteries of Otomat missiles. These weapons are currently on order.[19] In April 1983 the Saudis reportedly approached the French about purchase of two still larger frigates, but financial difficulties attendant upon a drop in oil demand left this contract in question.[20] The French have seconded 165 regular officers and noncommissioned officers to implement the Sawari agreement.

OMAN. Oman's inventory of missile attack craft is taking the same shape as those of other GCC states. Three 400-ton fast attack craft of British construction, each armed with six Exocet missiles, recently entered service, joining two smaller missile craft and four gunboats. Alone among the GCC states, however, Oman has developed a modest amphibious capability, made necessary by its long coastline and the need to support forces in the southern region. Oman has no minesweepers, nor in 1982 did it plan to buy any. Major naval bases are located at Muscat and Raysut.

Although Oman once deferred to Iran most responsibility for naval patrols in the Strait of Hormuz, in 1978 it began to develop its own base on Goat Island in the strait itself, as well as a new base west of Muscat and hence closer to the Musandam Peninsula. A new Sperry radar will go into Little Quoin Island in the strait and will enable the Omanis to spot moving vehicles across the full width of the strait.

19. Ibid., p. 52. The first of the four frigates is to be commissioned in January 1985. See "Trials for Saudi Ship," *Defense Week*, vol. 4 (November 21, 1983), p. 12.

20. On this so-called Sawari 2 contract, see Barbara Donnelly, "Saudi Arabia Again Turns to France For Frigates," *MEED*, vol. 27 (April 22, 1983), p. 40; and Paul Betts, "France Set to Sign Saudi Arms Deal," *Financial Times* (London), May 12, 1983.

Index

Abu Dhabi, 102, 103, 213. *See also* United Arab Emirates

Afghanistan, Soviet invasion of, 1, 9, 12, 13, 17, 19, 40, 41; forces deployed for, 25, 26, 30; lessons learned, 31, 33–34; mobilization, 26–27; political efforts before, 24–25

Air bases, U.S.: aircraft redeployment and, 62–63; critical importance, 55–58, 61, 85; protection, 63; uncertainties, 55–56

Airborne Division, *82*d, 66, 71, 79, 81

Airborne warning and control system (AWACS): in Saudi Arabia, 64, 135, 137, 138n, 145, 146, 147, 148, 149n, 215–16, 217; in Turkey, 56n

Aircraft: CENTCOM, 54–55, 57–58, 61, 62, 85, 203; GCC strike, 212–15; helicopters, 71; proposed U.S., 83; Saudi acquisition F-*15*, 55, 135, 138n, 168–70; Soviet, 27–29, 35–36, 38. *See also* C-130 aircraft

Air Force, U.S., 62, 83

Air interdiction campaign, U.S., 50, 53, 61; air base importance to, 55, 58–61; aircraft availability, 54–55; effectiveness, 54, 85

Airlift. *See* Strategic lift program

Allard, Kenneth, 27n

Amirsadeghi, Hossein, 71n, 102n, 150n

Anderson, Jack, 31n

Angola, 32

Anthony, John Duke, 102n, 123, 130n, 150n

Antiship missiles, 119n, 217, 219, 220

Arab American Oil Company (ARAMCO), 96, 107

Arabian Peninsula: coastal infiltrations, 129; diplomacy, 127; geographic factors protecting, 117–18, 125; internal conflicts, 92–95, 105–06, 128–32; military security problems, 91–92, 108; political factors protecting, 118–19; potential external military attacks, 119–24; regional power balance, 125, 150–51; Yemeni security threat, 108,

111–13, 116, 144–45. *See also* Military security, peninsular states; Military security policy for Peninsula, U.S.; Persian Gulf area

Arab-Israeli war, 3, 24

Arab League, 150

ARAMCO. *See* Arab American Oil Company

Army Reserves, U.S., 83

Army, U.S., 64

Asir tribes, 97

Aspaturian, Vernon V., 52n

Atkin, Muriel, 24n, 44n

AWACS. *See* Airborne warning and control system

Bahrain: GCC defense subsidies, 134; 1981 coup attempt, 100, 123, 131–32; purchase of defense equipment, 135; social welfare experiments, 100

Bandar ibn Sultan, 143n

Beaver, Paul, 137n

Bedouin warfare, 107, 135, 190

Berman, Robert P., 35n, 36n

Berry, F. Clifton, Jr., 81n

Betts, Richard K., 73

Bidwell, Robin, 134n

Bill, James A., 94n

Blechman, Barry M., 172n

Bowie, Robert R., 3n

Bray, Frank T., 118n, 137n, 140n, 141n, 210n

Breslauer, George W., 23n, 24n

Brzezinski, Zbigniew, 13n

Buchan, Alastair, 18n

Buraimi oasis, 106

C-130 aircraft: for intratheater lift, 68, 81–83; number, 80, 82; sortie rate, 80–81

Canby, Steven L., 71n

Carter Doctrine, 3, 13, 16

CBAC. *See* Combat Brigade, Air Cavalry, 6th

Central Command, U.S. (CENTCOM), 14, 53; air base access, 55–58, 61–62;